Interpreting Food at Museums and Historic Sites

INTERPRETING HISTORY

About the Series

The American Association for State and Local History publishes the *Interpreting History* series in order to provide expert, in-depth guidance in interpretation for history professionals at museums and historic sites. The books are intended to help practitioners expand their interpretation to be more inclusive of the range of American history.

Books in this series help readers:
- quickly learn about the questions surrounding a specific topic,
- introduce them to the challenges of interpreting this part of history, and
- highlight best practice examples of how interpretation has been done by different organizations.

They enable institutions to place their interpretative efforts into a larger context, despite each having a specific and often localized mission. These books serve as quick references to practical considerations, further research, and historical information.

Titles in the Series

Interpreting Native American History and Culture at Museums and Historic Sites by Raney Bench
Interpreting the Prohibition Era at Museums and Historic Sites by Jason S. Lantzer
Interpreting African American History and Culture at Museums and Historic Sites by Max van Balgooy
Interpreting LGBT History at Museums and Historic Sites by Susan Ferentinos
Interpreting Slavery at Museums and Historic Sites by Kristin L. Gallas and James DeWolf Perry
Interpreting Food at Museums and Historic Sites by Michelle Moon

Interpreting Food at Museums and Historic Sites

Michelle Moon

ROWMAN & LITTLEFIELD
Lanham • Boulder • New York • London

Published by Rowman & Littlefield
A wholly owned subsidiary of The Rowman & Littlefield Publishing Group, Inc.
4501 Forbes Boulevard, Suite 200, Lanham, Maryland 20706
www.rowman.com

Unit A, Whitacre Mews, 26-34 Stannary Street, London SE11 4AB

British Library Cataloguing in Publication Information Available

Library of Congress Cataloging-in-Publication Data
Names: Moon, Michelle, 1969– author.
Title: Interpreting food at museums and historic sites / Michelle Moon.
Description: Lanham : Rowman & Littlefield, [2016] | Series: Interpreting history | Includes bibliographical references and index.
Identifiers: LCCN 2015028258| ISBN 9781442257207 (cloth : alk. paper) | ISBN 9781442257214 (pbk. : alk. paper) | ISBN 9781442257221 (electronic)
Subjects: LCSH: Food habits—Exhibitions—Methodology. | Gastronomy—Exhibitions—Methodology.
Classification: LCC GT2850 .M66 2016 | DDC 394.1/2—dc23 LC record available at http://lccn.loc.gov/2015028258

Printed in the United States of America

Food history is as important as a baroque church. . . . A cheese is as worthy of preserving as a sixteenth-century building.

—Carlo Petrini, founder, Slow Food movement

Contents

Preface

A Mug-Up

THIS book begins with a mug-up.

One snowy Thanksgiving weekend, I brought my parents to visit Mystic Seaport, the maritime-themed outdoor history museum where I was working. Following the aroma of fresh-brewed coffee, we climbed aboard the 1921 fishing schooner *L.A. Dunton* and made our way below deck to the ship's galley. An interpreter colleague was at the galley stove, baking apple pies. Redolent of cinnamon, they were hard to ignore as we made introductions. The interpreter allowed us a taste.[1] At the first forkful, my mother asked, "How did you make this crust? It's just like my mother's!" Knowing that her oven had turned out another Proustian madeleine, the interpreter answered, "*Lard.*"

By insisting on the lard-shortened crust, the interpreter had revived a taste of the past. Once the most common cooking fat in the United States, lard isn't familiar to many people today—even though it has less saturated fat and cholesterol than butter. It was crowded off grocery shelves in the early twentieth century to make room for new hydrogenated fats. We all agreed that neither butter nor synthetic shortening created the same rich crust that so well offset warm apples.

As we finished the last crumbs, the interpreter explained why baked goods—pies, coffee cakes, muffins, and cookies—were served on vessels like this. Calorie-laden snacks, eaten during a short coffee break called a "mug-up," revived fishermen's spirits during numbing eighteen-hour days of icy waters, wet lines, and slick fish. As welcome as the treat was to us, how much more appreciated must it have been for those men, who needed up to five thousand calories a day? The setting linked us to an even wider past. The schooner spoke of the insatiable demand for fresh seafood, which fueled a relentless scouring of the oceans still impacting fisheries today. It spoke also of pride, skilled labor, and strong communities, qualities that continue to characterize the small-scale fishing industry. The stove's warmth highlighted the vessel's protection from the dangers this form of food labor has always entailed. At tables like this one, racial and ethnic histories of African American cooks and Yankee, Irish, and Portuguese fishermen played out. In our conversation aboard the *Dunton*, we were learning, connecting, and contributing, honoring the past while acknowledging its harsh truths, learning about our own lives and those of others from a different time.

Food is like that. From any taste, innumerable histories extend like roots through soil. In her survey of food in the American past, *How America Eats: A Social History of U.S. Food and Culture*, historian Jennifer Jensen Wallach positions food in history as both a reflective mirror and shaping force, recalling historian Felipe Fernández-Armesto's assertion that food may be "the world's most important subject . . . what matters most to most people for most of the time."[2] Wallach points out a relative dearth of historical scholarship on the topic, noting that it's often "a backdrop to other forms of human behavior . . . so basic and so constant as to seem almost invisible."[3] The same might be said about the interpretation of food in history museums. It's often a side dish, playing a supporting role in the epic of "real" history.

The history of food *is* real history. What if, in museums, food didn't merely illustrate? What if historic sites and history museums looked at food as a central organizing topic? This book aims to assist interpretive planners by identifying large-scale themes in food history that link past to present, cross disciplinary boundaries, and have strong contemporary relevance. It's addressed to the people who shape what visitors experience: the interpreters, planners, exhibition developers, museum educators, and institutional leaders charged with making meaningful connections between physical assets, information, audiences, and mission. One caveat: *Interpreting Food at Museums and Historic Sites* is about food history, but it is not a history *of* food. Unlike the many talented colleagues who have informed this work, I am not a food historian or a culinary historian. My work centers on museum education, interpretation, and community engagement. As much as I like to eat—and I do—I have never immersed myself in the historical details of any one type of food, time period, cultural cuisine, or regional style. Instead, I write from the perspective of an interpretive professional and a supporter of the contemporary movement to reform the food system.

Searching for a food-related metaphor for the structure of this book, I imagined it as braid of challah. A sweet yeast bread introduced to America by European Jewish cooks, challah is shaped by braiding strands of dough in an intricate pattern,[4] reflecting the way this book's historical themes, each discussed in its own chapter, follow a single topic as it weaves through the centuries. The introduction provides justification for the idea that the time is ripe for a new approach to food interpretation. Chapter 1, "Starting from Scratch," offers a brief historiography of food interpretation, surfacing assumptions about food interpretation that may still be with us. Thematic strands begin with chapter 2, "Who's at the Table?" on food and identity. Chapter 3, "It's Good for You!" traces linkages between food and wellness. Chapter 4, "Local Flavor," examines food as an expression of American regionality. Chapter 5, "Food—New and Improved!" explores how Americans have pushed for (and resisted) transformations in food. Chapter 6, "Edible Activism," deals with food politics. Finally, chapter 7, "Food Interpretation," offers practical suggestions and resources. Interpreters might imagine taking knife in hand to slice crosswise through these topics, seeing how these strands come together in a specific period. Or they might follow a single

Figure P.1. A traditional challah, made by interweaving six strands of dough. (WikiMedia Commons/Yoninah, March 30, 2006)

strand, tracing its journey as it contributes to the shape of the whole. The chapters can be read in sequence, or else broken out to stand alone. Not all themes will perfectly suit all sites or all projects. Implementing any of them will rely on additional research relevant to the interpretive project. They are designed to expand the scope of food interpretation. Instead of beginning and ending with the local and specific, they point to larger observations about the role food played in history (and still plays in our lives today).

Notes

1. This was itself an unusual event at the time, as most visitors were unable to eat food prepared in historic cooking demonstrations. This tasting was only possible because I worked at the museum. For more discussion of health regulations, see the final chapter.
2. Felipe Fernández-Armesto, *Near a Thousand Tables: A History of Food* (New York: Free Press, 2002), xi.
3. Jennifer Jensen Wallach, *How America Eats: A Social History of U.S. Food and Culture* (Lanham, MD: Rowman & Littlefield, 2013), xii.
4. Joan Nathan, "Jewish American Food," in *Oxford Companion to American Food and Drink*, ed. Andrew Smith (New York: Oxford University Press, 2007), 331.

Acknowledgments

THEY SAY too many cooks spoil a broth, but they definitely improve a book. I would like to express my gratitude to all of those who offered their ideas, resources, and encouragement in support of this project. It would not exist without Bob Beatty, who suggested I take on the topic and kept me supplied with news on food interpretation from around the museum world. Debra Reid generously shared resources and ideas at a critical early stage, and the American Association for State and Local History (AASLH) community and fellow series authors served throughout as a source of inspiration. I am also grateful to editor Charles Harmon for the opportunity to be part of this important series. I'm likewise indebted to Nicole Moore for some well-timed suggestions and Sarah Scully for helping to track down hard-to-find articles. Special thanks go to John Forti, Deb Friedman, Michael Twitty, Kathleen Wall, and Liz Williams for key insights shared in their "Fresh Ideas" interviews. Thanks as well to the talented interpreters, too many to name, who spellbound me with creative food interpretations and introduced me to the possibilities of food history. Friends from Connecticut to Vermont provided much-needed "writing retreats" and made helpful suggestions. Finally, I owe the greatest thanks to the generous-hearted cooks in my life—pecan pie bakers, Christmas bread makers, pizzaiolos, home preservers, white perch fryers, relish-tray perfectors, and minestrone soup stirrers—who fed me with love and ideas: my grandparents, parents, brother, and sister-in-law, and my husband. Together you have taught me how much meaning can be mixed into a simple meal.

Introduction

Why It's Time to Rethink Food in History Interpretation

ONCE, MOST PEOPLE had some role in food production. Today, almost all of our food is produced far from our homes by an astonishingly small number of professional food producers. This industrialization of the food supply is one of the most profound shifts in American history. Within this overarching narrative are countless personal stories that contributed to the shift—and resisted it. Museums are the keepers of those stories.

Today, Americans are wrestling with challenging questions related to that shift. How much of our own food should we—as a household, a state, a region—produce? What are the risks and benefits of industrializing the food supply? How can all people have access to good food, regardless of income? What are the negative effects of producing an over-supply of calories? What can we do to prevent foodborne illness? How can food help us maintain relationships with one another, with places, with cultural identities? These questions have roots in the past. History museums are realizing that the surge in food conversation represents a fresh opportunity to engage audiences on a topic of vital relevance. Food interpretation has the potential to bring historical thinking into public dialogue. This book suggests substantive ways of designing food interpretation. It advocates that food in history museums be restored to the centrality it has in history, and that the interpretations explore the kinds of sophisticated, nuanced, complex, and deeply interesting questions about food as it does about any other of the meaty historical topics that are museums' stock in trade. In a sense, this book poses a challenge to historic sites: to reach beyond simply being interpreters of *food* and to become interpreters of *food history*.

Food History and Culinary History: Making a Distinction

Aren't history museums already doing food history? Most touch on food in some way or another, but not all are presenting food history. Historian Ken Albala, tracing the roots of food scholarship, identifies a point around the eighteenth century when the field diverged into "two distinct approaches which still exist: *food history*, which covers the social, economic, intellectual, and cultural parameters of consumption, and *culinary history*, which focuses on ingredients, cooking methods, recipes, and the history of the cookbook, often accompanied by the reconstruction of historic cooking in situ." The split had far-reaching ramifications for history institutions, whose interpretive paradigms dictating a focus on ingredients, utensils, and methods put them on one side of a widening fissure. Museum interpreters generated experiential knowledge, but it circulated narrowly, rarely penetrating scholarly discourse. Meanwhile, the interpretive demand to focus on the local and particular prevented interpreters from seeking out broader historical narratives being articulated in academic food history. The result of such schisms, says Albala, is that "food history often neglects the kitchen, while culinary history often ignores the rigorous methods of textual analysis used by food historians."[1] Culinary history also ignores the themes and essential questions food scholars explore today.

Food history and its related interdisciplinary field of food studies[2] are relatively young fields. Albala traces the current wave to the 1960s and 1970s, when scholars positioned food as an integral element of "social history and material life, economic history and world trade, the history of private life and the caloric reconstruction of human diets." The first Oxford Symposium for Food and Cookery convened in 1981. Since then, the rapidly developing field has produced dozens of major publications, journals such as *Food and Foodways* and *Food, Culture and Society*; university food studies programs; library collections; and online repositories. Never have so many professional historians delved into questions of food, and never have interpreters had so many resources available to them.

Unintended Messages

Visitors do enjoy presentations that use culinary detail to depict the past mainly as a phenomenon of difference-from-today. But this risks the loss of informed perspective on how we arrived at the present state of affairs. Writing about pioneer museums, historian David Lowenthal identifies problematic messages that can result from a narrow focus on tools and methods. Implying constant industry, these interpretations wordlessly suggest that the painstaking labor of people in the past led smoothly and directly to the general ease and prosperity many audiences experience today—and that the most important difference between past and present is how much physical effort is required in daily living. A watching visitor "both admires the laborious past and sees how much better off he himself is, because his present emerges out of that past."[3] The takeaway is a sense of the superiority of present-day life, evaluated in terms of personal comfort. The costs of industrializing food systems and mechanizing labor remain outside the frame of interpretation. The contrast of sweat, muck, and grit with contemporary ease obscures everything that happened between then and now, implying an uncomplicated march to the system we have today.

Paradoxically, even as visitors look askance at the struggles of producing food in the past, they are also encouraged to romanticize the same processes. Visitors in the warm, clean, appealing kitchens of historic house museums or living history sites walk away talking wistfully of that "simpler time" when "everyone grew their own food," "knew where their food came from," and "took care of themselves." If we hope to avoid a catastrophic failure of interpretation as an educational service, food history presentations must navigate between twin misunderstandings:

- The past was unrelentingly difficult, but through the perseverance of our forebears and the continuous advance of material progress, we now deservedly enjoy great comfort with few complications, *or*
- The past was pastoral, bountiful, and healthful, but the selfish actions of people in the recent past destroyed that way of life, suggesting that the only hope for a sustainable future is to go "back" to past ways of living.

Each of these narratives is inadequate. We should not be surprised that audiences are puzzled by the gap between their experiences about the past and their understandings of the food system we have today.

Rethinking Food Interpretation

Museums should engage with food history in the same way they have with other histories. Of course, an academic food studies approach is inappropriate for museums, where we value active, sensory, informal learning through object-based experiences. This book calls for a blend of the two, proposing an agenda that unites culinary history and food history. It draws on academic work in the social and technological histories of food to identify thematic strands that arc across time, each of which could inform the development of an interpretive project. The strands are starting points that can be applied and explored, modified or challenged, to progress interpretation at almost any museum or site.

Popular culture suggests that visitors are outpacing museum interpreters in engaging with the full complexity of food ideas. Best-selling books like Michael Pollan's writing on food politics, policy, and ethics in *Omnivore's Dilemma* (2006), *In Defense of Food* (2008), and *Cooked* (2013); Barbara Kingsolver's *Animal, Vegetable, Miracle* (2007); Anthony Bourdain's *Kitchen Confidential* (2000); and Gabrielle Hamilton's *Blood, Bones, and Butter* (2011) are book club favorites. Eric Schlosser's *Fast Food Nation* (2005) and Marion Nestle's *What to Eat* (2007) take unflinching looks at food health and safety. Films such as *Food Inc.*, *Super Size Me*, and *King Corn* unpack the realities of industrialized food production. These books and films are challenging and address serious issues and dilemmas in our changing relationship with food. Yet they have been enthusiastically received. Today's museum audiences are interested in food presentations and are demanding of content that is truthful,

Figure I.1. Farmers' market growth is one sign of Americans' increasing interest in food sourcing and quality. Over the past two decades, the number of farmers' markets has more than quadrupled. Here, shoppers browse the CitySeed Farmers' Market in New Haven, Connecticut. (WikiMedia Commons, public domain)

interesting, and immediately applicable. A study by Reach Advisors found that 51 percent of museumgoers had an "explicit interest" in food and were "attuned to opportunities to learn about food, where it comes from and how it reflects different cultures and the past."[4] In 2011, the American Alliance of Museums convened a symposium titled "Feeding the Spirit: Museums, Food, and Community." Seeing that the nation was "immersed in a reexamination of its relationship to food," organizers urged museums to "serve as catalysts for community action on food and nutrition" and to "reexamine their own attitudes and relationships toward food."

For history museums, this self-examination can begin by determining where the institution sits in Albala's formulation. Is food interpretation based on a creative blend of ideas and evidence from food history with material culture and skills from culinary history? Does it take into account the "social, economic, intellectual, and cultural parameters"[5] of food production, diffusion, and consumption, exploring questions of access, power, cultural development, and continuity? Or does it embrace one to the exclusion of the other?

Food and the Future

In this fertile moment, history museums can provide immediately useful services to the public on a defining issue of the age. It could be a strategic mistake to pass the opportunity up. In recent years, museum leaders have voiced concern over declining attendance and tepid interest in history.[6] Museums are not usually perceived as solution-oriented institutions, but they have critical knowledge—historical *and* practical—to share. Inviting new audiences and longtime visitors to roll up their sleeves and take part in growing, making, learning about, and eating food may change the public perception of history museums for the better. Food interpretation can also improve museums' communities, helping audiences gather knowledge and inspiration needed to reach community goals, solve problems, and contribute to community resilience. A concept borrowed from ecological science, *community resilience* refers to the ability of a community of organisms to tolerate changes and maintain a healthy equilibrium. "Resilience factors" help communities avoid collapse, adapt, and thrive. Recently, civic planners and community developers have brought the notion of community resilience into the human realm. Resilience thinking prepares communities to manage disruptions—climate changes, natural disasters, and transitioning economies—and increase the quality of life and well-being.[7] Museums can develop community resilience factors by building knowledge, connection, and social capital around issues with historical roots—like food.

Beyond the pragmatic, food interpretation elevates our humanity. Food builds bridges, crossing divides of class, language, culture, geography, gender, and age. We all eat, and in following the pathways of food production, we discover our interconnectedness. Museum guru Hal Skramstad envisions museums as places where people "can be a part of something larger and more important than their own individual lives."[8] Offering opportunities to support institutional sustainability, increase relevance, further museum missions, and strengthen communities, museum food interpretation promises to be much more than the flavor of the moment.

Discussion Starter: Take a Food Inventory

What role does food currently play at your museum or historic site? For better understanding of where you are beginning, work individually or with a group to create an inventory of your food interpretation.

Gather a large-scale map or simply drawn floorplan of your space or site, or multiple copies of smaller-scale maps for each person, and several colors of marker or highlighter. Post the map on the wall, or gather around a table and distribute smaller-scale maps. You'll be marking up the map in three different colored markers, so begin by creating a "color key" listing what kind of food experience each color stands for.

- Interpretive content (labels, demonstrations, displays, food animal livestock)
- Retail/amenity (picnic area, snack bar, gift shop, restaurant)
- Backstage (breakrooms, prep areas)

Imagine that you are a visitor moving through your space or site, encountering the presence of food, or food interpretation, wherever it appears. You may choose to map a typical day or a special event, changing the exhibition or seasonal interpretation. At each location where someone might be thinking about or learning about food because of the surrounding environment, star or circle that spot on the map. After everyone has completed their maps, step back to share and analyze your discoveries.

Topics to Discuss

- Where is the weight of the visitor's food experience? Mostly interpretive, mostly amenity, or both?
- Are there continuities between retail/amenity and interpretive food experiences? Do amenities offer a chance to link the present and past? Can interpretive experiences include amenities?
- Does retail support, harmonize with, or counter the messages about food on your site? Does retail food reflect interpretive and institutional values, visitor demands, or unquestioned assumptions (or a bit of each)?
- In "backstage" areas, are staff having food experiences that could be available to the public, if policy were not an issue? What behind-the-scenes experiences might make their way to the front lines to be shared with visitors?
- Do you make exceptions to the "food rules" for special events? What prevents those rules or structures from entering everyday use?
- Where is food missing? What is happening in the blank parts of the map? Do any overlooked areas have the potential to become part of a food story?
- Where are the links between separate locations of food interpretation? Could you create these linkages to reveal supply chains, relationships of exchange, or power differentials?

- Looking at all of the food experiences, mark which ones connect to or contain contemporary food practices or touch on currently relevant food questions. Are these ideas surfacing with visitors?
- Where could you use more research, or benefit from talking with scholarly advisers or food producers?

Notes

1. Ken Albala, "History on the Plate: The Current State of Food History," *Historically Speaking* 10, no. 5 (2009): 6–8.
2. Food history is only one of the disciplines that may fall into the field grouped under "food studies." In an introduction to the field, Ken Albala includes anthropology, sociology, history, communications, philosophy, and "most of the traditional humanities and social sciences" among disciplines generating critical scholarship on food. Ken Albala, *Routledge International Handbook of Food Studies* (New York: Routledge, 2013), xv.
3. David Lowenthal, "Pioneer Museums," in *History Museums in the United States: A Critical Assessment*, ed. Warren Leon and Roy Rosenzweig (Urbana: University of Illinois Press, 1989), 123.
4. Susie Wilkening, "Do Museums Need to Care About Foodies?" Center for the Future of Museums (blog), September 22, 2011, http://futureofmuseums.blogspot.com/2011/09/do-museums-need-to-care-about-foodies.html.
5. Albala, "History on the Plate," 6.
6. Since the 1990s, fieldwide discussion of the state of history institutions has focused on an overall decline in participation. Attendance dropped steeply in the year following the September 11, 2001, attacks on New York City and Washington, D.C., prompting the convening of two national meetings to confront and analyze changes in participation: the Kykuit Summit in April 2002, and Kykuit II in 2006 (for more information, see http://resource.aaslh.org/view/the-kykuit-ii-summit/). A series of articles over the course of the decade challenged history museums to face demographic and cultural change and to set a new course; among the most influential were "Are There Too Many Historic Houses?" by Richard Moe, president of the National Trust for Historic Preservation, in the group's *Forum Journal* 16, no. 30 (2002), and Cary Carson's "The End of History Museums: What's Plan B?" in *The Public Historian* 30, no. 4 (Fall 2008), and *Forum Journal* 16, no. 30 (2002). The effects of the 2009 banking crisis further tightened the financial vise, especially for small museums and historic houses. News articles covered the impact on the public in such pieces as "Struggling to Attract Visitors, Historic Houses May Face Day of Reckoning" (J. Freedom du Lac, *Washington Post*, December 22, 2012) and "The Great Historic House Museum Debate" (Ruth Graham, *The Boston Globe*, August 10, 2014). Finally, in "Attendance Slide: A Call to Action" (http:// reachadvisors.typepad.com/museum_audience_insight/2013/09/the-attendance-slide-a-call-to-action.html), the research and consulting firm Reach Advisers pointed to findings from a National Endowment for the Arts Survey of Public Participation in the Arts indicating that history museums had lost eight million visitors annually since their peak, warning that if this decline continues, "obsolescence lies ahead."

7. For further discussion of community resilience as applied to human societies, see Brian Walker and David Salt, *Resilience Thinking: Sustaining Ecosystems and People in a Changing World* (Washington, DC: Island Press, 2006), and Ayda Eraydin and Tuna Tasan-Kok, *Resilience Thinking in Urban Planning* (New York: Springer, 2012).

8. Harold Skramstad, "An Agenda for Museums in the Twenty-First Century," in *Reinventing the Museum: Historical and Contemporary Perspectives on the Paradigm Shift*, ed. Gail Anderson (Lanham, MD: AltaMira Press, 2004), 126.

CHAPTER 1

Starting from Scratch: The Origins of Food Interpretation

WHERE DID food interpretation *come* from? On one hand, it seems so obvious that food should be part of historic interpretation that we hardly ever think about the processes that brought it there. Nothing seems more natural than to see a display of eggs next to a mixing bowl in a historic house kitchen, or vintage advertising for a local product in a community museum. But like every museum methodology, food interpretation was invented. There was a time before people thought of food as an appropriately dignified topic for museums, and before audiences were interested in historic foodways. The edible past entered museums and historic sites gradually, as events in the culture slowly reshaped the way people thought about food. This chapter provides grounding for interpreters by outlining a brief historiography of museum food interpretation.

The treatment of food in history museums reflects intellectual trends in museums themselves. Through food interpretation, it's possible to discern the reigning ideologies that have governed the production of museum presentations. To discover how food interpretation began, we need to rummage through the distant past of history museums, sniffing for hints of food in the ideas they shared with the public. This chapter begins by exploring three "raw ingredients" that emerged between 1850 and 1930 to form the antecedents of museum food interpretation:

- The early historic preservation movement
- Large-scale industrial exhibitions
- Progressive reform movements

Next, it examines the place of food interpretation in the professionalization and expansion of museum interpretation, tracing its progress from the sidelines to a position near—but, until recently, not quite at—the center. Finally, we'll see how inclusion and accountability began to widen content and audience. This new genealogy of food interpretation is presented to encourage critical thinking about how social agendas inform interpretive messages about food, how strategies developed for a different past continue to permeate interpretation, and which strategies make sense for contemporary audiences.

Invisible Edibles: The Historic Preservation Movement

To ask how food history interpretation began is to ask how history interpretation began. History-focused museums are a relatively recent development. Self-conscious references to the United States' history began early, with pageants, *tableaux vivants*, and festivals, such as the 1712 Fiestas de Santa Fe, a Spanish colonial celebration,[1] and the 1801 "Forefather's Day" that launched Plymouth, Massachusetts's tradition of celebrating its colonial past.[2] Historical societies soon joined pageantry in championing history. These associations brought business leaders and prominent citizens together to preserve documents and build libraries. The earliest, like the Massachusetts Historical Society (founded 1791) and the New-York Historical Society (founded 1804), did not stoop to collect everyday objects, preferring the traditional subjects of classical study: books, paintings, sculpture, and ancient coins. Americans had few other opportunities to take part in organized public history experiences. The young nation was as active in destroying its own history as in celebrating it, as builders and speculators tore down old building stock to develop new projects. Preservationist impulses first emerged in the foment before the Civil War, when patrician women, "frightened that the republic seemed to be coming apart and persuaded that a memorialization of the nation's founders might serve as an antidote," began advocating to save sites linked to the nation's origin.[3]

At Washington's Table: Heroic Shrines

Preservationists' first project was the preservation of George Washington's Virginia plantation, Mount Vernon. Wealthy women from distinguished families formed The Mount Vernon Ladies' Association (MVLA) to manage the property, establishing preservation as a genteel form of democratic participation for upper-class women. Already the moral guardians of the home, women extended nurturing guidance to the nation.[4] The MVLA debated many potential uses for the site, but the vision that dominated was to "purchase Washington's country residence and Negro-houses . . . and to keep them forever in the state in which he left them." Washington's plantation would show future Americans "the state of agriculture at the period when the Republic was founded, and how the old Virginia planters and their slaves lived in the eighteenth century."[5] America's first historic house was also its first agricultural museum.

The movement's language equated patriotism and religion. Mount Vernon was a "shrine"; visitors made their "pilgrimage" to the "Mecca of liberty" to view the former president's "relics," describing its aura as "holy" and Washington's memory "sanctified."[6] The interpretive spotlight shone on the biographies of the famous inhabitants and the provenance of the objects on view—the most awe-inspiring being the ones Washington touched. In these idealizations, a topic as quotidian as food was unlikely to be featured. Mount Vernon's sophisticated facilities for food production, cooking, and dining won only glancing mentions. In one of the site's guidebooks, Elizabeth Bryant Johnston's commentary on Washington's dining room focuses on the "elaborately carved mantelpiece of Carerra marble,"[7] a present from an English gentleman. John Townsend Trowbridge, another visitor, noted in the same room a harpsichord "cherished as a wedding-gift from Washington to his adopted daughter."[8] Johnston briefly describes the "family kitchen, where the daily meals of the family, white and black, were prepared. The immense fireplace, the crane, the low Dutch range, the large hominy mortar, show that the requirements of the cook were neither small nor unheeded. In this room, also in tents outside, a good and a reasonable lunch can be had by the visitors, while from a stand near the door views of Mount Vernon are sold."[9] Johnston mentioned that the plantation's extensive food infrastructure—the milk-house, ice-house, meat-house, summer-house, and spring-house—were in ruins.

Mount Vernon's housekeeping and groundskeeping staff offered informal and unofficial interpretation, much of it from a personal perspective. Some of these earliest interpreters were people formerly enslaved by the Washington family. Trowbridge, in 1866, related a conversation with a cook working at the site:

> Looking in at the wash house I saw a pretty looking colored girl industriously scrubbing over a tub. She told me she was twenty years old, that her husband worked the place and that a bright little fellow, four years old around the door, handsome as polished bronze, was her son. She formerly belonged to John A. Washington, who made haste to carry her off to Richmond with the money the Ladies Mount Vernon Association had paid him on the breaking out of the war. She was born on the place but had never worked for John A. Washington. "He kept me hired out for I s'pose he could make more by me that way." She laughed pleasantly as she spoke and rubbed away at the wet clothes in the tub. . . . "After the war was over, the Ladies' Association sent for me from Richmond, and I work for them now," said the girl, merrily scrubbing.
> "What wages do you get?"
> "I gits seven dollars a month and that's a heap better'n no wages at all!" laughing again with pleasure.[10]

The cook was not the only formerly enslaved worker interpreting Mount Vernon. Johnston relates that "but a step outside the kitchen is the well from which it was the pride of West Ford, an old servant of the estate, to hand visitors a cup of cold water."[11] Mentioned in another account for sharing with visitors "much of interest about Mount Vernon and its associations connected with his own experience,"[12] Ford had been enslaved by the Washington family until freed upon the death of his owner in 1806.[13] He continued a lifelong association with Mount Vernon, working as a site manager and adviser. Ford's well water was a memorable visitor experience of numinous connection with Washington. Trowbridge enjoyed a draught from the "Old Oaken Bucket,"[14] writing, "I thought how often the old General had probably come up thither from the field, taken off his hat in the shade, and solaced his thirst with a drink from the dripping bucket." At Mount Vernon, food was everywhere, yet nowhere the centerpiece. Those who knew most about the plantation's food history from direct experience took their knowledge with them when they passed.

The Mount Vernon model spurred other patriotic preservation efforts and spawned the related historic house movement. Its interpretive precedents were widely adopted: lionization of prominent people and focus on object provenance.[15] All of these topics led away from

Figure 1.1. The kitchen at Mount Vernon had been installed as a period room by the time this photograph was taken. (Library of Congress/"The Old Kitchen Fireplace," Detroit Publishing Company, between 1900–1915)

food and the systems and relationships that produced it. What people ate, and how they grew and prepared it, remained a minor detail.

Success Stories: The Historic House Movement

After the Civil War, interest in preserving history spread through the middle and upper classes, who founded ancestral associations, historical societies, and preservation groups. Michael Wallace notes that as the nation celebrated its centennial in 1876, it had seventy-eight active historical societies, about half of them with a museum. Among them were an increasing number of house museums, skyrocketing from only twenty in 1895 to more than one hundred by 1910. Why the boom? Wallace theorizes that urbanization, industrialization, and immigration threatened the elite, whose numbers seemed to shrink relative to the expanding middle and working classes. As Wallace has it, "Elites fashioned a new collective identity for themselves that had at its core the belief that there was such a thing as the American inheritance, and that they were its legitimate custodians. . . . Patricians discovered in their historical pedigrees a source of cultural and psychic self-confidence."[16] Ancestral societies, like the Daughters of the American Revolution (founded 1890) and the Mayflower Society (founded 1897), preserved historic houses to venerate ancestors. History became a "moral armor," according to Wallace.[17] These museums focused on biography, though with a different accent than the patriotic shrines. The emphasis was on character, discipline, and ambition. "Sites were chosen for their ability to represent 'civic virtue' . . . largely defined by success in politics, the professions, or business. The stories that these museums told were invariably success stories." Central figures were moral examples, not quasi-deities. In these biographical interpretations, stories about food were only told if they illuminated an aspect of character, or illustrated wealth and status. Objects like imported china from the colonial era represented not dining conventions but ancestral provenance. Kitchens were usually not on view. At a time when middle-class and elite Americans rarely stepped into their own kitchens, they were unable to imagine those spaces as points of interest.

History on Display: Decorative Arts Installations

In the 1920s, interest turned to the purely decorative, aestheticizing the historic house. Preservationist William Sumner Appleton founded the Society for the Preservation of New England Antiquities (SPNEA) to protect "the architectural or aesthetic worth of historic houses"[18] as testaments to earlier ages of taste and craftsmanship. A site could now be preserved simply for its beauty and longevity. In these architecturally focused presentations, kitchens, cellars, outbuildings, and other workaday food-handling spaces were often hidden from view, lest their plain finishes detract from the houses' presentation as fine art. Historian Gary Kulik argues that a key moment in this aestheticization was the 1924 opening of the American Wing at the Metropolitan Museum of Art. Curated by author and collector R. T. H. Halsey, the wing presented a set of period rooms—a parlor from Ipswich, Massachusetts, a tavern meeting room from Alexandria, Virginia, and a dining room from Baltimore—as "stage sets for the best of high-style furnishing." Dishes, tables, and sideboards were displayed for their visual qualities and described with art-historical jargon. "The exhibition of the quaint and curious," Halsey commented with a degree of derision, "should be left to our historical museums." The notion that historical objects could be viewed through an art-historical lens had lasting impact. Halsey's project helped "define a new taxonomy for historical objects," introducing "categories of value—metalwares, ceramics and glass, textiles and costumes, furnishings" that would "determine the curatorial slots that history museums would feel compelled to fill."[19] Halsey's legacy lives on wherever dishes and glassware are shown without a mention of who washed them, what foods and beverages filled them, or who gathered around them.

Preservation's Legacies

These three early genres of the historic house museum—the heroic shrine, the monument to success, and the artistic gem—had different social, educational, and political ends, but they shared a disinterest in the flavor of everyday life. Their framing rendered food and food labor invisible and closed off discussion of the complex topics it might raise. They rarely discussed (or even named) servants and slaves, or depicted the work they did. Interpreters were relatively incurious about the systems of transportation that linked historic houses to the food supply, the organization of food preparation, hierarchies of labor and consumption, or the trends that influenced dining. The assumptions and intents, traditions and techniques of the earliest historic house interpreters profoundly shaped the way museums approached the topic of food: as a sidelight to the central story of great heroes, industrial successes, or bygone golden ages.

Food as Spectacle: The Great Exhibitions

As the preservation movement lifted off, great industrial exhibitions were also captivating the public imagination. These massively scaled international fairs were funded by governments and industries, which collaborated to display scientific and cultural accomplishments. Expositions presented compelling immersive experiences to convince audiences of national strength and technological progress.[20] With sprawling grounds and astonishing attendance, these exhibitions dominated public discourse long before their opening and after they closed. People of even modest means made the significant effort to travel to fairs and record their experiences for the benefit of those at home. Between the staggering participation and media saturation, exhibitions were influential cultural events.

Great exhibitions invited exhibitors from across the country, creating a platform for economic competition and cultural differentiation among the states. Companies and government agencies devoted vast sums to presenting products and messages, driving rapid innovation in public presentation. Eye-popping displays and experiential programs drew on techniques from formerly unconnected fields, from theater to sales. Stimulating and memorable, the great exhibitions deeply influenced museum practice by developing ways of communicating with "a society hungry for information and knowledge but wanting to get it in a digestible form."[21] Industrial exhibitions and museums grew in tandem. Objects from exhibitions form the basis of museum collections, including those of London's Victoria and Albert Museum and Chicago's Field Museum. George Brown Goode, a Smithsonian scientist who eventually led the National Museum of American History, oversaw exhibitions for the federal government. Drawing on his exhibit experiences, Goode crafted a new pedagogical tool, the "object lesson," which held that language was inadequate to convey knowledge, and that full understanding required the study of three-dimensional objects. Exhibitions offered a laboratory to test this methodology with a continuous stream of informal learners. The theory of the object lesson, eventually adopted in schools and museums, supported exhibition promoters' argument that their fairs were educational, not just recreational.[22]

Exhibitors pushed the boundaries of communicative design, each new exhibition topping the last. Anything could be put on view—even human beings. On the midway at Chicago's 1893 World's Columbian Exposition, fairgoers strolled through ethnological "villages" where Native American, Tunisian, Austrian, German, Turkish, Irish, Arabian, and Japanese cultural performers lived full time. Spoken of as "living museums," these human displays were early experiments in the museum genre eventually known as living history.[23] Food interpretation at the fairs included daily cooking in these village displays, but that was just one component. Commercial food concerns offered tastings and demonstrated gadgets. States promoted agricultural industries, like Minnesota butter and California grapes. Food manufacturers used the great fairs to build excitement about industrialization. At London's

1851 Crystal Palace exhibition, European food exhibitors promoted gastronomy and terroir, while "practical" American Gail Borden won a prize for his meat biscuit—"a functional food designed for efficiency rather than for taste or elegance."[24] At the same fair, Cyrus McCormick debuted his reaper, new technology that proved transformative for U.S. grain production. Processed food manufacturers promoted "canned meats, desiccated soups, evaporated milk, packaged gelatins, meat extracts," and fat substitutes.[25]

Fairgoers were not allowed to passively observe. Experts, barkers, assistants, models, salespeople, and craftspeople framed their experience. Exhibitors' educational agendas were not neutral; interpretive strategies were needed to help messages hit home.[26] At the Philadelphia Centennial, Gaff, Fleischmann and Co. presented a model bakery "to demonstrate to the public the superior qualities" of their new yeast cakes for leavening bread.[27] A sculptor transformed a large chunk of Arkansas butter "into the likeness of a slumbering maiden while thunderstruck visitors looked on."[28] The Heinz Company built demonstration kitchens at fairs from the 1870s to the 1890s, in which young women gave out samples of pickles, horseradish, mustard, ketchup, and celery sauce along with tiny, pickle-shaped charms.[29]

Looking Backward

In some displays, the product was regional nostalgia. Women's charitable groups developed historically themed installations at fairs to raise funds. A series of Sanitary Fairs (fundraising events for the U.S. Sanitary Commission during the Civil War) initiated the concept of the period kitchen.[30] Each new event improved on the last: "At every Sanitary Fair there were visiting representatives who came to observe, confer, and return home with ideas."[31] The basic design of the New England Kitchen at the 1864 Brooklyn fair could, with a few tweaks, transform into the old-Dutch-themed Knickerbocker Kitchen at the Metropolitan Fair, described on April 9, 1864, by a *New York Times* reviewer as "the jolliest, liveliest, pleasantest place in the fair; in fact, the only place that looks and feels comfortable." At the Baltimore Sanitary Fair of 1864, children visited "Grandma Cushing's kitchen corner" daily at 4 p.m. for a "tea party with plenty of fresh baked cookies."[32] At the Philadelphia Centennial's "Old-Time New England Farm-House of 100 Years Ago," women in quasi-colonial costume led guests through a simulated colonial house, "explaining with courtesy the wonderful articles of furniture and cooking utensils."[33] Already Americans were enjoying the combination of contrived domestic interiors, female hostesses, nostalgic themes, and traditional cooking. Audiences enjoyed the glow of the old-time hearth as a temporary refuge from the troubled present and awe-inspiring future on display in the technological exhibit halls. This display style would become another long-lasting contribution to what Kulik called "the vocabulary of history exhibits," migrating into museums from George Francis Dow's Ward House in Salem, Massachusetts, to the Colonial Kitchen at the DeYoung Museum in San Francisco.[34] Almost all museum methods of demonstration, display, and re-creation can be traced to antecedents at the great exhibitions. By the turn of the twentieth century, if an average American had seen a live demonstration of food being prepared, heard the virtues of a cooking implement extolled, and been welcomed into a re-created historic kitchen, it was very likely at the fair.

BROOKLYN SANITARY FAIR, 1864.
NEW ENGLAND KITCHEN.

Figure 1.2. Women in colonial-style costume staged historical presentations in simulated period environments as early as the Civil War era. In this lithograph, volunteers at the New England Kitchen of the 1864 Brooklyn and Long Island Sanitary Fair are shown dressing in colonial-style costumes and cooking traditional meals in an enormous fireplace. (Library of Congress. Brooklyn Sanitary Fair, 1864. New England kitchen/lithograph of A. Brown & Co., 47 Nassau St., New York, for Henry McCloskey's *Manual* of 1864)

Food Crusades: Domestic Science and Reform

At the 1893 World's Columbian Exposition in Chicago, a new kind of fair kitchen made its debut. The Rumford Kitchen dished out cutting-edge domestic science with its nutritionally optimized meals. This exhibit was the brainchild of Ellen Swallow Richards, chemist, food scientist, and the first woman to earn a degree from the Massachusetts Institute of Technology. Richards infused the fairground kitchen with scientific purpose, spreading the gospel of "the New Nutrition."[35] Named for Count Rumford of fireplace fame, Richards's kitchen was designed to teach principles of nutrition. Instead of antiques, kitchen walls were decorated with charts and diagrams, and "the menu card on each table gave the requirement for one-quarter of one day's ration, with the weight and composition of each dish composing the meal." More than ten thousand people sampled the kitchen's stews, bean dishes, and brown breads.[36] Richards was one of a vanguard of chemists, social scientists, reformers, and journalists who promulgated the disciplines of household management, domestic science, and home economics. These broad initiatives reframed every act of sourcing, cooking, and eating food—along with all other household activities—as perfectible endeavors governed by scientific principles. Home cooks could use food to influence wellness and improve their sense of self-worth in an economy that denied them other outlets for their intellect and skills.[37]

Earlier in the nineteenth century, reform activists, led by educated, affluent, white, native-born women, identified improper eating as a cause of social problems that threatened ideals of decency, health, and gentility. Poor diets, many believed, caused hunger, weakness, and malnutrition, and even alcoholism, political unrest, crime, and violence.[38] Historian Susan Strasser describes how activists proposing intervention "operated on the assumption that social progress depended on public attention to matters formerly considered private."[39] The new insistence on the value of women's work at home was a reaction to changes brought on by industrialization. "Housework was losing status" compared to wage-earning labor.[40] Seeking to reclaim women's work, writers such as Catherine Beecher filled women's magazines and housekeeping books with arguments for a scientific approach to what was now termed *household management*.[41]

Cooking Schools

Reform was partly spurred by the "servant problem," a labor shortage caused by the defection of working-class women from domestic service to manufacturing, managerial, and retail jobs that offered more independence and opportunity for advancement. This challenged middle-class expectations. Middling households in the mid-nineteenth century often employed one to three servants.[42] The shrinking pool of available workers lacked the skills housewives desired. Reformers hit upon the idea of training workers themselves, a strategy that promised to serve their own needs while aiding the working class. In 1874, cooking school pioneer Juliet Corson convened the first cooking class for servants, expanding in 1876 to open her New York Cooking School. Though her central motivation was to aid the poor, Corson segmented her clientele into tiers: free classes for poor women, "a 'plain cook's class' for working cooks and workers' wives, and a Ladies' Class teaching 'the elegances of artistic cookery,'" which subsidized the tuition-free programs and the publication of cookbooks such as *Fifteen-Cent Dinners for Workingmen's Families*.[43] Cooking schools popped up in other urban centers. Famed Boston lecturer Maria Parloa, sometimes thought of as America's first celebrity chef, cofounded the Boston Cooking School, a charitable project of the Women's Association of Boston, in 1879.[44] The school offered free classes to immigrants, taught nutrition to Harvard medical students, and tutored nurses in invalid cooking. In Philadelphia, Sarah Tyson Rorer launched a school after attending a short cooking course and soon became a national figure.[45]

Scientific cooking was also seen as a lever for the economic and social advancement of African American women, for whom domestic service comprised an outsized proportion of available jobs because white employers excluded them from most other fields. Educational leaders Mary MacLeod Bethune and Nannie Helen Burroughs, among others, offered training in scientific cooking, along with other skilled trades. Though students often preferred to concentrate in other fields, between 1880 and 1930, 52 percent of African American women nationwide, and up to 90 percent in some northern cities, worked as domestic servants.[46] Educational leaders felt an obligation to prepare students for this reality, but they also saw domestic science as a means of countering negative stereotypes, using "'home uplift' as a route to 'racial uplift.'"[47] The Settlement House movement was another cooking-focused meeting point between the middle and working classes. Settlement houses were charitable hubs in poor urban neighborhoods, where volunteer workers participated in an intentional community with poor residents. The first American settlement house, Neighborhood Guild in New York City, was founded in 1886; in 1889, Jane Addams and Ellen Gates Starr formed Hull House in Chicago. Settlement house programs offered cooking in a broad curriculum including parenting education, cultural and artistic events, and civic activism. Settlement workers were slightly more open than other reformers to a two-way exchange of food culture. Milwaukee settlement teacher Lizzie Black Kander worked with Jewish immigrants to create *The Settlement Cookbook* (1901), a compilation of recipes published as a fund-raiser. The book was embraced by both new immigrants and Americanized audiences.[48]

Cooking in the Classroom

Reformers also trained children in public schools, YMCAs, and churches. They "capitalized on the fact that the children of immigrant families could be made to feel ashamed of appearing different from their classmates and thus could be convinced to abandon family food traditions in the name of fitting in."[49] Teachers demonstrated "how to properly boil oatmeal, rice, and potatoes, how to make pea soup, mutton stew, creamed codfish, biscuits, and gingerbread."[50] Public school cooking classes were a way to teach new habits to the poor through their children, deputized as "missionaries" for American foodways.[51] A 1918 public school enrolled immigrant students in "Food Scouts," asking students to keep food journals and police one another's meals.[52] Cooking also went to campus. The Morrill Act of 1862 created the nation's land grant universities, opening instruction in household management and domestic science to women students. Iowa State University offered its first cooking courses by the 1870s, and Kansas State Agricultural College soon followed with cooking chemistry. These programs attracted women who went on to expand the field as instructors and research scientists.[53]

Cooperative Kitchens

Some reformers tried to liberate women from cooking. Edward Bellamy advanced the idea of cooperative kitchens in his 1888 speculative novel *Looking Backward*, as did Charlotte Perkins Gilman in her 1898 treatise *Women and Economics*. Author Melusina Fay Peirce published articles outlining a plan to outsource housework to communal kitchens and laundries.[54] Americans never fully adopted the schemes, largely because, as critics charged, they were "basically incompatible with the American ideal of family life."[55] Ellen Richards experimented with a central kitchen program, Boston's New England Kitchen. She resisted displacing the family supper, declaring that "home and family are our strongholds . . . the

Figure 1.3. Public school children practice cooking with a home economics teacher in a model "housekeeping flat" in New York in the early twentieth century. (Library of Congress/National Photo Company Collection/Home economics in public schools, kitchen in housekeeping flat, New York)

food must go to the families, and not the people to the food."[56] The New England Kitchen's domestic scientists devised and tested recipes for "inexpensive, plain American fare," sold as take-out meals to working-class immigrants. The menu, featuring Anglo-American dishes such as chowder, Indian pudding, baked beans, oatmeal, and succotash, had little appeal for customers. Richards deplored immigrants' "decided preferences for the looks and flavors of food to which they have been accustomed. They will not try new things, and are exceedingly suspicious of any attempt to help them."[57]

Reforming Minds, Not Meals

Reformers and domestic scientists reenvisioned American food culture. They created a new branch of applied science, forged paths for women in technical fields, and established the importance of food in public health. But the impact of their social change agenda was limited—not only by pupils unwilling to drop their cultural traditions but also by incomplete understandings of nutrition science, often shaded by cultural biases. Mabel Kittredge, author of the widely assigned textbook *Practical Homemaking*, "saw little use for vegetables," and she discouraged Jewish children from eating pickled vegetables and Italian children from using olive oil, both now known for pronounced health benefits.[58] Reformers were blinded by assumptions about the inherent superiority of their own foodways, as well as inadequacies in research. Historian Alice Ross, critiquing cookbooks of the period, cautions that "by modern nutrition standards they were compendia of contradictory science and folklore."[59] The dietary reformers of the day also failed to take on systemic issues that more powerfully determined access to food and health. They challenged malnutrition and poverty by teaching thrifty cooking, rather than addressing inequality of access. They attempted to change society through individual choices and habits, not by restructuring the political and economic systems that framed those choices.[60] Finally, Richards and her fellow scientific crusaders were unable to make much difference in what people actually ate. Though diets did change, other influences—new commercial foods, migration to urban centers, transportation growth, increasing purchasing power, and "the elimination of elemental home food production"—ultimately had more impact on American foodways.[61]

Museum-ifying Food: Professionalization

Fair exhibitors, food reformers, and domestic science pioneers established the basic vocabulary of food interpretation. Collectively, they created or adapted the systematic recipe, the cooking demonstration, the product sample, the comparative tasting, the instruction manual and "how-to" pamphlet, the participatory cooking class, the thematic exhibit, and the interpretive food display. By World War I, nearly every adult American understood and expected that food experiences could be educational and entertaining. It remained only for history entrepreneurs to marry these tactics to the preservation impulse, creating the history museum movements of the twentieth century.

History Goes Outdoors

In the 1920s, a small set of powerful history enthusiasts hatched grand designs to achieve more impact than a single historic house could offer. This generation of museum founders began by collecting objects of everyday life: tools, furnishings, and agricultural implements. Professional historians dismissed material culture as antiquarian, but in the early twentieth century, as power lines and streetcars transformed American landscapes, collectors wanted artifacts that reminded them of a simpler age.[62] In a quest to house and display their enormous collections, they established the outlines of what would eventually be known as the outdoor history museum. The idea was in the zeitgeist. The individuals who founded the earliest of these organizations were not part of a shared network, and they had no common model. Yet the projects they launched between 1920 and 1950—Colonial Williamsburg (1924), Mystic Seaport (1929), Greenfield Village (1929), Conner Prairie (1934), Old Sturbridge Village (1936), and Plimoth Plantation (1944), among others—share commonalities. All began as the projects of wealthy men, conceived as restoration and collection projects, with public education as a secondary and assumed benefit. And all presented preindustrial Americana, material that seemed to express something fundamental about the American spirit menaced by modernization. These deep-pocketed founders crafted a vision for "bringing history to the masses on a grand scale."[63]

The "Model T" Museum

Wallace credits two pioneers with "decisive transformations" in the presentation of public history: J. D. Rockefeller Jr. and Henry Ford. Rockefeller's interest in preservation had lured him to the city of Williamsburg, Virginia, which, unlike other colonial cities, retained a large number of original structures. Rockefeller restored the buildings and streets as they might have looked during the city's heyday, creating the illusion of time turned back to a pivotal moment in the nation's history. Ford, who once famously declared that "history is more or less bunk . . . the only history that is worth a tinker's damn is the history we make today," had experienced a change of heart. Believing society was in decline, Ford crafted a fantasy "early American Village" out of hodgepodge historic structures, creating an imagined past "saner and sweeter" than the present day.[64] Ford's installation, like his Model T, set an enduring precedent. Nostalgic, celebratory, and safe, Greenfield Village was a history museum for the common American, a place to be entertained and comforted by the past, not to examine its painful moments.

Crafting a Past

Rockefeller and his planners wanted to present "colonial life from the inside."[65] Newly restored spaces became platforms for historically themed entertainments, with "a seasonal calendar of concerts, recitals, sing-alongs, dances, theater performances, film showings, indoor and outdoor games, and other special events."[66] Leaders at other sites "reacted enthusiastically to the idea of a total historical environment," reported Jay Anderson, and they followed suit, led forward by the convincing realism of the places they had made.[67] After a taste of a re-created past in buildings and collections, audiences and staff wanted more— more activities, more costumes, more opportunities to pretend they had really escaped into another time.

Food interpretation was unimportant compared to the need to impress guests' eyes with costumes and furnishings. Even food-related sites, like Colonial Williamsburg's Raleigh Tavern (one of the first buildings restored), focused on leading men gathering for music, conversation, and politics—not on the food and drink served there by colonial hospitality workers. Emphasis fell instead on craft demonstration. Industrialist founders saw in craft a tradition of dedication to labor they missed in these days of worker unrest and mechanization. The public, too, found "something comforting and appealing to seeing a broom, chair, blanket, or andiron created by the skilled hands of a patient craftsperson . . . such demonstrations symbolized what was lost in the transition to the modern urban-industrial world." Old Sturbridge Village "did not initially include a farm, even though most New Englanders were farmers. Yet the museum featured four craft shops when it opened in 1946."[68] Skilled craftsmen were shown as producers, obscuring other facets of their daily lives. Most demonstrations focused on work traditionally performed by men, skewing perceptions of historical labor. Leathercraft, metalwork, pottery, and woodwork offered a certain complexity of process and abundance of tools that appealed to visitors. Demonstrations of professional food preparation or preservation, though also crafts and trades, did not feature prominently. The result was a pronounced gender imbalance in the representation of skilled trade and economic production. Visitors would not encounter an interpretation of a domestic cook that acknowledged levels of achievement equal to a master craftsman's.

Privileging shopcraft over food labor also rendered invisible entire categories of people. At Colonial Williamsburg, the most obvious omission was the enslaved population who performed the bulk of the colony's food labor. "Hostesses" welcomed visitors into most houses; the absence of interpreters representing slaves or hired workers made it impossible to present an accurate picture of social relationships and divisions of labor. When African Americans did interpret food history, visitors saw them through the lens of the Jim Crow South. Restoration partner W. A. R. Goodwin, visiting Colonial Williamsburg shortly after its opening, described the Governor's Palace kitchen, where "two old Negro women, in fitting costume, preside over the Palace kitchen with a courtesy they learned from those whom they affectionately recall as 'Ole Missus.'"[69] It's impossible to know whether visitors left with the interpretive messages about Palace cooking that the staff intended to deliver, but the exchange he shared in the pages of *National Geographic* focused on the illusion of a peaceful capital where elite and impoverished, free and enslaved, coexisted in harmony by adhering to prescribed roles. At Colonial Williamsburg and the many other institutions that followed their model, insights and questions that might have been sparked by focusing on the processes of cultivating, procuring, preparing, and distributing food were long left unexamined.

Inventing Interpretation

After World War II, the startup era behind them, museum administrators were leading history organizations of unprecedented scale and complexity. The next task was to ensure their passage into the future by regulating operations. Founders handed off their legacies to a rising corps of leaders with expertise in history, education, or business, charging them with professionalizing museum organizations, an activity that would remain "the dominant focus of museum culture for most of the twentieth century."[70] Museum leaders in this era invented historic interpretation as we know it today.

In the 1930s, the National Park Service (NPS) introduced and standardized the basic elements of historic site interpretation. They created classes and training materials, conducted visitor research, and supported Freeman Tilden in preparing the seminal work *Interpreting Our Heritage*. Well in advance of widespread living history, NPS sites experimented with re-created settings, including food preparation. A 1936 brochure described an "Indian camp" at Yosemite, where "an old squaw demonstrates the weaving of baskets, preparation of foodstuffs, and sings Indian songs. This 'live exhibit' has proved to be of great interest to visitors."[71] Other museums were also working to codify and structure interpretation, asking basic questions about what should happen during a visit. What should interpreters be doing? Should they recite a script, or speak conversationally? Should they give guided tours, or station themselves in a single location? How could historic spaces be "activated" by museum staff?

Museum leaders referenced other institutions, developing an "industry standard." Mystic Seaport Museum, for example, used benchmarking to evolve interpretation during the 1950s. In internal correspondence, interpretation managers sketched out new goals aimed at depicting "some of the everyday life of a seafaring community." Planners realized that the ideas they wanted to share could not be communicated by words alone: "Statements about 'free enterprise,' 'self-reliance' and 'hardihood' as the characteristics of our seafaring folk become mere phrases which can result in empty phrases through repetition. That the individual had to be a man of enterprise can best be illustrated if what he did every day is demonstrated." In 1955, planners coined the term *activists* to describe a job role in which staff members would activate spaces with the "vitality of dramatic presentation." They sent a delegation to the Farmers' Museum (Cooperstown, New York) for inspiration. There, they were impressed with the Bump Tavern. As a Seaport observer wrote, "They feel so strongly about activation that they are contemplating actually serving meals, similar to those served years ago when the Stage Coach stopped over to change horses—possibly their own home-baked bread and cakes, their own cheese, milk, imported Chinese tea, etc., even light lunches of smoked meats, etc. I think this is a terrific idea." The Lippett Homestead also drew praise, as "here the attendant bakes bread, cakes, etc., and makes butter, cheese, etc., and actually works in and through the house and barnyard just as always. Nothing more could be added—it is, in my mind, perfect." Envisioning a similar plan at Mystic Seaport, the observer wrote, "I strongly believe we must have our hostess in Buckingham House doing something—we must have a fire going—the smell of food, animals, candles, etc., is all part of it." The Buckingham-Hall house was soon outfitted for "activation." Guided tours ended in the house's parlor, where visitors enjoyed tea and cookies by the fire. An internal report raved, "It is the prize of our houses, it is the center of our winter program, and it has the most conspicuous record of approval from visitors."[72]

These "activation" strategies predate widely accepted origin stories for "living history." In Jay Anderson's conception, the dawn of living history broke at Plimoth Plantation in the late 1960s and early 1970. To the contrary, the study of interpretive development at major sites argues that living history techniques were not the invention of a single individual or organization, but of the wider network of history organization planners and interpreters in professional relationships that included informal collaboration, competition, and iteration. Its basic methodologies, including depictions of food culture, were in place by the mid-1950s, fifteen years before Anderson's starting point. Recognizing that static displays, even if presented by hosts and hostesses, did not create visceral experiences, midcentury sites took a leap into previously untried forms of interpretation. The activation of domestic settings with live demonstration, food preparation, food consumption, and even food for sale progressed the interpretation of food. It was now recognized as an area that required a particular body of content, requiring technical know-how and interpretive skill and necessary to a realistic depiction of an organized society. No longer an afterthought, food became the specialty of a new class of historic site interpreters.

Museums for the American Century

Despite these leaps, food demonstrations lacked rigor. Nostalgia reigned, and food was still set as dressing for central topics—mainly, patriotic messages about the American character, felt to need shoring up as the Cold War hummed in the background. Museums highlighted qualities thought to represent the best in the American character—boldness, activity, and vigor—aiming presentations at white middle-class families with school-age children, who, enjoying postwar prosperity, were seeing a plucky and heroic version of the United States in their Chevrolets. The quality of food interpretation was uneven. The benchmarking and borrowing that rapidly progressed interpretation also minimized the need to research the specific food history of each site. Warren Leon and Margaret Piatt warned of this homogenizing risk: "A new museum might make the same brooms as the broom shop at Old Sturbridge Village without ever researching whether the same style of broom was used in the region the museum represented or even whether any brooms were produced there at all."[73] Food was like the broom—if it was good enough for Old Sturbridge Village, it was good enough for a local historical society. In generic kitchen interpretations, staff sizzled corn pones and churned butter without original research or regard for details of the food culture of that place and time. Conditions were ripe for a scholarly revolution.

History's Counterculture: Museums and Food in the Social History Revolution

In the 1960s and 1970s, history museums began engaging with intellectual trends in the academy as advanced humanities graduates joined museum staffs.[74] Proponents of "the new social history," their methods called for examinations of the past "from the bottom up," looking not at heroic figures but at regular people. Central to this practice was the questioning of narratives—especially nationalistic ones whose triumphalism was strained in a time of war, corruption, and human rights activism. Michael Wallace observes that history museums' "celebratory certainties" began to seem full of holes, their "selective and distorted character" in need of review and revision. Activists from previously marginalized groups "began producing history in order to grasp the deep-rooted nature of the processes they were protesting against and to dismantle those readings of the past that provided powerful justifications for the status quo."[75] Collections yielded new discoveries about people who had been excluded from the documentary record but left something of themselves in the objects they used.[76] The quality of emerging scholarship forced history museums to adapt their content. Museums were pushed to set standards of rigor and accuracy and to present a "more pluralistic conception" of the past.[77] New social history thinking also pervaded the study of food. For the first time, museum historians and museum interpreters could pursue their work in an environment that treated food as a serious topic of inquiry. From this point forward, museum interpreters would begin to have access to carefully researched, sophisticated investigations of food as symbol, communication system, and cultural object.

Food Becomes Foodways: Living History

Furthering the "activation" tactics of the 1930s to the 1950s, the next generation of interpreters explored the boundaries of verisimilitude. How far could a museum go to create a vivid impression of life in the past? Food interpretation could not be an afterthought, as food organized the routines of daily life, and it could not be generic, aping ingredients, equipment, or methods from other sites. The requirement of specificity drove the development of interpretive content through direct experimentation. Demonstrators tested recipes, brewed beer, and "back-bred" livestock to simulate historic breeds.[78] Though proponents of living history were undertaking more serious inquiries into food history than their "activist" predecessors, like them they exploited the reliable human interest in food to rouse attention. They were probably not consciously aware of it, but they replicated the presentation vocabulary of industrial expositions and domestic science movements by adding a new element: the ideal of total cohesion and continuity. For the first time, interpretive activities linked phases of food production, revealing interrelationships of agriculture, exchange, trade, and social interaction. It was now possible to follow the path of food through a community.

Plimoth Plantation often receives credit for being the first history museum to officially embrace this form of interpretation. Until the mid-1960s, Plimoth Plantation used a "presentational approach in which costumed docents used lecture-style demonstrations in front of, or within, historical buildings." In a now-legendary incident, staff archaeologist and anthropologist James Deetz, before the opening of the 1969 season, went on a "raid" through the re-created Pilgrim Village, pulling out "wax mannequins, signage, and inaccurate antiques." Deetz and his staff set a new course, outlining a vision of historic interpretation as total immersion. Demonstrations would fit into the naturalistic depiction of a normal day; crafts would be done when they would have needed doing, and meals cooked when it was time to eat. Interpreters were doing, not demonstrating.[79] Once they were following the daily routines of people from 1620, the imaginative leap to embodying them as characters was short. In the words of staff historian Carolyn Travers, "A reproduction village with reproduction furniture sort of calls out for reproduction people." "Full-fledged characterization of and intentional identification with the Pilgrim role" was the base interpretation strategy by 1978.[80]

On Pilgrims' Plates

There was no way to achieve this realism without serious investigation into historic foodways. Life in the pilgrim settlement revolved around the food supply and the hope of generating surplus for trade. Interpretation planners understood the importance of food study. Their exacting research used frameworks from archeology and anthropology, including the concept of *foodways*. The term, "used to denote the general food habits of a familial, regional, cultural, or ethnic group," originated in the study of folklore and anthropology, where it was in use by the 1940s to denote "forces that shape how people prepare and serve food, especially attitudes, customs, traditions, and ritualistic protocol," as well as the "various historic, symbolic, political, social, religious, economic, and cultural factors that influence food choice and use."[81] Plimoth Plantation's daunting, but unavoidable, food history task was to deconstruct the national myth that turned a thinly documented event between Pilgrim settlers and Wampanoag residents into the idealized "First Thanksgiving." Foodways researchers combed the documentary record and tribal oral histories, evaluated climate and seasonal availability, and examined archaeological evidence to recast understandings. Food history had revised a national myth. As Rayna Green recounts:

> The new approaches enabled an interested public to know what was and was not served (deer and eel, not turkey; baked pumpkin and squash, not pumpkin pie), the social and political nature of the occasion (perhaps including a thanksgiving, practiced by both peoples), what foodstuffs and what cooking practices were available to both the English and the Wampanoags (corn, of course, fresh and dried, but not much sugar, dairy, or wheat flour), and which

group was likely responsible for what at the feast (ducks and geese from the English, dried fruits such as blueberries, cranberries, some nuts from the Wampanoags, some fresh vegetables, such as cabbages and carrots, from the settlers), in each instance, all quite different from the story recounted in popular narrative. The new story rebalances the relationships between Pilgrims and Indians, making a more realistic and less self-serving, less "colonial" history of the English settlers on Native lands. The new story is as much about interdependencies and Native agency as about the satisfactions of a successful "conquest" . . . the story of Thanksgiving foods, as reimagined in Plimoth, is embedded in a significant tale of environmental history and change in New England.[82]

In adopting a foodways framework, museums like Plimoth Plantation led the field toward sophisticated, research-supported explorations of edible culture in all its dimensions.

Cultivating Historic Farms

The 1970s also saw the birth of a new museum genre: the farm museum. These sites were intensely active in researching and presenting food history. Old Sturbridge Village (Sturbridge, Massachusetts) was an early epicenter. Old Sturbridge Village (OSV) had grown into a townscape of relocated buildings representing a generic rural New England village of the 1830s. In the 1970s, influenced by social history, OSV "sharpened its concern with historical authenticity," basing interpretation on primary research and the study of period objects.[83] Cultural geographer and agricultural historian Darwin Kelsey advanced these goals in developing a new interpretation of the site's Freeman Farm. Kelsey's program of research ensured that "his farm at Sturbridge was based on the most complete body of evidence his architects, curators, horticulturists, and social historians could provide."[84]

In 1970, government, museum, and agricultural specialists converged on OSV to pursue a common vision: a nationwide network of living history farms. The concept grew from discussions in the USDA about preserving America's farm history. Agricultural economist Marion Clawson and John Schlebecker, then curator of agricultural history at the Smithsonian Institution, had proposed the creation of twenty-five to fifty historical demonstration farms dotted across the nation. Though that vision was never realized, Clawson's charge to interpret agricultural history was taken up at the 1970 conference of the Agricultural History Society at OSV. At that event, the Association for Living History, Farms, and Museums[85] was signed into being. ALHFAM held annual meetings, published a journal, and created a professional network for academic historians, museum interpreters, and independent researchers. Robust and driven by the zeitgeist, its energetic, "how-to" style turned old sites to new ends. Their influence empowered interpreters to undertake and share research and push for more fully realized depictions of the past. As Michael Wallace describes, under their influence, "structures developed a lived-in look; chickens and sheep wandered in and out of the buildings, which consequently became (as they once had been) fly-ridden and smelly. Abandoning Howard Johnson standards of cleanliness allowed a marked gain in historical accuracy."[86] Engaged and active interpreters at farm sites drove the living history movement forward. With large staffs, these sites encouraged specialization in agricultural and domestic skills, and ALHFAM helped disseminate the resulting knowledge. Topics and techniques developed on living history farms traveled into historic houses and even urban and industrial sites, supporting food history interpretation everywhere. Though their rhetoric sometimes bordered on utopian, they shared a commonality with the pre–World War II industrialist founders: the desire to transcend, for a time, a modernity many people experienced as being in decline. But they differed from those founders in their political ideals, taking a more democratic approach congruent with social history's focus on ordinary people.

A Costumed Straitjacket

Living history is a compelling interpretive mode, but it has inherent biases that can mislead audiences. These pitfalls can make living history interpreters victims of their own success: the illusion they create is so complete, so rich in detail, that visitors can forget to use their critical-thinking skills. What they are seeing just seems like reality. Ironically, the reputation of museums for research and accuracy can exacerbate this. Taking museums at their word, visitors assume that what they see is all heavily researched, fully descriptive, real, and reliable. Where food appears, visitors can end up constructing inaccurate understandings of the food of the past. Three of the most significant risks to understanding are outlined here.

Exclusion

As a group, living history sites exclude many individuals from their tellings of the American story. Depicting communities that are overwhelmingly white, rural, Protestant, middle and upper class, and agrarian, they give the public "an unrepresentative sample of past Americans." As if planners and interpreters "found certain pasts more in need of rebuilding than others," their choices about the kind of community to feature in living history presentations are oddly uniform.[87] For example, Leon and Piatt point out that several museums depict nineteenth-century Shaker communities, a small minority in their time, but very few populate a site with much more numerous "Irish immigrant laborers, black slaves, coal miners, and Polish-American steel workers." Nineteenth-century agricultural life is a far more popular topic for a living history museum than twentieth-century industrial life.[88] Social structures and power relationships can be excluded as well. As Michael Wallace observes, the visitor-centric bias toward constant activity urges interpreters to spend time "sowing and reaping" instead of "examining tenantry, foreclosures, world markets, commodity exchange . . . and the agrarian movements that responded to these processes."[89] Few interpreters portray rabble-rousers, dissenters, protesters, profiteers, or authoritarian figures. Nor are there economic or social outcasts struggling on the margins of society—even though such people existed in most communities. In general, characters depicted have a home, an occupation, and good mental and physical health. Visitors seeing full larders, bubbling kettles, and appetizing smells easily imagine that all people ate similarly in quantity and quality. Yet historical data suggest that hunger and want were familiar to most people in American history. Even relatively affluent families' eating patterns varied dramatically with the seasons, geography, and vagaries of transportation. Times of hunger, nutrient deficiency, or numbing monotony are not as common in interpretation as they were in daily life. The risk is that visitors can walk away with the sense that food inequality is a modern problem. Tackling the uneven distribution of food, inequalities of access, inadequacy of supply, dependency on imports, the sheer difficulty of labor, and other uncertainties would give visitors a better chance of understanding some of the vexing challenges and trade-offs of food pricing, distribution, and access today.

Romanticization

Where kitchens are always cheerful and warm, dining tables neatly set, visitors encounter an ideal of home and hearth rather than franker representations of the kitchen as workplace. Kitchens were sites of everyday drudgery, challenging and repetitive labor, rigid social hierarchy, and even conflict. Nor were dining spaces universally benign, any more than they are today. Tables were sites of consumption but also of social performance, enforcement of behavioral standards, and, at times, debate, disagreement, and even control and intimidation. Because it is rare to depict these sides of everyday life, Thomas Schlereth called living history museums "peaceable kingdoms," in which generic, impersonal stories "tended to downplay aspects of community life that were dysfunctional or produced conflict."[90] Food sourcing can lead to false impressions of overall healthfulness and quality. Contemporary food used in historic cooking demonstrations is a far cry from what was available in the past. Commercial produce is bigger and brighter, free of blemishes, differently colored and flavored. Meats are different in cut and consistency. The repetition of leftovers, and use of food threatening to spoil, is not often shown. Vermin and pests aren't visible, apart from a few flies in the flycatcher. Dooryard gardens suggest a degree of household self-sufficiency inconsistent with records of trade and exchange. Time is built into the day for interpretive staff to clean, sweep, organize, and arrange food production; spaces are neat and "put back" at the end of each day, rather than turned upside-down to accommodate multiday processes of food production, housecleaning, or preparation for the change of seasons. It can be instructive to compare interpretation to oral histories and to experience historically themed environments with those who knew about similar places firsthand. Jay Anderson relates the impact of a twentieth-century farm setting at Iowa Living History Farms: "Grandmothers would notice the intense heat of the 1900 kitchen, driven up into the nineties by the wood-fired range, and comment that the good old days really weren't ideally pleasant. Retired farmers would run their hands along the familiar lines of an antique cultivator and ruminate about the drudgery of cultivating corn long into the summer evenings."[91] By researching and presenting fuller, more direct accounts of food labor, food quality, and food safety, interpretive conversations could become more real and honest.

Disconnection with the Present

The marketing language of living history often promises to do the impossible: "bring the past to life," or send visitors "traveling in time." Some living historians believe that the illusion they are creating is just a few small details away from being indistinguishable from an actual past. Staff and visitors can forget that a living history site is a contrived interpretation of the past, not a perfect re-creation of it. Verisimilitude can forestall conversations that link past and present. Visitors are wooed by a magical strangeness, admiring the skill and intensity of the performance, the richness of the illusion, and the sensory input—an experience not dissimilar from walking into a circus tent or haunted house attraction. Noticing this domination of the senses at Colonial Williamsburg, Leon and Piatt write that "what people see and experience in living history museums is generally more important than what they read or hear. Costumed staff members may talk about contentious Virginians, some of whom had to struggle to attain the simplest necessities of life and to maintain basic human dignity, but the visitor is likely to remember contented, friendly, well-fed and well-clothed men and women who live in an unusually pleasant and pretty town."[92]

Public historian Cathy Stanton has identified a paradox of interpretation at living history sites. On one hand, by isolating their discussion to issues and conditions in the past, they create a static sense of "pastness" that relegates those issues to another time; yet, on the other hand, in considering the past from the perspective of the present day, they run the risk of being accused of "presentism," or dismissing the need to evaluate the choices and actions of people in the past in historical context. Living history farms "created environments where visitors could simultaneously escape the complexities of the contemporary world and see that world as desirable by comparison."[93] The past-focused approach of living history museums leads away from "political, presentist neo-agrarianism" that might become the basis for discussing contemporary issues. In cutting off conversation between past and present, living history sites take a step away from offering useful skills, information, and insights to people struggling to negotiate the hazards of the industrial food system, while at the same time incorrectly convincing audiences that they are living in a time of decline from an abundant past. The combination, without additional interpretive supports, leaves visitors with the general sense that history has little to say to contemporary concerns.

Multicultural Flavors: The Age of Accountability

By the 1980s, museums had been federally defined as educational service institutions, and they were asked to accept more direct responsibility to a broad and diverse public. In 1992, the American Association of Museums published "Excellence and Equity: Education and the Public Dimension of Museums."[94] In strong terms, the document argued that education and inclusion were essential to any meaningful measure of excellence, espousing three core principles: a commitment to education, dynamic leadership, and the idea that museums should "reflect our society's pluralism," becoming "more inclusive places that welcome diverse audiences." Museums were asked to move from focusing narrowly on content to using their resources to build an "enlightened, humane citizenry," or, in the words of Stephen Weil, "from being *about* something to being *for* somebody."[95] "Excellence and Equity" called attention to the limited scope of history museum interpretation to date. It pushed museums to widen audiences, improve scholarly foundations, incorporate a range of cultural and class perspectives, and create intellectual access for people of all backgrounds. Historic houses opened kitchens, basements, and servants' and slave quarters to "behind the scenes" or "upstairs/downstairs" tours. Multiculturalism prompted staff to reinterrogate site history and collections to develop resources on immigration, Native American histories, or the Underground Railroad. Museums broadened foodways research, absorbing more of its anthropological flavor. Interpreters saw food as embodying learned behaviors that defined culture, and they used its presence and appeal as a way of presenting dissemination, cultural hybridization, cultural difference, and resistance. The "foodways" framework remained the dominant standard for food history presentations through the turn of the twenty-first century.

As the discipline of food studies broadened its critical sweep, "foodways" began to seem constrained by its focus on individual and community behaviors, frequently to the exclusion of larger contexts of power, economics, technology, and beliefs. This opened a disconnect with visitors, as these topics increasingly characterized Americans' thinking about food. Shallow approaches to multiculturalism have been critiqued from both within and outside of dominant cultural communities, with many noting that it can present a glossy sheen of social equivalence without unpacking the complex issues beneath diversity. The foodways approach can devolve into presentations that position cultures as dishes on plates or facile correspondences ("everyone eats some kind of flatbread!") that elide important variations. An associated effect can be an unintentional othering, even patronization. Edmund Barry Gaither spoke of this in a discussion of the deep levels of belonging that every individual in American culture has a right to claim. "We belong inseparably both to ourselves and to the whole. We are our own community while being part of the larger community. . . . Museums must honor America's diversity without paternalism and condescension."

The professional standard represented by foodways-informed approaches was a great leap forward. It moved food off the sideboard and made it a centerpiece of interpretation, where it could reveal cultural practices, hidden economies, and interpersonal connections. It drove compelling research, and for the first time it foregrounded food as a source of new questions about the past. Though it was unquestionably an advance, it must be used thoughtfully and in consideration of the problematics its framing may engender. Foodways is one tool in the exploration of complex food histories.

Food Interpretation for the Twenty-First Century

Today, we find ourselves at another flexion point. History audiences are conversant with food, passionate about it, and instrumentalist in their orientation to it. They want to know not only how things were done "back then" but also whether historical research can help us identify better ways to do them now. By not drawing clear lines between the food history we exhibit and the tumultuous and dynamic climate that has always surrounded food issues, we cut off visitors' ability to understand that food has always been a contested resource, the subject of cultural anxiety, obsessive planning, exuberant celebration, and hotly debated policy. Michael Wallace decries a history presentation that "diminishes our capacity to make sense of the world through understanding how it came to be."[96] The responsible presentation of history, Wallace says, "informs people about the matrix of constraints and possibilities they have inherited from the past and enhances their capacity for effective social action in the present." Presentations that mislead people about the past are, he says, not historical but "historicidal." Unless museums present the topic in its fullness, we will be unable to achieve the goal set forth in "Excellence and Equity": to nurture an informed citizenry capable of making wise and historically informed decisions. Museums around the country are already developing principles for good food interpretation. Among them are the following:

- Food interpretation is specific to time and place, and it is individual, not generic.
- Food interpretation is framed in terms of interdisciplinary scholarship in food history, including sociological, technological, cultural, environmental, and economic dimensions.
- Food interpretation is comprehensive in its inclusion, honestly depicting the variations within its scope, including not just culturally specific food practices but also their intersections with status hierarchies of consumption.
- Food interpretation avoids nostalgia and links past to present in concrete and meaningful ways that will help visitors make sense of contemporary food issues and understand more about how the American food system developed.

Fresh Ideas: Kathleen Wall on Museum Foodways

Kathleen Wall has been shaping food interpretation at Plimoth Plantation for thirty-five years. When she arrived at the re-created seventeenth-century site in 1980, its living history interpretation had been developing for over a decade. Plimoth could hardly help having a foodways program, she jokes, because "we had Thanksgiving—the other thing that makes Plimoth unique. Everybody knows who we are because of a meal that didn't happen the way everybody thinks it happened." A lively interpreter and painstaking researcher, Wall continues to unearth new knowledge and pilot new approaches as the colonial foodways culinarian.

Plimoth Plantation has long been a pioneer of foodways interpretation. Looking back to the early days, what stands out to you?

We were so serious at the beginning. We knew the myths, and we felt a responsibility to counteract them. We went for years without saying the "T word"—[as Pilgrims] we only know the word *wildfowl*, so we must not say turkey! I've been accused of being a turkey denier, but I know that people assume turkey; I wanted to make sure that other things got a mention. We were really focused on daily life. We had herb gardens that were no longer maintained by the "little green men," as we called them—men in uniform who took care of the herb gardens in the 1960s. Suddenly, people in costume had to take care of their gardens, as if they were their own gardens. And when you get that radish or carrot to grow, you want to eat it! And then you get interested in the questions "How did they grow it? How did they eat it?" You start to take it personally. We weren't just an exhibit or a demonstration. We presented food as part of daily life. With every question—curatorial decisions, garden decisions—we asked ourselves, if you really did live here then, how did you feel about these things? How did you do these things? We were inventing it. It took us a few years—we were young, we were stupid, we didn't know. We just knew the answers were out there, and we could find them.

How did you decide what merits a place in interpretation, and what to rule out?

Since the museum started, even when it was static interpretation, there was an emphasis on going to the original sources. Arthur Pyle, the first employee of the museum, was a history teacher, and he put together a program based on Mourt's Relation, all the court records, and all the public documents. That collection was always our source. When James Deetz came along, he brought archeology to the mix. So those reference points became the alpha and omega: the word was "go out, and find what you will but whatever you bring back, it must fit." There's a temptation to seek out sources to justify things you want to do. For instance, in the early 1990s, we had a woman who wanted to portray a blacksmith. She found a source describing a female blacksmith in seventeenth-century France. We had to say no; that's too unusual. Just because somewhere, sometime, someone once did something, that is not enough to say you should do it, too. You have to be specific to your own site. I think that's what makes it interesting! I don't want to have the same twelve activities that every other living history site seems to have. Sometimes you can "steal" from other people, but when ideas become too widespread, history becomes generic.

In the 1980s, there were relatively few scholarly books or articles about food in social history. How did you find information to develop your interpretation?

In a book I reviewed recently, the author describes her book as "an intellectual pantry."[97] We should all have an intellectual pantry, and a way of organizing it. Your pantry has *sources* and *resources*, and you need to know the difference. *Sources* are peculiar to you, your character. Deeds, public docs, private documents, your place and your people. Interpretive content has to fit to that, not the other way around. *Resources* are sources that are applicable, but less specific to you. Resources help you interpret your sources. For example, let's say you have a farm site with a farm diary from 1836. It's great, but it doesn't tell you what the family had for dinner. But if you can find a cookbook from that region, now you have a resource that fits your source. Never use a resource without understanding how it ties in with your source. Sources are true always; resources are tools you use to flesh your sources out. Here's an example of how the resources have changed: in the 1990s, when I was learning how to butcher the seventeenth-century way, there were very few primary sources to work from. They knew how to butcher, so they didn't write about it a lot. So I looked up Merle Ellis, who used to do butchering on TV. He had a book on butchering, but it's not written like you're actually going to *do* the butchering. You're going to go to the grocery store and buy the cuts he described. Ten years later, it was the opposite problem. Now there are books on whole-hog butchering, how to raise pigs, how to kiss the pig goodnight before you butcher it, nose-to-tail cookery. And now, there's a book only on hog testicles, describing forty-seven different ways to prepare them. It's gotten to the point where I've said to myself "It's getting too focused—I need to read more general histories again." Some of the recent publications are really good, and some are trying to ride the wave. I think it's harder now—you're flooded with information, and you don't know what's good. You're always balancing, looking for insights you can use.

Aside from cooking daily meals in character, what are some creative ways Plimoth Plantation weaves food history into the interpretive experience?

The Pilgrim Village foodways programs are seasonal, and they take place in real time. If you come at 3:00 in the afternoon, we're washing up the dishes. So we plan demonstrations on other parts of the site—so you might see someone making a salad at 4:00, and talking about what seasonal greens are available. We do workshops, and recently added one we call "Hardcore Hearth Cooking." It takes place in February in a seventeenth-century house, so your only heat is the fire. With a small group, we cook a full meal and then sit down and enjoy it, talking about all the aspects of the experience. In the last three years, we've hosted our farmer's market here once a month. During the market we participate in a program called "Culinary Insights." I show a seventeenth-century recipe that uses things available at the market, so people can learn that arugula, which seems so modern, was called "rocket," and Englishmen used it in salad. It travels well and grows easily, so it did very well early on in English gardens. For these programs, I'm not in character—I'm standing behind a hot plate cooking. That's when you realize how important smoke is to draw people into an open-hearth experience; you realize some things translate better than others.

What changes have you seen in the audience since you began interpreting food? Where are we headed next?

There are two interesting changes in the audience, and they're divergent. First, people are looking for what's local, and history can help with them that. They're interested in how things are grown, how they're sourced. Those are our locavores, one of our base audiences. The other group is people who do not cook at all. For them it's so foreign they ask, "How can you possibly cook over a fire?" I connect it with what they see on *Top Chef*: "They have a gas stove. The fuel source is different, but it's still a fire." They'll walk into a house, walk right by the hearth, and say, "Where's the cooking?" It's where the fire is! Smell. Trust yourself. But we have a fairly international audience, including people who know how to cook over the fire because they still do it. The modern American House Beautiful kitchen is not a way of life that's as loved internationally as in urban America.

What relevance can a historic foodways program have for today's audience?

A few years ago a reporter from the paper came around asking visitors whether they thought living history was relevant. I'm in costume, at the bread oven, lighting a fire, as she's asking, "How can anyone relate to this? Who even knows how to bake bread anymore?" A crowd gathers around the oven, and I see an older woman standing there, staring at the fire. She says, "I haven't seen an oven like this since I was a girl. I used to help my mother gather wood. Then the tanks came. Then we came to America." There were fifty people there who now knew something about this woman's childhood, that there were people not long ago who did this. There was also a Caribbean man, who said, "When I was young, my mother was the baker. She had an oven like this and she made coconut cakes. Then the hurricane came, and we all had to leave." These were memories from only fifty years ago for the Polish lady, twenty years for the Caribbean man. They came to Plimoth Plantation to see the seventeenth century. They didn't know they'd be seeing their own past—and it was the American past, too.

Discussion Starter: Is Your Food Interpretation Frozen in Time?

Plimoth Plantation's current interpretive approach blossomed along with living history, informed by the archeology and anthropology backgrounds of its leaders in the 1970s and 1980s. The museum committed to exploring seventeenth-century foodways, and it continues to do so today. But, as Kathleen Wall's discussion shows, the museum continuously reupdates its food interpretation, experimenting with new formats. Some of the interpretive paradigms of the past remain powerful and well adapted to their settings. But sometimes old interpretive commitments may cause museums to get stuck in interpretive modes that no longer connect well with audiences. Where does your project or institution fall? Working on your own or with a group, complete the following checklist, identifying food interpretation strategies found today in your project or on your site. Then compare notes and discuss.

Preservation Shrines

___ Focus on the biography and object provenance
___ Food is not a central topic, or is invisible
___ Food interpretation illustrates the heroic virtues of the main characters
___ No interpretive resources on food are available to staff

Model T Museums

___ Focus on the "common man" and industriousness
___ Craft demonstrations more common than food demonstrations
___ Food-related objects displayed in production, not in use context
___ Little research or interpretive content on food available to staff

Aesthetic and Decorative Arts Museums

___ Focus on visual beauty of objects and architecture
___ Objects presented in art-historical categories defined by material and period

__ Contextual displays of interiors are pristine and orderly as if never used
__ Research and interpretive materials focus on fine art qualities of food-related objects

Museums for the American Century

__ Focus on American character and democratic values
__ Contextual displays of interiors are naturalistic, but static
__ Food is used mainly to enliven spaces with activity
__ Research and interpretive support for food topics is conjectural and nonspecific

History's Counterculture

__ Focus on realism, attempt to create complete illusion of a past time
__ Site uses livestock, gardens, and more, to illustrate food sources and multiple phases of food production and consumption
__ Focus on culinary detail, re-creating exact methodologies
__ Research is rigorous and site specific; incorporates primary sources and experimental archaeology

The Age of Accountability

__ Focus on identity and culture, and American diversity
__ Food interpreted through cultural lens with focus on cultural transmission of foodways
__ Food a central topic, used mainly to demonstrate cultural and class specificity and variation
__ Research incorporates oral histories and secondary literature in food history

Questions for Discussion

- Does your site fall largely into one category, or use a mix of strategies from a few earlier paradigms?
- Is your current mix of interpretive strategies helping to reach current goals for audience and experience?
- What holdover formats or assumptions from the past are limiting your food interpretation?
- What "classic" elements of site interpretation do you never want to give up?

Notes

1. Dennis J. Carroll, "Fiesta de Santa Fe," *Santa Fe New Mexican*, August 22, 2013.
2. Stephen Eddy Snow, *Performing the Pilgrims: A Study of Ethnohistorical Role-Playing at Plimoth Plantation* (Jackson: University Press of Mississippi, 1993), 13. Snow identifies an 1801 "Forefather's Day" celebration as "the first actual performative representation of Pilgrim History" known to date.

3. Michael Wallace, "Visiting the Past: History Museums in the United States," in *Presenting the Past: Essays on History and the Public*, ed. Susan Porter Benson, Stephen Brier, and Roy Rosenzweig (Philadelphia: Temple University Press, 1981), 138.

4. Wallace, "Visiting the Past: History Museums in the United States," 138.

5. Charles Lyell, *A Second Visit to the United States of North America* (London: John Murray, 1855), 267.

6. Charles Edwards Lester, *The Light and Dark of the Rebellion* (Philadelphia: George W. Childs, 1863), 24–28.

7. Elizabeth Bryant Johnston, *A Visitors' Guide to Mount Vernon*, 16th edition (Washington, DC: Gibson Brothers, 1889), 28.

8. John Townsend Trowbridge, *The South: A Tour of Its Battle-Fields and Ruined Cities, a Journey through the Desolated States, and Talks with the People* (Hartford, CT: L. Stebbins, 1886), 7.

9. Johnston, *A Visitors' Guide*, 38.

10. Trowbridge, *South*, 95–96. The "John A. Washington" referred to here is John A. Washington III, great-grandson of George Washington's brother. John A. Washington III was the last family member to own Mount Vernon.

11. Johnston, *Visitors' Guide to Mount Vernon*, 62.

12. Joel Tyler Headley, *The Illustrated Life of Washington* (New York: G & F Bill, 1859), 512.

13. WGBH Educational Foundation, "Mount Vernon Responds to the Ford Family," from supporting material for episode "Jefferson's Blood," *Frontline*, 2000. West Ford was born a slave to John Augustine Washington, brother of George Washington. George Washington left Mount Vernon to his nephew, Bushrod, son of John Augustine Washington. Bushrod moved to Mount Vernon in 1802, taking West Ford with him, though Ford was then the property of his mother, Hannah Bushrod Washington, John Augustine Washington's widow. According the terms of her will, Ford was freed in 1805, but he continued in Bushrod's employment as manager at Mount Vernon and other family properties until he died in 1829, having become "the second wealthiest free black person" in the county. Among Ford's duties were supervising slaves and offering interpretive tours of the site for visitors and journalists, many of whom, like Trowbridge, wrote about him. See http://www.pbs.org/wgbh/pages/frontline/shows/jefferson/video/tofords.html.

14. Martin Gardner, *Best Remembered Poems* (Mineola, NY: Dover Press, 1992). The mention of the "Old Oaken Bucket" is probably a reference to a wildly popular nostalgic poem written in 1818 by Samuel Woodworth, and set to music in 1843 by George Kiallmark.

15. Wallace, "Visiting the Past: History Museums in the United States," 139–40.

16. Wallace, "Visiting the Past: History Museums in the United States," 140.

17. Wallace, "Visiting the Past: History Museums in the United States," 141.

18. Edward P. Alexander and Mary Alexander, *Museums in Motion: An Introduction to the History and Functions of Museums*, 2nd ed. (Lanham, MD: AltaMira Press, 2008), 127.

19. Gary Kulik, "Designing the Past: History-Museum Exhibitions from Peale to the Present," in *History Museums in the United States: A Critical Assessment*, ed. Warren Leon and Roy Rosenzweig (Urbana: University of Illinois Press, 1989), 12–17.

20. Robert W. Rydell, *All the World's a Fair: Visions of Empire at America's Great Industrial Expositions, 1876–1916* (Chicago: University of Chicago Press, 1984), 2–3.

21. Harold Skramstad, "An Agenda for Museums in the Twenty-First Century," in *Reinventing the Museum: Historical and Contemporary Perspectives on the Paradigm Shift*, ed. Gail Anderson (Lanham, MD: AltaMira Press, 2004), 119.

22. Rydell, *All the World's a Fair*, 44.

23. Rydell, *All the World's a Fair*, 56.

24. Warren Belasco, *Meals to Come: A History of the Future of Food* (Berkeley and Los Angeles, CA: University of California Press, 2006), 167.

25. Belasco, *Meals to Come*, 168.

26. Rydell, *All the World's a Fair*, 16.

27. Gaff, Fleischmann, and Co., trade card, "Centennial Exhibition, Vienna Model Bakery," No. c110290, Centennial Exhibition Digital Collection, Philadelphia Free Library, http://libwww.library.phila.gov/CenCol/Details.cfm?ItemNo=c110290.

28. Karal Ann Marling, "The Origins of Minnesota Butter Sculpture," *Minnesota History* 50, no. 6 (1987): 218–28, accessed August 5, 2014, http://www.mnhs.org/market/mhspress/minnesotahistory/featuredarticles/5006218-228/.

29. Nancy Fowler Koehn, *Brand New: How Entrepreneurs Earned Customers' Trust from Wedgwood to Dell* (Boston: Harvard Business School Publishing, 2001), 46.

30. New York Public Library Archives & Manuscripts, United States Sanitary Commission Records, http://archives.nypl.org/mss/3101. New York Public Library archivists describe the U.S. Sanitary Commission as "a civilian organization authorized by the United States government to provide medical and sanitary assistance to the Union volunteer forces during the United States Civil War, 1861–65."

31. Beverly Gordon, *Bazaars and Fair Ladies: The History of the American Fundraising Fair* (Knoxville: University of Tennessee Press, 1998), 77.

32. Maryland State Archives, "The Long Awaited Event," in *A Record of Heroism: The Maryland State Fair for U.S. Soldier Relief*, 2002, http://msa.maryland.gov/msa/speccol/sc5400/sc5494/html/fair.html.

33. J. S. Ingram, *The Centennial Exposition Described and Illustrated* (Philadelphia: Hubbard Bros., 1876), 44; and Laurel Thatcher Ulrich, Justin Florence, Rebecca Goetz, Rick Bell, and Eliza Clark, *Inventing New England: History, Memory, and the Creation of a Regional Identity* (course website), http://sites.fas.harvard.edu/~hsb41/index.html, accessed April 26, 2015.

34. Kulik, "Designing the Past," 23; for discussion of the Ward House, see Warren Leon and Margaret Piatt, "Living History Museums," in Leon and Rosenzweig, *History Museums*, 66. For an extended discussion of Colonial Revival kitchens as they transitioned from fairs into historic houses, see Abigail Carroll, "Of Kettles and Cranes: Colonial Revival Kitchens and the Performance of National Identity," *Winterthur Portfolio* 43, no. 4 (2009): 335–64.

35. Kiyoshi Shintani, "Cooking up Modernity: Culinary Reformers and the Making of Consumer Culture, 1876–1916," dissertation, University of Oregon, 2008, 6.

36. Belasco, *Meals to Come*, 168; excerpts from Report of the Massachusetts Board of World's Fair Managers, Boston 1894, from "The Rumford Kitchen Exhibit at the World's Columbian Exposition, Chicago, 1893," in MIT Institute Archives digital exhibition *Ellen Swallow Richards*, http://libraries.mit.edu/archives/exhibits/esr/esr-rumford.html, accessed April 26, 2015. Richards considered eighteenth-century inventor Count Rumford "the first to apply the term 'science of nutrition' to the study of human food, and the first to apply science to the preparation of food materials."

37. Sheila Rowbotham, *Dreamers of a New Day: Women Who Invented the Twentieth Century* (Brooklyn, NY: Verso Books, 2010), 125–47.

38. Jennifer Jensen Wallach, *How America Eats: A Social History of U.S. Food and Culture* (Lanham, MD: Rowman & Littlefield, 2013), 126–28.

39. Susan Strasser, *Never Done: A History of American Housework* (New York: Pantheon Books, 1982), 206.

40. Strasser, *Never Done*, 185.

41. Strasser, *Never Done*, 180–201. Catherine Beecher was a lifelong educator who had founded the Hartford Women's Seminary in 1823. Beecher advised women to redefine household work as a divinely ordained, demanding intellectual responsibility, no less important than men's work outside the home. A widely read authority after the 1841 publication of her *A Treatise on Domestic Economy*, Beecher presented housekeeping as a "scientific study" requiring the understanding of principles in "architecture, pneumatics, hydrostatics, calorification, floriculture, horticulture, animal husbandry, botany, hygiene, physiology domestic chemistry, and economics." In 1869, along with her sister, author Harriet Beecher Stowe, Beecher published *The American Woman's Home*, expanding on her philosophy of the home as the fount of patriotism, middle-class decency, and regularity, and including specific instructions for running a household efficiently. The sisters laid out plans for redesigned kitchens that maximized convenience and prolonged food's shelf life, and they reworked fixture placement with the eyes of time-and-motion experts, appropriating ideas from mechanized industries. Direct instruction and clear plans were needed, because, as Beecher saw it, the typical woman was as prepared to "take charge of a man-of-war" as to run a household.

42. Harvey Levenstein, *Revolution at the Table: The Transformation of the American Diet* (Berkeley and Los Angeles: University of California Press, 2003), 61–64.

43. Strasser, *Never Done*, 204–305; Wallach, *How America Eats*, 125–26.

44. Laura Shapiro, *Perfection Salad: Women and Cooking at the Turn of the Century* (New York: Farrar, Straus, and Giroux, 1986), 52–53.

45. Shapiro, *Perfection Salad*, 192–94.

46. National Women's History Museum, "Progressive Era: 1880–1930," in online exhibit *A History of Women in Industry* (2007), accessed April 26, 2015, https://www.nwhm.org/online-exhibits/industry/7.htm.

47. Victoria W. Woolcott, *Remaking Respectability: African American Women in Interwar Detroit* (Chapel Hill: University of North Carolina Press, 2001), 21.

48. Jane Ziegelman, *97 Orchard: An Edible History of Five Immigrant Families in One New York Tenement* (New York: HarperCollins, 2010), 160–65.

49. Wallach, *How America Eats*, 126–27.

50. Zeigelman, *97 Orchard*, 161–62.

51. Ziegleman, *97 Orchard*, 165.

52. Wallach, *How America Eats*, 127–28.

53. Virginia Railsback Gunn, "Industrialists not Butterflies: Women's Higher Education at Kansas State Agricultural College, 1873–1882," *Kansas History* 18, no. 1 (1995): 2–17.

54. Strasser, *Never Done*, 195–201; Wallach, *How America Eats*, 113–15.

55. Levenstein, *Revolution at the Table*, 66.

56. Ellen Swallow Richards, "The Wholesale Preparation of Food," in *The Science of Nutrition*, ed. Edward Atkinson (Boston: Damrell & Upham, 1896), 197; Levenstein, *Revolution at the Table*, 67.

57. Wallach, *How America Eats*, 130.

58. Ziegelman, *97 Orchard*, 163–65.

59. Alice Ross, "Health and Diet in Nineteenth-Century America: A Food Historian's Point of View," *Historical Archaeology* 27, no. 2 (1993): 46.

60. For a critical evaluation of the legacy of scientific culinary reform, see Shintani, "Cooking up Modernity," 212–18.
61. Ross, "Health and Diet in Nineteenth-Century America," 47.
62. The appeal of the mundane was part of a wider shift in collecting priorities. See Teresa Barnett, *Sacred Relics: Pieces of the Past in Nineteenth-Century America* (Chicago: University of Chicago Press, 2013), 181, on the move "from the association item to the evidentiary object and from the singular and auratic to the generic and everyday."
63. Wallace, "Visiting the Past: History Museums in the United States," 144–45.
64. Wallace, "Visiting the Past: History Museums in the United States," 144–49.
65. Cary Carson, "Colonial Williamsburg and the Practice of Interpretive Planning in American History Museums," *The Public Historian* 20, no. 3 (1998): 16.
66. Carson, "Colonial Williamsburg and the Practice of Interpretive Planning," 15.
67. Jay Anderson, *A Living History Reader: Volume One: Museums* (Nashville: American Association for State and Local History, 1991), 19.
68. Leon and Piatt, "Living History Museums," in Leon and Rosenzweig, *History Museums*, 67.
69. W. A. R. Goodwin, "The Restoration of Colonial Williamsburg," *National Geographic Magazine*, April 1937, 443.
70. Skramstad, "An Agenda for Museums in the Twenty-First Century," 123.
71. Barry Mackintosh, *Interpretation in the National Park Service: A Historical Perspective* (Washington, DC: History Division, National Park Service, Department of the Interior, 1986), chap. 1, online book accessed April 26, 2015, http://www.nps.gov/parkhistory/online_books/mackintosh2/index.htm.
72. Miscellaneous correspondence, Mystic Seaport Museum institutional archives: Education, Programs and Interpretation (Called Activation), 1952–1966, Boxes 13, 14, and 15.
73. Leon and Piatt, "Living History Museums," in Leon and Rosenzweig, *History Museums*, 68.
74. Anderson, *A Living History Reader*, 195.
75. Wallace, "Visiting the Past: History Museums in the United States," 155.
76. Barbara Melosh, "Speaking of Women: Museums' Representations of Women's History," in Leon and Rosenzweig, *History Museums*, 183–84.
77. Wallace, "Visiting the Past: History Museums in the United States," 157.
78. Jay Anderson, *Time Machines: The World of Living History* (Nashville: American Association for State and Local History, 1984), 195.
79. Scott Magelssen, *Living History Museums: Undoing History through Performance* (Lanham, MD: Scarecrow Press, 2007), 86.
80. Snow, *Performing the Pilgrims*, 40.
81. Polly Adema, "Foodways," in *The Oxford Encyclopedia of Food and Drink in America*, 2nd edition, ed. Andrew Smith (Oxford: Oxford University Press, 2013), 817.
82. Rayna Green, "Public Histories of Food," in *Oxford Handbook of Food History*, ed. Jeffrey Pilcher (New York: Oxford University Press, 2012), 84.
83. Mark Ashton and Jack Larkin, "Celebrating 50 Years of History Part I: How the Village Came to Be," *Old Sturbridge Village Visitor* (Spring 1996).
84. Anderson, *Time Machines*, 43.
85. The Association for Living History, Farm, and Agricultural Museums, "The History of the Association for Living History, Farm, and Agricultural Museums," accessed April 26, 2015, http://www.alhfam.org/?cat_id=226%20-%20also&nav_tree=101,226%20-%20also,

accessed April 26, 2015; Marion Clawson, "Living Historical Farms: A Proposal for Action," *Agricultural History* 39, no. 2 (1965).

86. Wallace, "Visiting the Past: History Museums in the United States," 156.

87. Thomas J. Schlereth, "History Museums and Material Culture," in Leon and Rosenzweig, *History Museums*, 307.

88. Leon and Piatt, in Leon and Rosenzweig, *History Museums*, 65.

89. Wallace, "Visiting the Past: History Museums in the United States," 157.

90. Leon and Piatt, "Living History Museums," in Leon and Rosenzeig, *History Museums*, 69.

91. Anderson, *Time Machines*, 80–81.

92. Leon and Piatt, "Living History Museums," in Leon and Rosenzeig, *History Museums*, 74.

93. Cathy Stanton, "Between Pastness and Presentism: Public History and the Local Food Movement," *Oxford Handbook of Public History*, ed. James Gardner and Paula Hamilton (New York: Oxford University Press, forthcoming), 12.

94. The American Association of Museums, "Excellence and Equity: Education and the Public Dimension of Museums," ed. Ellen Cochran Hirzy (American Association of Museums, 1998).

95. Stephen E. Weil, "From Being about Something to Being for Somebody: The Ongoing Transformation of the American Museum," *Daedalus* 128, no. 3 (1999).

96. Michael Wallace, "Mickey Mouse History: Portraying the Past at Disney World," in Leon and Rosenzweig, *History Museums*, 58.

97. Kathleen Wall, review of *Seeking the Historical Cook: Exploring Eighteenth Century Southern Foodways*, by Kay K. Moss, *ALHFAM Bulletin* 44, no. 2 (2014): 23.

CHAPTER 2

Who's at the Table? Interpreting Food and Identity

STRONG FOOD INTERPRETATION begins by thinking first about who was at the table, not what was on it. Food behavior, now and in the past, is a complex expression of the intersections of identity, culture, taste, access, and status at a given moment. Food interpretation that begins with a specific, well-researched individual, family, or community can create stronger empathy for people of the past and build more concrete understandings about the "the labor, resourcefulness, and exchange that historical actors brought to the everyday challenge of addressing their own hunger."[1] Interpretive planning should center human beings in food narratives, asking how the conditions of their lives and in the larger world defined the food choices available to them, and how their own creativity and ingenuity transformed food culture. This chapter will introduce broad themes from food history that can support specific interpretations and suggest avenues for further research. Using these themes, interpreters can diversify and refine their understandings of the people at the heart of any food story.

Key Interpretive Concepts

1. *Food and identity are tightly interwoven.* The foods people have had access to, aspired to eat, and enjoyed intersect with their ethnic, racial, gender, and class identities, among others.
2. *Diversity and variation are usually present even with a shared food culture.* Avoid generalization and assumptions; recognize individuality, multiple identities, and personal preferences.
3. *America's cuisines are constantly shifting and reforming.* Iterative processes of exploration, negotiation, and assimilation result in a continuing creolization of the nation's foodways. There has never been a single "true" American cuisine.

Creole Cuisines: Ethnic and Racial Identity

American cuisine has been called "a mirror of history," and that history is complicated.[2] Countless interactions between distinct cultural communities—voluntary and involuntary, peaceful and forceful—made almost all American foodways "creole" foodways.[3] Ubiquitous and adaptable, food cultures lend themselves readily to dissemination. Calling human beings "omnivore-generalists" because "the number of their potential foods is high," historian Knut Oyangen notes that most people "exhibit neophilia, the persistent desire to add new foods to the culinary repertoire," as well as "neophobia, a reluctance or skepticism toward new foods." Americans experienced both, but the churn of American history guaranteed a continual mixing of food practices.[4] From the nation's beginnings, appetite and curiosity have overcome neophobia and demolished culinary purism, making culinary creativity through creolization the nation's great contribution to world food culture.

Native Landscapes

In 1539, Hernando de Soto landed on the coast of Florida, expecting a virgin wilderness but finding fields of "maize, beans, calabashes, and other vegetables, the fields on both sides of the road extending across the plain out of sight."[5] North America was already a place of cultivated foodscapes. Many museumgoers are unaware of the extensive agriculture of pre-contact North America. Indigenous people were not passive recipients of nature's bounty. They actively shaped the environment to increase and regulate the food supply. Millennia before European arrival, indigenous North Americans adopted agriculture, and they continuously expanded the food supply, using cultivation (manipulation of landscape to support desired plants), domestication (gradually altering plants' genetic makeup through selective breeding until they must be supported by humans), control of wild animal populations, and trade. New cultivars, and new ideas, traveled freely.[6] Constantly changing conditions demanded adaptation, generating new eating patterns. Archaeological studies of one village site in Arkansas reveal variations over time. In the fourteenth century, the community relied on maize, but by the seventeenth century people were eating more sunflower seeds, pecans, hickory nuts, acorns, persimmons, and plums. Fourteenth-century residents ate a great deal of deer meat; two centuries later, they had shifted to alternative proteins like fish and turtles. Archaeologists speculate that these changes were partially caused by social factors such as spikes in warfare that made deer hunting unsafe and prevented field cultivation. In this as in many other communities, the food supply fluctuated, and so did human diets.[7]

Culinary Contact

Contact between the Old and New Worlds transformed eating for the entire planet. Hunger for new products spurred the most infamous point of contact, Columbus's 1492 voyage of exploration. Columbus's documentation contains the earliest written accounts of North American foodways, including cassava bread, "cooked roots that had the flavour of chestnuts" (likely sweet potatoes), beans, wild birds, crabs, fruit, and fish.[8] Voyages of exploration revealed to the powers of Europe the wealth of land and products on the other side of the Atlantic, sparking traffic between the hemispheres. The resulting transfer of people, languages, religions, goods, and diseases, termed by historian Alfred Crosby the "Columbian Exchange," permanently revolutionized global food culture.[9] From Europe came wheat, barley, rice, and turnips, while American maize, potatoes, sweet potatoes, chilies, coffee, chocolate, and tomatoes were introduced to Europe.[10] Settlers followed explorers. Population booms in Europe (partly fueled by increased calories from New World foods) and economic competition among nation-states led to colonization. In the coastal Southeast and Southwest, Spanish colonists built missions complete with self-sustaining agricultural facilities. British and Dutch colonists spread across the Northeastern seaboard and mid-Atlantic coasts. In each region, distinct foodways unfolded as colonists' customs met and mingled with locally available ingredients and the foodways of other Europeans, enslaved Africans, and Native Americans. Creolization had begun.

A Hybrid Diet

Hunger was the first challenge colonists faced. Despite gifts of food from local native people, the Jamestown colony was forced into survival cannibalism within two years.[11] Nearly half of the original Plymouth colonists died of hunger and exposure. Colonists were reluctant to use native foods. British settlers seesawed between considering the New World an inert growing medium for their preferred crops—wheat, oats, turnips, and apples—and celebrating a natural paradise stocked with deer, fish, and wildfowl. Maize quickly replaced wheat in colonists' diets, despite what Wallach calls "ambivalence" to what they saw as an inferior grain that "nourisheth but little," but their wheat refused to thrive. "Due to their recent experiences with hunger and scarcity," Wallach writes, "they could not afford to dispense with this reliable food source regardless of how unpalatable some found it." Colonists instead tried to "disguise corn" by using it in English-style recipes. Settlers brewed corn beer and blended rye with Indian corn meal to create a "peculiarly New World bread" they nicknamed "rye-and-injun." As settlements matured, colonists had so thoroughly integrated indigenous foodways that any awareness of their Native origin was erased from memory. Beans, corn, maple sap, cranberries, quahogs, crabs, sweet potatoes, and squashes became simply "American."[12] In 1672, naturalist John Josselyn wrote that the English on Martha's Vineyard had learned to boil cranberries into a sauce for meat from local Wampanoag people; by 1800, Anglo-Americans considered cranberries a "New England" food, and Wampanoag descendants now competed with whites to harvest the cranberry bogs they had been maintaining for centuries, even having to petition the state legislature to reserve cranberries for "the most Indigent of the Women and Children" for whom it was "a Staple means of support throughout the winter."[13]

African foodways were a third pillar of the hybridizing American diet. Wallach notes that "culinary encounters between Europeans and Africans began on the coast of Africa," as slave merchants provisioned ships according to captives' ethnicity: rice for captives taken from Senegambia, for instance.[14] Slave traders or captives themselves also carried okra, melon, and sesame. Once in the colonies, Africans created new culinary combinations.

According to culinary historian Michael Twitty, "enslaved Africans and their Afri-Creole and African American descendants had to cope with new realities just as Europeans did. They applied whatever knowledge they had learned from home, to awarenesses gained in their American experience, and actively sought to understand the landscape they lived in."[15] In the kitchens of planters' homes, slaves followed the European-style recipes of white mistresses, but they had access to a range of ingredients and equipment. As able, they introduced African techniques: cooking bitter greens with acid to mellow flavor, frying fowl in oil, spicing foods with pepper.[16] Historian William Pierson believes that enslaved cooks "improved the nutritional habits of many of their masters" by increasing the vegetables in their diet.[17]

Though they did not all enjoy equal status, all cooks in the colonial period experimented, improvised, and borrowed to create cuisines that could arise nowhere else in the world. Every new arrival brought another contribution to the changing foodscape. Some influences were more pronounced than others, but no community maintained a "pure" ethnic cuisine wholly of their place of origin. These new ways of eating forged a shared identity for a newly forming nation.

According to some estimates, by 1775 British North America was the wealthiest society the world had ever seen. Southern planters and Northern merchants "established a consciously European cuisine, seeking to equal or outdo European aristocracy."[18] William Hugh Grove, an Englishman visiting Virginia in 1732, wrote that "the gentry at their tables have commonly five dishes or plates, of which pigg meat and greens is generally one, and tame fowl another. Beef, mutton, veal and lamb make another. Pudding, often in the mid[dle], makes the fifth. Venison, wild fowl, or fish a fourth. Smal[l] beer made of molasses with Madera wine [and] English beer [is] their liquor."[19] This elite dining was the cuisine of the 1 percent. For every person who feasted at an elite table, a dozen or more faced leaner rations.

Food and Slavery

Enslaved and indentured people generated much of the surplus that purchased Madeira, currants, and lemons, elevating eighteenth-century elite diets. The Caribbean sugar supply flavored desserts and sweetened punches and appeared in table sculptures at fashionable dinners.[20] Culinary inequality became more pronounced. Indentured servants complained of having "scarce any thing but Indian Corn and Salt to eat."[21] Witnessing the rations allotted to enslaved people during the Revolutionary War, a European military man remarked:

> They are called up at day break, and seldom allowed to swallow a mouthful of hominy, or hoe cake, but are drawn out into the field immediately, where they continue at hard labour, without intermission, till noon, when they go to their dinners, and are seldom allowed an hour for that purpose; their meals consist of hominy and salt, and if their master is a man of humanity, touched by the finer feelings of love and sensibility, he allows them twice a week a little skimmed milk, fat rusty bacon, or salt herring, to relish this miserable and scanty fare. The man at this plantation, in lieu of these, grants his negroes an acre of ground, and all Saturday afternoon to raise grain and poultry for themselves. After they have dined, they return to labor in the field . . . it is late in the evening before these poor creatures return to their second scanty meal, and the time taken up at it encroaches upon their hours of sleep, which for refreshment of food and sleep together can never be reckoned to.[22]

Many of the foodways identified with today's American South initially reflected the necessity of preparing sustaining food from few ingredients. Corn was the "backbone of the slave's diet," along with "much smaller quantities of meat, generally fatty pork or . . . salted fish." Slave-owners calibrated food rations, spending not "a penny more than necessary" for enslaved people to continue to work.[23] Wherever they were allowed, enslaved people improved their food supply by tending gardens, foraging, and hunting or fishing.[24] Museums sometimes inadvertently mislead visitors by presenting the entire range of dietary possibilities for enslaved people at once. Twitty says that when he demonstrates "cooking as the slaves did," what visitors encounter "should really be me serving a visitor or student a bowl of mush or rice or a corncake with no frills except perhaps some salted meat or fish, and water, for several meals a day. That might be the most jarring and authentic way to transfer the message: Enslaved foods were supposed to be filling and blandly satisfactory, not tasty and comforting."[25]

Expanding Foodscapes

The Louisiana Purchase brought into America "approximately 827,000 square miles of proportionately equal new food possibilities." Its already robust cuisines blended indigenous foodways with colonial influences from France and Spain and flavors from the Caribbean. French colonial cooks applied classic techniques to local ingredients, replacing wheat with corn, roux with Choctaw filé, and adopting freshwater fish, raccoons, persimmons, crawfish, and wild rice.[26] The famous jambalaya may derive from an American version of Spanish paella.[27] Dishes now icons of "authentic" Louisiana cuisine began as culinary experiments.

The Plains drew land-poor migrants from the East to establish grain farms. Homesteaders faced a dearth of familiar foods.[28] Many settlers "depended on the willingness of the Native Americans to trade with them" or introduce them to wild foods. Later mythologized as self-sufficient "pioneers," homesteaders were "crucially dependent on supplies and markets, advice and culture."[29] They rapidly established, and then relied upon, transportation links to bring in staples—bacon and salted meats, dried codfish, cornmeal, sugar, coffee, and crackers. The diets most impacted by westward expansion were those of indigenous residents. In the Great Lakes, manoomin (wild rice), fish, and game were replaced by European-American foods as native people lost access to land and waterways. In the far west, bison fed hundreds at a time. Settlement, disease, and near extermination by federal policy gutted this food source.[30]

In 1848, the end of the Mexican-American War again expanded the United States.[31] The Southwest's corn-based food culture mixed indigenous and Spanish preparations, combining tomatoes, aromatics, onions, fresh cheeses, poultry, and meat. Chiles were a unique contribution, "powerful cultural symbols" and a food of royalty. *Chile con carne* migrated into Anglo-American diets in the late nineteenth century, when women sold it from stalls in San Antonio's Military Plaza in the 1890s. In 1892, German immigrant William Gebhardt developed a dried spice mix known as "chili powder," selling it from his Texas beer garden. The prepared mix could be shipped long distance, allowing "chili" to travel nationwide.[32]

Continuing Displacement

The spread of the United States displaced native people throughout the nineteenth and twentieth centuries. With the loss of land went access to customary foods, traditional food knowledge, and practices. Rationing systems and boardinghouses pushed a commercial Anglo-American diet on communities now disconnected from the ecosystems that had sustained them. Today, Native communities struggle with a legacy of diet-related health impacts. More than 16 percent of American Indians and Alaska Natives have type 2 diabetes, double the rate of the general U.S. population.[33] Many Native communities are updating agricultural traditions to build capital and improve health. For example, before the industrial era, the Mississippi Band of Choctaw Indians traded food from the Great Lakes to the Atlantic. Today, the band manages Choctaw Fresh Produce, a project developed with the USDA to establish farms, run CSAs, teach organic gardening, and produce food for Choctaw-owned businesses.[34]

African American Eating After the Civil War

At the Civil War's end, food supply was an immediate issue for millions of newly freed African Americans. Planters still tried to use food to control and profit from the black population. One strategy was to lease plantation land to former slaves in a tenant system called sharecropping. One-sided contracts controlled choices, prices, and credit, preventing sharecroppers from getting ahead. Tenant farming re-created a devastatingly familiar quasi-slave state. Still, black families found ways to survive. Gardening and raising poultry or hogs limited the need to interact with white merchants. In multigenerational homesteads, younger adults farmed while the elderly supervised children, cooked, and gardened.[35] Rural Southern black families ate "simple meals": bacon and corn cakes flavored with molasses, augmented in season by sweet potatoes, turnips, and collards. In winter, families cut food consumption by up to 30 percent.[36]

Migration offered hope. As the Southern economy collapsed and Jim Crow codes took hold, African Americans left farming in great waves for industrial cities across the North and Midwest. The burgeoning processed food industry offered employment, but bias reigned. In meatpacking plants, "few blacks worked as butchers, a skilled job requiring the use of a knife. Instead, they unloaded trucks, slaughtered the animals, transported intestines, and generally cleaned the plants."[37] Black entrepreneurialism was one response to limited opportunity. Where an individual or group could pull investment capital together, African American cooks opened catering companies and eateries. The black elite saw food behavior as a visible way to counter racist stereotypes. Dining customs migrated from wealthy white households into well-to-do black households, often carried by the "legions of African-Americans [who] served white households as domestic, cooks, and service laborers."[38]

Still, African American leaders debated the merits of joining the "cult of domesticity." Some saw reform as a path to racial uplift, incorporating cooking, nutrition science, and home economics into vocational curricula.[39] But some thinkers rejected white, middle-class moralities, declaring black lives "not bound by either the strictures or the privileges of gender

Figure 2.1. Sharecroppers in the early twentieth century used kitchen gardens as a survival strategy, making up nutritional gaps left by low and irregular wages. (National Archives and Records Administration/U.S. Department of Agriculture Extension and Home Demonstration Activities, 1920–1954)

or age," and promoting the freedom to pursue economic advancement in any profession.[40] W. E. B. Du Bois worried that "training black women in domestic science only served to reinforce the demeaning image of servitude" and disdained the "pseudoprofessionalism" of domestic science, attacking the very idea of a gendered division of labor as fundamentally sexist, an assertion few whites of the time dared to make. In the doctrine of "separate spheres," Du Bois saw an echo of the constraints of slavery: "We cannot abolish the new economic freedom of women. We cannot imprison women again in a home or require them all on pain of death to be nurses and house-keepers."[41]

Character and Caricature

The disproportionate representation of African Americans in professional food labor resulted from constraints on freedom, and it played into stereotypes of an inferiority redeemed by a few special gifts, like culinary skill.[42] At the same time, African American cooks recognized culinary mastery as an avenue to advancement, navigating between prejudice and aspiration. Advertising imagery reinforced the association of African Americans with cooking. Some caricatures were negative depictions experienced by white audiences as comic, while others presented a somewhat "more positive image as an accomplished cook."[43] Marketers played on white nostalgia for the pre–Civil War past, illustrating food packaging with images of old-timey black cooks that "needed no explanation to Victorian eyes."[44] Aunt Jemima, named after a minstrel song, became a brand presence for the Davis Milling Company's demonstrations at the Chicago World's Columbian Exposition in 1893. Seeking an actress to portray Aunt Jemima, the flour company selected Nancy Green, a storyteller and performer who donned the character's headscarf and served thousands of pancakes to fairgoers. Green received a showmanship award for her work at the fair and represented the brand until her death in 1923.[45] Born into slavery, Green built a modern performance career bringing life to its caricatures. Demeaning and cartoonish representations of African Americans remained common through the nadir of race relations in the 1920s and 1930s. By World War II, "faces became more human and more like blacks encountered in everyday life," although still presenting character types dating back to the minstrel era.[46] Until the civil rights movement of the 1960s "gave voice to all those anonymous faces," white Americans mostly saw African American food marketing images as uncomplicated. From the 1950s through the present day, numerous studies have analyzed the semiotics of race in advertising, noting a continuing reliance on stereotypes of African American relationships to food and a tendency to target African Americans with advertising for fast food, an effort characterized by activists as a form of food oppression.[47]

Toward Equality

The Great Migration of the early twentieth century improved African American diets. The quantity and variety of food increased: "Fresh red meat in metropolitan areas could be purchased for about the same price as salted and smoked pork fat, and cornmeal was more expensive than flour."[48] The rural diets migrants had left behind were recalled and embellished in a syncretic African American cuisine that coalesced as blacks from different regions of the South met and mingled in the segregated neighborhoods of industrial cities. Before World War II, most of its components had been "far from prominent on African American tables, even in the rural South." Beans, rice, and chicken were rare. Collard and mustard greens, basic to the "soul food" tradition, were found in only about 25 percent of dietary studies done in twenty African American households in Tuskegee, Alabama, in 1895.[49] In the 1960s, politically conscious black culinarians renamed this cuisine "soul food," a "symbol of black urban culture, self-awareness, and ethnic pride."[50] Activists in the 1970s debated the merits of soul food as opposed to a more West African–derived cuisine, stripped of European and New World influences. Soul food is reinterpreted with each generation; Bryant Terry's 2009 *Vegan Soul Kitchen* presents an "Afro-Vegan" cuisine, amplifying the plant-based foods of the traditional south.

African American cooks in urban settings found ways to turn food into financial power, working as restaurant cooks, waiting tables, and creating home-based food businesses. Eateries were sharply segregated until the 1960s, a fact best illustrated by the fact that a groundbreaking moment in the civil rights movement, the 1960 sit-in in Greensboro, North Carolina, took place at a lunch counter. Eating places were so rarely integrated that a series of travel guides listing restaurants, gas stations, and hotels that would accommodate black travelers was published between 1936 and 1966. Conceived by World War I veteran and postal carrier Victor Green, the Negro Motorist Green Books helped black travelers avoid dangerous or embarrassing situations.[51]

Though African Americans had as long a history in the New World as most European Americans, their forced dispossession during slavery, followed by mass migrations and new community formation, mirrored some of the displacement that defined the experiences of the nation's immigrants. Their foodways, too, featured stories of adaptation, survival, and resilience.

Food Beyond the Golden Door: Eating and Immigration

Immigration can be thought of as continuous in American history, but it hit a peak between 1860 and 1920, when twenty-eight million immigrants, drawn by seemingly limitless work opportunities in the industrial economy, flooded into the United States. Food scarcity in countries of origin has often contributed to the push-pull effect that powers immigration. Wallach notes the irony that many immigrants "had reasonable fears about their ability to continue feeding themselves in their countries of origin,"[52] but they brought with them an intangible bounty of "knowledge of elaborate food traditions that long predated the founding of the United States."[53] Across past and present, immigrants have used that knowledge in their reinventions of American cuisine.

Melting Pot—or Not?

In 1908, immigrant playwright Israel Zangwill titled a new play *The Melting Pot*. Often misunderstood as a stew pot, Zangwill's original analogy referred to metals in a foundry, with immigrants being a different type of metal and America "God's crucible, where all the races of Europe are melting and re-forming."[54] Ethnic and national affiliations were impurities to be purged, creating a wholly new American identity. For generations, historians have critiqued this metaphor, many offering food-related replacements, such as the "salad bowl" (in which components mix but retain their individual identities) or "tomato soup" (in which added ingredients enhance the tomato without altering its basic character).[55] None truly address the complexity of interchange between immigrants and the food cultures they interacted with in America. Immigrant foodways were reshaped, and Americans appropriated and absorbed incoming ideas, offering yet a different food matrix to the next arrivals. No cultural or ethnic cuisine in the United States—not even the mainstream Anglo-American one—would remain unchanged.

Three processes ensue from encounters between food cultures, put in motion as people confront, adapt, and integrate new food ideas:

- Exploration, including awareness, curiosity, and assessment
- Negotiation, including resistance and the formation of gustatory identities
- Assimilation, including experimentation, adoption, appropriation, and adaptation

Exploration

When two food cultures meet, each explores the other's food. Anthropologist Shannon Lee Dawdy, in a study of colonial Louisiana, identifies diplomatic exchanges as a frequent venue for first food encounters, noting that "the politeness required of reciprocal hospitality provided a catalyst for the exchange of food ideas."[56] Wallach describes the exploratory phase as one characterized by twin responses of curiosity and xenophobia, with assessments based on food values already encoded in each culture.[57]

Finding Familiar Food

The first shared food experience many immigrants have is displacement. Though willing to accept tremendous lifestyle changes, immigrants have generally been unwilling to abandon familiar foods. In new environments, immigrants used a common set of strategies to find food they could accept:

- Experimenting with substitutions
- Expanding home food production
- Developing a culturally specific food supply

Substitution

Substituting a traditional food with an American analogue was one way to maintain a semblance of the familiar. Laura Schenone's memoir *The Lost Ravioli Recipes of Hoboken: A Search for Food and Family* illustrates one example of this flexible sourcing. Tracing the history of a family ravioli recipe, Schenone investigates its presumably Italian origins, discovering that her ancestors swapped out Genoese ingredients for Philadelphia cream cheese and American ground beef.[58] The popularity of cream cheese in America is partly due to this substitution by immigrants from dairying cultures. Lithuanian immigrant Isaac Breghstein arrived in 1882 and opened a dairy, making traditional farmer's cheese and selling it to Jewish markets. He renamed the business Breakstone's, modifying and mellowing his formula. Cream cheese became the basis for American-style cheesecake, once a holiday food associated with Shavuot, a Jewish spring celebration.[59]

Home Production

In many cultures, professionals usually made staples like bread, pickles, cured meats, and dairy products. Separated from that infrastructure, immigrants often had to start making these foods at home. German and Eastern European housewives scoured crockery each fall to prepare sauerkraut, an important source of nutrients.[60] Jewish housewives in city tenements turned patches of dirt behind their buildings into goose farms to ensure a supply of goose fat, since dietary restrictions prevented them from using butter.[61] Italian immigrants grew traditional herbs in back lots, window boxes, and on fire escapes.[62]

Ethnic Entrepreneurs

Some immigrants found a way to make a living by selling culturally specific food. They understood cultural preferences, and they had the language skills to build distribution networks. Street peddling was "the fallback occupation of new immigrants. It required little capital, no special work skills, and scant knowledge of English. All immigrants needed were a basket and a few dollars to invest."[63] Italian pushcart vendors sold vegetables Anglo-Americans found foreign—"cow peas, cucumbers, celery (distinct from American celery), fennel, peppers, tomatoes, eggplant, onion, garlic, chickweed, beet tops, lettuce."[64] In Louisiana, citrus trade linked Palermo, Italy, with the port of New Orleans. Fifty thousand Sicilians arrived between 1880 and 1910. Soon they were selling oranges and lemons from carts or setting up wholesale operations for "kin or countrymen, who peddled the produce in the neighborhoods or sold it from stalls in the French Market."[65] Giuseppe Uddo, founder of Progresso Foods, started his business delivering cheese, olives, and oil by horse cart to Italian customers in New Orleans.[66]

In multiethnic areas, cultural groups often dominated specific food trades. Germans often worked as grocers, butchers, and bakers; the ring-shaped kranzkuchen morphed into the American "coffee cake."[67] Germans also established the delicatessen. Selling "a limited stock of sausages, cheeses and sweets," these stores were welcomed by working people of all backgrounds who appreciated ready-to-eat suppers. Jewish food retailers adapted the delicatessen, and their brisket, pastrami, and cold salads migrated beyond the Jewish community, becoming comfort foods for other Americans. Joel Russ, a Jewish immigrant from Spain, sold groceries from a horse and wagon before opening a Manhattan store. Now called Russ and Daughters, the legendary store still deals in lox, pickles, and deli meats.[68]

Italian immigrants who had fled farming under feudal conditions transformed the produce industry as growers, packers, and shippers. By 1860, California's fields were home to the largest concentration of Italians in the United States. These *giardinieri* grew rosemary, fennel, and oregano, popularized the zucchini, and introduced the plum tomato. Their farms generated so much surplus that they needed wider markets, and Italian manufacturing and distribution entrepreneurs stepped in. One of them was Marco Fontana, a produce clerk. Noticing how many bruised vegetables were thrown away, Fontana began canning them, eventually employing more than a thousand Italian women at a factory that grew into the Del Monte Corporation.[69] On the East Coast, too, Italian immigrants specialized in truck farming, supplying urban markets. In 1900, two hundred and sixty Italian families in Vineland, New Jersey, raised "garlic, peppers, cauliflower, cabbage, beets, fennel, cardoons (a relative of artichoke), chestnuts, figs, plums, and ten varieties of grapes" for fellow immigrants in Philadelphia, Baltimore, and New York.[70]

Tens of thousands of Chinese immigrants, drawn by mine and railroad labor, made their way to California in the mid-nineteenth century. Chinese importers ordered shiploads of "oranges, dried oysters, mushrooms, dried bean curd, bamboo shoots, duck eggs, sausages [and] ginger" to sell to these immigrants, and Chinese food producers supplied the network with chicken, pork, duck, and *choy*—cabbages, mustard greens, and spring onions.[71] Chinese immigrants also found success opening restaurants. Adventurous white customers found their soups, noodle dishes, and dumplings fascinatingly different and "exceedingly palatable." Restaurateurs tweaked menus to please Western palates, creating Chinese American hybrids like "egg foo young, shrimp fried rice, spareribs and sweet and sour pork."[72]

In many cities, restaurants were outgrowths of specialty stores. In the 1880s, New York City Italian restaurants were "hidden within the Italian groceries . . . the provisions lined up on one half of the room, the other half set aside for tables."[73] Restaurants were often opened to feed single male immigrants. Having rarely cooked at home, they were hard pressed to feed themselves even if they could find familiar foods. Oyangen relates the tale of Prussian immigrant Theodor Van Dreveldt, who in the winter of 1848 survived on a "mixture of flour, water, and fat" until he became sick. Van Drevelt decided that in moving to America without a wife, he "had purchased many privations for a great deal of money," and he made plans to return to Europe.[74] For those who stayed, ethnic restaurants offered a taste of home—and some literally were homes. A 1930s American Writers Project article describes restaurants in Barre, Vermont, where northern Italians immigrated in the 1880s to work in the granite industry. Some died early, leaving widows who "turned for support to the art they knew best, cooking." Fifty homes in Barre doubled as restaurants, including that of Maria Stefani, where a daughter served customers baskets of "long golden Italian loaves, sliced, and revealing generous centers of spongy white," followed by prosciutto, salami, pickled veal, celery, ripe olives, and "the favorite antipasto, a savory achievement incorporating mushrooms, pearl onions, tuna, anchovies, broccoli—all permeated and tinctured with a tangy red sauce." The meal culminated with spaghetti and ravioli with hand-grated Parmesan.[75]

After World War II, Greek immigrants bought cafeterias and diners from earlier Irish, German, or Jewish operators selling out of that demanding business. Twentieth-century

Lebanese and Syrian immigration brought Arab and Mediterranean influences into the United States, introducing yogurt, hummus, and other foods. Chinese American communities expanded; America's Chinatowns became pan-Asian capitals where multiple languages and foodways mingled. Indian and Bangladeshi immigrants arrived in the 1960s and 1970s as England, formerly a popular destination, enacted stricter immigration limits. Their restaurants enjoyed crossover appeal from Americans broadening their global awareness.[76]

Xenophobia

America's reception of new cuisines was not always positive. Foodways were contaminated by association, as the foods of people assigned lower social status took on lower status themselves. Occasionally, Americans feared that literal contamination was spreading through immigrants' participation in food manufacturing. In the late nineteenth-century Northeast, Italian and Polish women in candy manufacturing often brought piecework home, enlisting families to help wrap candy and pack boxes. Moralizers declared these candies "a threat to public safety," possibly "contaminated by the same germs that flourished in her tenement home."[77] The rejection was, in essence, a rejection of immigrants' inclusion in the American mainstream. As Oyangen observes, "If eating food implies acceptance of those who cook and serve it, rejecting someone's food and foodways implies the opposite."[78] Immigrant cuisines have often been thought of as unsafe and repellent. A common motif was concern about taboo ingredients, such as vermin or pets; those suspicions have been levied against various groups whose food practices were obscure to the dominant culture. A comic song of the late nineteenth century, "Johnny Vorbeck,"[79] tells the story of a German immigrant whose mechanical sausage maker secretly grinds up "pussy cats and long-tailed rats," until one night, while trying to fix the machine, he falls into it and comes out as sausage himself. The song expresses both a satirical commentary on the mechanization of meat production and a fundamental distrust of one immigrant community.

Some food encounters disoriented in welcome ways. People entering the United States through Ellis Island had a first taste of America when, on barges carrying them to the island, "each passenger was handed a cup of cider and a small round pie, the quintessential fast food of turn-of-the-century America." In Ellis Island cafeterias, travelers were offered "pork and beans, beef hash, corned beef with cabbage and potatoes, Yankee pot roast, and boiled mutton with brown gravy." The menu introduced American tastes: bland, heavy on meat and starch, rich with sugar and dairy.[80] New immigrants allowed curiosity—and hunger—to lead their experimentation with American food.

Negotiation

Immigrants and Americans negotiated over the introduction of food ideas. The unspoken goal was to determine whether, in the new cultural context, traditional cultural foodways should be celebrated, modified, or abandoned.

Gustatory Identity

One might think transplantation would dilute traditional cuisines. In fact, they often intensified. In America, traditional diets were no longer the cultural default but markers of belonging to an ethnic community. Particularities of diet stood out to outsiders, and they also took on stronger valence for insiders. Kurt Oyangen describes Scandinavian immigrants who were embarrassed that their foodways identified them as foreign; at the same time, they found their foods to be a comfort, an assertion of identity, and a source of solidarity. Discussing how immigrants "both resisted and participated in their own displacement from old food habits, trying to find an acceptable combination of tradition, acculturation, and innovation," Oyangen identifies three processes that engaged them. *Displacement* refers to the disorientation of new environments, the "environmental and social conditions that made reproducing the cultural practices of a different place inconvenient, imprudent, or impossible." *Placemaking* "resulted from the effort to read the new environment, identifying novel foods as well as correlates to traditional cuisines, and creating personal ties to the landscape." *Gustatory identity* developed as immigrants began to "define their identities by contrasting their food habits with the food habits of others." Responding to displacement through placemaking and the construction of gustatory identity, new immigrants asserted their belonging to, and ownership of, new places and identities.[81]

Reform and Rejection

At the turn of the twentieth century, reformers and domestic scientists worried that failure to adopt an American diet indicated a dangerous unwillingness to assimilate. Activists visited immigrants' homes, investigated their lunch pails, and added up household food spending. Entire bodies of time-honored practice came in for review. Jewish families were counseled to avoid salami and pickles as "bad for the digestive system."[82] The Italian "salad habit" raised concern about the difficulty of digesting raw vegetables.[83] Reformers promoted middle-class eating: bland, mild foods in separate portions. In cooking schools, settlement houses, and public schools, they taught students how to "make toast and brew coffee . . . boil oatmeal, rice, and potatoes . . . make pea soup, mutton stew, creamed codfish, biscuits and gingerbread." Jane Zeigelman evaluates cooking-reform classes as "only a modest success" for the simple reason that most immigrants "already knew how to cook"—just not to the tastes of middle-class reformers, whose palates must have seemed frankly numb.[84] Italian Americans were among the most recalcitrant. In reformers' eyes, profligate Italian Americans were frittering away money on expensive imports. Italians only clutched their preferences more tightly; their new access to "once scarce and coveted ingredients had transformed them into fiercely proud American eaters."[85]

Newcomers gave, as well as received, dietary critique. Oyangen relates the 1894 reaction of Danish immigrant Niels Hansen to the rich Midwestern diet: initially, shock that children were allowed to indulge in "roast and cake, everyday," gradually giving way to an appreciation of American white bread, butter, and meats. Meanwhile, Caja Munch, a Norwegian housewife in the Midwest, maintained a traditional diet of meatballs, cabbage, soups, and gravy, dreading the "dry wheat loaves" she found inferior to Norwegian rye and looking down on the "Yankee habit of having 'pork, coffee, and pie morning, noon, and evening.'"[86] Each individual negotiated with American foodways but arrived at differing stances.

Adapting to Abundance

The sheer abundance of food in America reshaped cultural cuisines, sometimes amplifying Old World foodways into richer versions of themselves. The evolving cuisine of Italian American and Irish American communities, both pulled to America largely by food insecurity in their countries of origin, offer contrasting case studies. Wallach characterizes most of the four million Italians who arrived between 1880 and 1920 as peasants fleeing hunger and poverty in a homeland where they rarely enjoyed pasta, meats, and cheese. Italians in America rejoiced in "a diet that was unimaginably luxurious by working-class Italian standards."[87] The once-rare feast day became a regular event, "a nightly celebration of the triumph over hunger."

> By the 1920s, a midweek dinner in a working-class Italian kitchen included soup, then pasta, followed by meat and a salad. At the end of the week, Italian families sat down to a banquet of stunning extravagance. Sunday supper began in the early afternoon with an antipasto of cheese, salami, ham, and anchovies. Appetites now fully awake, the family moved through multiple courses, leading them to the heart of the feast. If the family were Sicilian, that might include a ragu made from marrow bones, chicken, pork sausage, and meatballs, stewed veal and peppers, and braciole, a thin filet of pounded beef or pork wrapped around a stuffing of cheese, bread crumbs, parsley, pine nuts, and raisins.[88]

These exuberant food expressions were associated with Italian heritage, though they really reflected an explosion of purchasing power and a conflation of regional and festival traditions with everyday eating under conditions occurring only in the Italian diaspora, not in Italy itself.

Irish Americans were also staggered by abundance, but they did not develop as strong a gustatory identity, instead adopting and assimilating Anglo-American foodways. Food was the impetus for Irish people to emigrate from a land terrorized by famine. In their book *Empires of Food*, Evan D. G. Fraser and Andrew Rimas describe ancient Irish pastures as "the lushest in Europe," rich in beef, milk, butter, and cheese, complemented by seafood, produce, and grain. English colonizers confiscated much of this bounty, exporting food to England, where Irish beef fueled the Industrial Revolution. Irish peasants increasingly depended on potatoes, a reliable crop that "grew well in the wet Irish soil and yielded more vitamins and protein than corn, wheat, or oats." Each person ate seven to twelve pounds a day, complemented sporadically by bacon, buttermilk, greens, and oats.[89] In 1845, an invasive fungus arrived in a seed shipment from New England, turning potato plants into "black sludge" overnight.[90] Nearly a quarter of Irish people died of famine-related causes; a million survivors departed, many for the United States.[91] They arrived with "skeletal" food traditions, amounting to "a single carbohydrate and a handful of condiments."[92] Compared to other immigrants, they had little to preserve. Immigrating allowed the Irish to reintegrate traditional fare lost through colonization: butter, cream, produce, wheat, and meat.

Many food customs now thought of as Irish American originated in Anglo-American households, borne back to Irish families by women working in domestic service. Irish servants dominated domestic service during the late nineteenth century, living in intimacy with their employers even though they were often despised as ignorant and dirty and mocked for cooking "blackened steaks, scorched coffee, gummy puddings, [and] leaden pastries."[93] As Ziegelman points out, their struggles resulted largely from lack of experience; famine and poverty limited their culinary repertoire. Irish cooks "received a crash course" in American foodways from their time in service and applied them in their own family kitchens. Due to these influences from servitude, their ability to speak English, and the paucity of food traditions they brought with them, the Irish never developed a "parallel universe" of ethnic culinary enclaves.[94]

Assimilation

The tensions of negotiation relax into assimilation, as the initial strangeness of others' foodways is gradually overriden. The lasting legacies of introduced cuisines are their eventual adoption and adaptation by others. In "a shadow food economy," nineteenth-century tenement neighbors shared food frequently; "an Italian housewife fed minestrone to the Irish kids who lived on the second floor, while Russians brought honey cake to the old Slovak lady across the airshaft."[95] Regional cuisines, distinct in the old country, blurred and elided as people from different regions shopped at the same food stalls and import grocers. In Germany, every community had its own local sausage and baked desserts like jelly doughnuts, stollen, or gingerbread.[96] In the German neighborhoods of the United States, these traditions mingled, losing associations with specific villages and becoming known simply as "German."[97] Native-born Americans wandered into ethnic enclaves, where restaurants "served as culinary classrooms."[98] By the mid-twentieth century, Americans' awareness of the wider world sparked an interest in culinary novelty. Urban centers became culinary bazaars in which immigrants and longtime citizens sampled the many options before them, mixing and mingling traditions.

The American Potluck

No one ever succeeded in "melting down" Americans and their varied cuisines. The best metaphor for America's polyglot and ever-evolving food culture is not a melting pot but a potluck supper. That collaborative and unpredictable feast, staple of the church supper, barn raising, and community festival, appears across American history. Each attendee brings his or her own dish, which represents some combination of history, taste, creativity, and what is available, but each diner samples many others—and often asks for the recipe. Cultural omnivorousness may be the most American component of our eating habits.[99] Though some critics deplore the improvisational, disorganized, and spontaneous disassembling and reassembling of foodways in America, calling it incoherent, others celebrate the creative chaos. Cyclical exploration, negotiation, and assimilation give American cuisine its inexhaustible energy.

Best Practices: Interpreting Food, Race, and Ethnicity

- Be inclusive. Use census and other population data to understand who was present within the scope of your interpretation, and represent them in discussions, exhibits, and live activities.
- Develop culturally specific interpretations with the participation and collaboration of descendant communities and related communities. Seek support from community organizations, culturally linked food businesses, and knowledge-bearing individuals.
- Explore the surrounding environment for evidence of past foodways—"walk the land," as Michael Twitty puts it. Work with botanists, biologists, foragers, and other experts to identify the flora and fauna of your region, reconstructing wild and cultivated foodscapes of the past to discover how they may have been reshaped and adapted by newcomers.
- Use specific stories and evidence to combat misperceptions and stereotypes of ethnic and racial communities.
- Interpret foodways and the communities that practiced them as constantly changing, not static replications of culinary practice from one generation to the next. Explore both continuity and change, and look for incidences of individual agency.
- When interpreting settlers, colonists, migrants, and immigrants, research foodways of the specific locality, region, and cultural context from which they originated. What habits, tastes, preferences, and prejudices did they bring with them? How did they modify and add to them once resettled?
- Be aware that Eurocentric notions of timelines and the evidentiary record are not the only relevant knowledge when it comes to many communities. Be open to exploring other ways of knowing, such as tribal oral histories and cosmologies.
- Include recent history. The newly introduced immigrant cuisines of the 1960s, 1970s, and 1980s are now thoroughly embedded in American culinary history. Similarly, Angolan, Ethiopian, Vietnamese, Guatemalan, and other new cuisines making inroads today will have their own future impact. Look at food stories thematically, relating the experiences and activities of newer immigrants to older ones.

Mama's in the Kitchen: Food and Gender

If asked about gender roles and food in history, many Americans might venture something like this: men hunt, fish, and grow food; women work in the kitchen. Simple statements like these reveal deeply embedded assumptions about food and gender. Indeed, maleness and femaleness have been the main variable determining one's relationship with food, but underneath that statement lays a greater complexity.

Most preindustrial societies used gender to assign food labor. Women's responsibilities tended to center near home sites and focus on food processing, while men's involved more wide-ranging, public elements of food production. But that rubric underemphasizes the interdependence of their labor. Archaeologist Nicole Waguespack, examining the eating patterns of Paleoindian communities at Clovis, found that although game hunting and wild plant gathering were both essential food production activities, hunting left more visible residue in the archaeological record. Bones and stone tools, slow to degrade, speak more clearly than sinew, reed, bark, and leather, the perishable materials used for food gathering. Her analysis suggests that hunting and foraging were deeply interdependent strategies. Women's production made the critical difference to survival when game was scarce.[100] Gender also played a role in transitions to settled cultivation. Archaeologists Barbara Roth and Andrea Freeman argue that women initiated the conversion from foraging to maize agriculture in the Southwest. They theorize that maize was planted in a seasonal niche between wild saguaro collecting and the onset of summer rains, and was harvested after the gathering of mesquite beans. Maize fit into existing food production patterns, giving women the "flexibility to experiment with and incorporate new plant resources into the subsistence base."[101]

European Divisions of Labor

Europeans brought their own gendered patterns of food labor to their settlements. Men took on crop work, butchering, herding, and fishing. Women tended gardens; kept poultry, cows, and pigs; and supervised preservation and cooking. However, their work was not sharply separated. In *A Midwife's Tale: The Life of Martha Ballard, Based on Her Diary, 1785–1812*, historian Laurel Thatcher Ulrich reconstructs the household economy of Martha Ballard and her husband, demonstrating that both were instrumental in managing the food supply. Ulrich's work illuminates what historians have termed the family labor system, a pattern in which married couples with children used their household resources to generate income. As Wallach describes it,

> men played an active and highly visible role in the preparations necessary before cooking could begin. They grew the wheat that was transformed into bread. They gathered fuel necessary to keep the hearth heated . . . the men in the family crafted many of the items used in the kitchen, such as the wooden trenchers that held the prepared food. They cared for and slaughtered the animals that found their way into the family's cooking pots. Men and women worked in close proximity and in collaborative ways to make sure that the members of the household would have enough to eat.[102]

Women also brought food production equipment to their households with dowries, endowing them with the means of subsistence. Historian Jane C. Nylander describes how one New Hampshire man outfitted his five daughters. For the wedding of his oldest in 1762, he gathered "pewter plates and platters . . . a frying pan, a kettle, a teapot, tea cups . . . a dozen plates . . . nutmeg, tea, molasses and rum." All the daughters received earthenware, punch bowls, tin and wooden wares, bread pans, milk pails, a butter churn, spoons, and knives.

Each also got a cow, which could be the basis of a reliable revenue stream.[103] Not all families could outfit their daughters so well; historian Jack Larkin describes families of the same era who had "only one article to cook with, a dish-kettle."[104]

Remaking Marketing and Mealtime

The shift to manufacturing dismantled the collaborative family labor system almost before society could recognize the repercussions of removing a laborer from the household. Many of today's gendered expectations about food labor date from this era. With industrialization, men, older boys, and single women took cash-paying work, while married women, the elderly, and young children remained at home. A cultural ideal emerged to assign women the expanded role of companion, nurturer, and moral guide. Historians have termed this complex of values, emerging by the 1820s, the *cult of domesticity*, codified in the "doctrine of separate spheres" for men and women.[105] Women's labor, once practical and productive, now became largely emotional; they were to create peaceful, comfortable homes to refresh and reenergize wage earners. Reverence for the domestic was a two-edged sword. Housekeeping tasks were elevated to near sacraments, but housework "lost its status as a productive activity more or less equal with men's productive activities."[106] Industrialization also shifted women from producer to consumer. The cult of domesticity amplified the importance of discriminating product selection and menu planning. In preindustrial economies, men often did food shopping, but by 1850 marketing was clearly incompatible with business schedules. Women took on the shopping, a public activity that cohered with domestic values. They were now were expected to develop a "sophisticated knowledge" of ingredients, differentiating between products, alert to the nuances of status and quality.[107]

Industrial-era lifestyles bifurcated the daily routines of men and women, reformatting the cadence and structure of meals. The biggest change was the midday meal. In preindustrial society, calories were concentrated at midday, complemented by a very light breakfast—toast, porridge, or leftover cold meat—and a light "supper."[108] The main meal of the day, hot and substantial, was "dinner," served around noon for laborers, or as late as 3:00 or 4:00 p.m. in elite homes. Under industrialization, most families were unable to continue this pattern. The midday meal, once a family occasion, was polarized into a single-sex one. Middle-class women repurposed the meal as "luncheon," an occasion to gather with other unoccupied women,[109] opening a space in which middle-class women's political identities flourished. Luncheons and teas allowed women to express ideas among themselves, feeding women's activism in social reform—abolition, suffrage, improving conditions for prisoners, the poor, and immigrants. The activist organizations and charitable experiments they developed served as prototypes for programs later enfolded into government and industrial practice. Men of all classes now ate dinner in the company of other men. The managerial class enjoyed a growing number of restaurants, while working-class men carried "lunch" pails and ate on the job site. Working women also toted food to work, but, even there, they often felt the impetus to re-create a semblance of home dining. Textile worker Ora Pelletier recalled how in the 1920s, she and her fellow workers used their factory space for shared sit-down lunches. "In a corner [of the sink room] was a great big, long sink. It always had a little water in it, and there was a steam pipe going into the water, so it was boiling hot. We'd bring soup, cans of corn, cans of tomatoes, and heat them in there for our meal."[110]

Domestic Service

Women comprised the majority of domestic servants. Beliefs about their limitations walled off other fields, but cooking, cleaning, childcare, and nursing fell squarely within women's sphere. For most of the nineteenth century, hiring at least a cook and maid was within reach of the middle class. The more affluent could add additional maids, housekeepers to take on the supervisory burden, and perhaps a butler for serving. The presence of a male servant in the dining room was in itself a statement of wealth, since men earned more by default.[111] Domestic servants usually received room and board, often of better quality than they might have been able to find if paying out of pocket. But for many, the pressures of service were harder to bear than those of the factory floor. Servants were subject to their employers' whims, personalities, and habits, and sometimes they were at risk of sexual harassment. White women began opting out by the late nineteenth century, causing a shortage known as "the servant problem." They left for jobs in retail, manufacturing, or clerical work. Black women, barred from those opportunities by discrimination, increasingly entered domestic labor, raising standards for domestic employment in the process. Because more black women were married and had children, they negotiated "nonresident domestic service" on a "take-it-or-leave-it basis," and shorthanded employers accepted.[112] By 1930, black women represented almost half of the women in domestic service nationwide. Eventually, home technology and changing definitions of "middle class" combined to reduce the demand for servants.

Gendered Tastes

Gender also dictated what people should eat. Male and female eating codes flourished in the nineteenth century. As Laura Shapiro describes in *Perfection Salad: Women and Cooking at the Turn of the Century*, middle-class women's food was expected to be dainty, demure, sweet, and delicate, reflecting ideals for the diners' behavior. Women were thought to have naturally weak appetites, meaning that food had to be small, brightly colored, or sweet to attract their interest. A typical early twentieth-century luncheon menu featured four spears of asparagus on a lettuce leaf, a small tomato stuffed with chopped celery, "tiny parsley biscuits," and "lime and cherry sherbet with pink tea cookies." Men, at the opposite extreme, embraced "large meals of meat, stews, breads, and potatoes." Steakhouses and chophouses became business haunts, reflecting a growing association between maleness and meat. Now distant from preindustrial roles as hunters and home butchers, men identified meat as more symbolic than ever before, "culturally linked to power and strength."[113]

European-style restaurants and steakhouses had hired only men. In 1929, Howard Johnson insisted that only women would wait tables in his new restaurant chain, calling up associations of maternal care. Johnson's restaurants were part of a trend toward "home" cooking, serving dishes becoming rarer as fewer people had time for "slow-cooked dinners, cookies baked from scratch, and homemade bread." Historian Samantha Barbas describes how restaurateurs created "surrogate homes" that aimed to "restore to the middle class the old-fashioned domesticity that urbanization, modernization, and culinary standardization had stolen away."[114] Women were indeed cooking less. Manufacturers had been fine-tuning food to streamline cooking. Barbas reports that in 1890, most households baked their own bread, but by the 1920s, they purchased 55–70 percent of it prebaked. Spending on canned goods increased nearly ten times from 1909 to 1929. Women experienced these changes as "an important step forward," but despite labor-saving devices and convenience foods, they were spending more time on housework.[115] In 1926, women reported spending an average of twenty-three hours a week preparing food; by 1929, this had increased to twenty-six hours. More were also working outside the home and looking to inexpensive restaurants for some relief. In 1910, Barbas reports, women made up fewer than 20 percent of restaurant diners, but by 1926 they represented almost 60 percent.[116] Still, women who juggled office or factory life with home chores were indicted for "laziness and selfishness, rather than industriousness." Advice columnists lectured women that "can opener cuisine" and "delicatessen dinners" drove husbands to adultery.[117]

Women on the Home Front

During World Wars I and II, women found themselves in a culinary battle zone. In World War I, they were asked to plan menus around Meatless Mondays and Wheatless Wednesdays, to refrain from hoarding, and to join the Women's Land Army (WLA), an agricultural labor force created to relieve men for military service. The YWCA, women's colleges, and garden clubs recruited more than twenty thousand young women for the WLA, most with no prior experience of farming. After a brief training, these "farmerettes" were deemed "as capable as men workers" and sent into fields.[118] The concept returned in World War II. Between April 1940 and July 1942, as more than two million men left farms to join the military, women's groups mobilized to revive the WLA. By June 1943, three million women were working on farms—27 percent of the agricultural labor force. At war's end, despite a massive decrease in the on-farm population, food production had increased by 32 percent.[119]

Propaganda cast women as "domestic soldiers who could combat the enemy from the safety of their own kitchens."[120] Women were being recruited into defense industry positions normally restricted to men, making some Americans feel uncomfortable with sudden changes to ideas about work and gender. To muffle this concern, propaganda featured women in kitchens, with children, cheerfully managing the gardening, rationing, and preserving, doing what the government asked of them. Home canning was seen as "a properly feminine way to aid in the war effort." Most women had left preserving a generation or so behind them in favor of commercial canned goods, so they needed direct instruction. That demanded leisure time and money for equipment, leaving out working-class women. Canning became more symbolic than practical, "a middle-class means for demonstrating food piety and patriotism."[121]

Figure 2.2. Members of the Women's Land Army, known as "farmerettes," march in a World War I–era parade, carrying signs reading "We Carry Hoes, They Fight Foes" and "Bonds Buy Bullets and Beans—We Raise Beans, You Buy Bonds." ("Farmerettes," Library of Congress/Bain News Service Collection, n.d.)

Reshaping Roles

When men returned from World War II, leaders feared a labor glut and widespread unemployment. Federal policies and social pressure pushed women to return to their prewar sphere, the home and kitchen. Women who did so found themselves cast back into the nineteenth-century role of cook and nurturer—this time, with a dizzying set of new imperatives. Bombarded with commercial images of the happy housewife, who, with the help of appliances and processed foods, could easily live up to domestic ideals, women once again took on the responsibility to plan, cook, serve, and clean up from meals. Some embraced the role, while others discovered in it a tension not easily resolved. As Wallach observes, the idealized housewife archetype was "particularly burdensome to those whose real lives deviated the most from those images: members of ethnic and racial minorities, gays and lesbians, unmarried people, and the working poor."[122] Even the middle-class women who were targets of this rhetoric struggled with expectations. A seminal work of the women's movement, *The Feminine Mystique*, had its inception in Betty Friedan's sense of emptiness in this prescribed role.

Meanwhile, the number of women working outside the home continued to rise. Women made up 32 percent of the wage labor force by 1957, a higher percentage than during World War II. The money they earned, Wallach notes, made it possible for many to purchase the labor-saving devices and branded foods that defined the middle-class lifestyle.[123]

But working women had less time to meet the demands of home life—which kept rising, as new kitchen technology translated to higher standards for cooking.[124] The food industry offered a solution: more convenience foods. Frozen TV dinners, fish sticks, frozen orange juices, Spam, cake mixes, and boxed crackers were always ready in a flash. But the idea of investing eating with so little time and sentiment did not jibe with expectations for women as nurturers. Magazines and food packages began to feature recipes that added complexity back into convenience foods. By combining several different soups, canned fruits, sauces or other products into a new casserole or salad, Wallach observes, "Mrs. Consumer could be creative and add her own personal touch to the items . . . by combining various ingredients the illusion of cooking just as previous generations had done could still be preserved."[125]

Men as Cooks

With women taking on so much food labor, where were the men? Often, in the backyard. Postwar housing styles incorporated an ideal of indoor-outdoor living. The backyard barbecue became a form of entertainment cooking by the 1950s, with men as the grillmasters. The association of men with outdoor cooking, especially meat, is an enduring motif with long historical roots. Sheila Phipps asserts that "the cultural connection between masculinity and meat simultaneously elevates the status of both subjects."[126] Today's food press often observes that professional cooks, especially restaurant chefs, are predominantly men, while women still do most domestic cooking. Historical evidence suggests a greater nuance. Both men and women cooked professionally, as is made obvious by the cooking schools, boardinghouses, and institutional kitchens where women have presided. But they cooked in different settings and for different diners. Women cooking professionally have been best accepted in settings that re-created the atmosphere of family, reinforcing beliefs that even women being paid to cook should not stray too far from their sphere. "Mom and pop" restaurants, school and hospital kitchens, and boardinghouses were close analogues to home settings. Men, meanwhile, specialized in environments seen as very different from home. The overall pattern looks something like this:

Men cook	Women cook
For other men in work settings	In domestic and family-like environments
In single-gender (male) settings	For mixed-gender groups
In extreme conditions	In controlled conditions
With extreme or expensive foods	With everyday foods
As performance	As instruction

Occupational Cooking

The gender-segregated nature of most manual labor meant that women were simply not around to cook; men had no choice but to fill the role. On schooners and whaleships, in mining and railroad camps, men cooked for one another. Male cooks were seen as somewhat exceptional; the United States did not share Europe's history of "professionalized cooks and court cuisine," making cooking such a feminized activity that the task of working with food was often assigned to categories of men who, like women, were accorded lower status: African Americans, immigrants, the very young or old.[127] Lumber camps were one such all-male setting. Teenage boys and young men were drawn to camp kitchens "by the mystique of logging, the promise of warm, indoor work, and, more often, the opportunity to secure steady employment at decent pay." These "flunkies," a breed apart from the skilled workers they cooked for, "waited on the lumberjacks or crews, washed dishes, and cleaned tables and floors."[128]

Military units posed a special problem. On naval ships, cooks occupied specific positions in a hierarchy, but in land armies, food was almost an afterthought. Regulations in 1825 specified that the army would hire a cook for each regiment, but it provided no training or directives. The Civil War was a pivotal point. Soldiers were mustered in camps in larger units than ever before. Few recruits had food preparation skills. One reporter visited a Union unit in which cooking chores rotated among members of a mess group, and where

> he could hardly stifle a laugh at the sight of six-foot-tall young men struggling to figure out a coffee grinder that they had likely seen their mothers operate effortlessly for years . . . often breaking into unbecoming profanity when the mill slipped from their grasp and all their precious little store of grounds fell into the dirt. It proved more hilarious yet to stand beside the fires and watch the neophytes try to figure out what was supposed to happen to all the stuff they had thrown into the cauldrons and pans, and their chagrin at the result. "I saw the cook, his face beaming like the coals, the perspiration streaming down his cheeks, watching a huge fat mass of salt junk [pork] bubble up and down in the great pot." The cook kept looking at his watch to assess how long the congealing blob of pork had been cooking and then looking up at the sky, scratching his head, and muttering under his breath that he wondered "if the d----d thing was done yet."[129]

Union soldiers accepted the help of the U.S. Sanitary Commission, which served food in camps and on the battlefield. But this help was spotty and insufficient, driving James Sanderson, a sanitary volunteer and professional hotelier, to offer his hospitality expertise. In 1861, he proposed to the War Department that

> a "respectable minority" in each company be expertly trained in the essential basics of cooking. For every 100-man company, the skilled cook would be appointed two privates; one position would be permanent and the other would rotate among the men of the company. The skilled cook would be given the rank of "Cook Major" and receive a monthly salary of $50. It would be the Cook Major's responsibility to ration the food, prepare it, and delegate tasks to the company cooks.

Sanderson was commissioned to reorganize the army food service, and he wrote its first cookbook, *Camp Fires and Camp Cooking; or Culinary Hints for the Soldier*.[130] Sanderson included a "Cook's Creed" praising cleanliness and sharing words of wisdom like "Beans, badly boiled, kill more than bullets."[131] The food-supply failures of the Civil War convinced the reunited military to take feeding the troops seriously. Because "no officer could possibly come out of the conflict without the endless complaints of the men over their meals echoing

Figure 2.3. An army cook contemplates the day's victuals near City Point, Virginia. The kettles and tripods he is cooking on were not widely available before James Sanderson called attention to the need for special training and provisioning for military cooks. Standard fare for soldiers was boiled salt pork or beef, beans, and cornbread or hardtack. (Library of Congress/Photograph from the main eastern theater of war, the siege of Petersburg, June 1864–April 1865)

in his memory,"[132] the War Department undertook serious plans for provisioning, producing the 1879 *Manual for Army Cooks* that remained standard for decades.

Festival and Outdoor Cooking

Men also tended to take over cooking in public celebrations. Occasions like pig roasts, crawfish boils, and booya and pilau feasts gave men an opportunity to demonstrate mastery of techniques with some component of the extreme—heat, volume, weight, or skill— in a "festal pattern of male cooking."[133] From maple sugaring to clambakes to deep-fried turkey, outdoor cooking has often been the domain of men. The traditions of festival cooking and work camp cooking came together in the early twentieth century, when outdoor cooking found new venues in the scouting and recreational camping movements. In suburbanized areas, the backyard came to stand in for the wilderness as men brought outdoor cooking projects home. Magazines and cookbooks urged men to cook over flame, keeping alive their "connection to fire, meat, and the primal strength of primitive humanity." As the world increasingly removed middle-class men from subsistence activities like hunting and fishing, backyard barbecuing encouraged them to recapture "true masculinity."[134]

Restaurants and Catering

The association of masculinity with cooking at the extremes translates to the exacting atmosphere of the high-end restaurant kitchen. The face of professional restaurant cuisine in America has almost always been male. During the eighteenth century, tavern keeping was a predominantly male profession. In elite homes, the presence of a male chef was a status symbol. By the 1840s, German immigrants were known for their beer-hall hospitality, but it was still rare for native-born men to specialize in food service. The expanding restaurant culture of the late 1800s brought more men into the field as hoteliers and cooks. African American men, barred from employment that required land or capital investment, found in catering an industry with low entry costs but high prospects for profit and independence.

Women Chefs

Men's domination of professional kitchens likely has more to do with the doctrine of separate spheres than with culinary skill. As Phipps observes, the culture told women that "cooking was not only what they were trained to do, it was what they were born to do. Yet, somehow, regardless of this 'natural' inclination, the proliferation of restaurants in the United States beginning in the 1920s was not an invitation for women to be paid for the same work they had performed in the home for generations."[135] She identifies another irony in the fact that the eminent Culinary Institute of America was founded by two women, Frances Roth and Katherine Angell, "whose sex would have prevented them from being enrolled in their own school until 24 years after they established it." The first woman was admitted to the school in 1970.[136] A 2014 Bloomberg report found that women still make up a minority of executive chefs in restaurants—as few as 6 percent.[137] This gap will likely narrow. In 2015, women represented 45 percent of students at the Culinary Institute of America. Cooking at home is somewhat more equitable, but it is still imbalanced. Though men have widely embraced cooking as a hobby, a 2013 study by the Bureau of Labor statistics found that 68 percent of women reported doing regular food-related work in the kitchen, as compared with only 42 percent of men.[138] Time pressures on the home kitchen may continue to drive even more people, both male and female, from the stovetop.

Best Practices: Interpreting Food and Gender

- Be wary of the tendency to project modern gender stereotypes and assumptions onto the past.
- Avoid defaulting to ahistorical nuclear family presentations. Reveal complex labor relationships in household hierarchies.
- Wherever appropriate, depict the work of men and women as a dynamic collaboration, with specialization and separation becoming more pronounced at some times and places than others.
- Create links between kitchen interiors and the outside world. Integrate food and production activities outside the house to activities in the kitchen.
- Depict foodways and cooking practices associated with men—military and work-site cooking, festival and outdoor cooking—as well as those generally managed by women.
- Treat the domestic environment as seriously as a workplace; for most people, it was one.
- Be cautious when drawing on "prescriptive literature," including cookbooks, etiquette books, and women's magazines. These present ideals, not always life as it was lived. Balance such sources with evidence from job advertisements, instructions to staff, receipts and account books, court records, diaries and letters, and archaeological study.

Economic Position

Another determinant of what people eat is wealth—or lack of it. It's impossible to pinpoint when food began to express class status. As Fernández-Armesto speculates, it was likely "at a remote, undocumented moment when some people started to command more food resources than others. . . . There was never a golden age of equality in the history of humankind."[139] Dining habits diverge along economic lines as working classes and the poor struggle to stay out of hunger and enjoy the occasional celebration, while middle and upper classes deploy wealth for health and pleasure, to communicate status, and to experiment with novelty.

Survival Strategies: Poor and Working-Class Eating

Food is the first necessity. Precontact indigenous migrations were spurred by the search for food security. Movements of seventeenth- and eighteenth-century colonists, nineteenth-century immigrants, and expansionist setters also rested on the hope of eliminating hunger, equating success with food bounty. Tennessee-born musician and songwriter Uncle Dave Macon, around the turn of the twentieth century, used food to paint a vision of rural food security in his song "Gray Cat on a Tennessee Farm":

Talk to the man who can if you will prosper in the valley of the Tennessee hills.
. . . Cattle in the pasture, hogs in the pen, sheep on the ranch and wheat in the bin.

Wagon in the shed, porter in the yard, meat in the smokehouse, big can of lard.
Fruit in the cellar, cheese on the board, big sack of coffee and sugar in the gourd.[140]

Around 1800, most ordinary people "spent on average seventy to eighty percent of their income on food alone."[141] This "nutritional class distinction" stratified further during the nineteenth century, as the middle class pulled ahead of the poor.[142] A variety of strategies helped stretch food dollars.

Quantity over Quality

Trading nutrient density for volume, poor people evaluated food "firstly by its capacity to fill the stomach, how much could be used without waste, the ease with which it could be prepared (utility value) and its cost (exchange value); secondly, for its social prestige value, and only finally its taste and nutritional value."[143] They relied on cheap but filling ingredients. In nineteenth-century urban settings, that meant "bread, potatoes, crackers, salt pork, and blood pudding, filled out with onion, cabbage, and cheaper proteins like herring."[144] Rural people relied on cornmeal, greens, rabbits, and beans. Stretching and substitution helped the poor approximate richer foods. Scraps of meat were diced into hash or meat pies.[145] The Great Depression prompted cooks to "adapt traditional recipes, eliminating costly ingredients like sugar, butter and eggs," resulting in recipes like "Depression Cake," sweetened with molasses and studded with raisins.[146]

Food Recovery

Poor people made use of discarded scraps and subpar groceries passed over by other buyers. Jane Zeigelman describes hungry nineteenth-century New Yorkers sorting through the castoffs of butchers, produce vendors, and fishmongers, "eating some of what they gathered and selling the rest for profit."[147] The very ability of wealthier Americans to throw away food stunned recent immigrants, who could "make a living off American's leftovers."[148] The poor gleaned frostbitten produce from field margins, turned bruised tomatoes into sauces, trimmed rotten bits away from vegetables for soup, and boiled mushy fruits into jam.

Buying in Small Quantities

Variable cash flow, lack of refrigeration, and cramped kitchens limited the ability to stock the larder. Cooks made just-in-time purchases in small amounts. Pushcart vendors offered housewives "half a parsnip or a handful or barley, not a single ounce more than she needed."[149] Frustratingly, smaller quantities often come at higher unit cost.

Boarding

A fourth tactic, especially for those without families, was to group together to eat. Boardinghouses, found across the country, provided a cost savings by cooking in volume, and they usually offered rented rooms as well as meals. Working-class families frequently took in boarders, using their homes as "a resource that could be used for generating extra income, for paying debts, for staying out of poverty, and for maintaining autonomy in old age."[150] During the nineteenth and early twentieth centuries, a large proportion of working-class households included boarders. Boardinghouse cuisine was reviled by those who had little choice but to eat their "tough steaks, greasy, waterlogged vegetables, and insipid stews."[151]

Relief

Poor people also accepted food relief when available, negotiating a tangle of possibilities emerging by the mid-nineteenth century: charitable soup kitchens, reformist programs, and, eventually, government relief. Government agencies began offering food support during the Depression, attempting to address the twin problems of surplus farm production and widespread hunger. The government bought and redistributed commodity farm products like apples, cheese, beans, and beef; set up school lunch programs; and, in 1939, introduced the nation's first food stamp program.[152] Over its four years, the stamp program provided food aid to more than four million Americans. The nation returned to relief in the 1960s when the public became more widely aware of crises in nutrient deficiency among poor Americans. Lyndon Johnson's "War on Poverty" revived the idea of using government surplus to feed

Figure 2.4. Migrant farmworkers and others line up for food relief distributed by the Surplus Commodities Committee in St. Johns, Arizona, in October 1940. Relief programs like this aimed to ameliorate both poverty and falling farm prices by diverting surplus agricultural production to those in need. (Library of Congress/Lee Russell, photographer/U.S. Farm Security Administration/ Office of War Information Collection)

hungry families. As historian of dietary science Marion Nestle reports, these programs drove down the incidence of malnutrition, but in the 1980s, food insecurity began rising again, making many of these survival strategies—along with new ones, such as reliance on cheap, mass-produced convenience foods and fast foods—a continuing necessity.[153]

Striving for Gentility: The Middle-Class Table

Most Americans today, whether affluent or barely getting by, consider themselves "middle class."[154] But until the end of World War II, being middle class was not the statistical norm but a status never achieved by a majority of Americans. During the late nineteenth century, the middle class represented no more than about 15 percent of the total population.[155] The very rich occupied a few percent at the top; the rest of the population was working class or impoverished. The middle class had emerged in the eighteenth century, but, as Tannahill describes, it expanded when the urban, manufacturing economy

> needed the services of lawyers, bankers and insurers, shippers and carriers, engineers and architects, managers and clerks, while growing towns needed more shops, more schools, more doctors, and more clergymen . . . all had a margin, however slight, of income over expenditure. They were not forced to eat what was cheapest but were able to exercise some choice, and their choice when they entertained (if not every day) was governed by the Jones factor: the middle-class dinner menu was an economy-conscious reflection of what people ate on the next level up the social scale.[156]

The dining table became a theater for the performance of prosperity and aspiration. The middle class strove to emulate the wealthy elite who employed them, and to distinguish themselves from the masses. Dining etiquette was one way to make these distinctions, allowing middle-class people to "display their knowledge of gentility." Hostesses consulted manuals and magazines to be sure their tables were properly set and their habits sufficiently gracious. Changes in fashion periodically upended norms. Archaeologist Robert Fitts describes a major revolution: the switch at the middle of the nineteenth century from "English"-style service, in which "food was placed in uncovered serving pieces on the table at the start of each course," to "service a la Russe," in which the table was set only with place settings and an ornamental centerpiece. Food was placed on a sideboard, usually in covered dishes, and served to each diner by servants.[157] The showier service a la Russe required careful orchestration and great dependence on the skills of servants.

In conjunction with mass manufacturing, interest in finer dining fueled a proliferation of diningware. Victorians saw eating as "a base act which brought humans down to the level of animals," and they countered its embarrassing earthiness by focusing attention on decorative tablewares.[158] According to Fitts, a household aspiring to genteel dining

> needed a basic tableware set consisting of dinner plates, soup plates, twifflers, muffin plates, sauce tureens, a soup tureen, a variety of platters in different sizes, covered serving dishes, open serving dishes, bakers, a butter dish, a pitcher, and a gravy boat. Tea sets were often included with the set, but were also sold separately. The basic tea set included cups, saucers,

a tea pot, a slop bowl, a sugar, a creamer, and often muffin plates. In total these basic sets contained about 20 different vessel forms. These basic sets could be supplemented by numerous forms with specific functions, such as relish dishes, breakfast bowls, compotes, egg cups, punch bowls and cups, coffee cups, chocolate cups, and custards.[159]

Appliances proliferated as well. During the latter half of the nineteenth century, cookstoves, water boilers, iceboxes, and other labor-saving devices went from being cutting-edge innovations to ordinary accoutrements in middle-class kitchens.

A Cut Above: Elite Dining

The foodways of the "1 percent" differed in quality and kind from those of the surrounding society, shedding light on the ways dining functioned among the upper class. High-end dining has long served to express distinction. The very wealthy have few constraints on the food budget, and they set themselves apart by showcasing novelty and rarity, indulging in excess, and, paradoxically, eschewing certain foods in a display of chosen austerity.

Novelty and Rarity

On eighteenth-century tables, serving foods utterly unavailable to most—for example, citrus, meats, and produce out of season—was a way of demonstrating purchasing power and access to networks of exchange. As the scope of trade widened, bringing more new foods within reach of the masses, the rich were forced into a continual quest for ever more unusual foods, locked in a "culinary arms race with the middle class."[160] Rarity of skill was also desired. Diners were impressed by confectionery towers and trompe l'oeil dishes. By the late eighteenth century, French chefs skilled in producing these effects were a status symbol in the homes of statesmen and merchants. James Hemings, a chef enslaved by Thomas Jefferson, trained in Paris in 1784 to prepare dishes in the French style, passing his knowledge on to other enslaved cooks at Monticello.[161] Jefferson continued highlighting French cuisine as president, introducing Americans to champagne, lightly cooked vegetables, and crème brûlée.[162] In the following century, French "cuisine bourgeousie" was an expected expression of membership in elite society.

Displays of Excess

From precontact feasts to contemporary parties, an overabundance of food and drink has been a means of demonstrating resources, generosity, and reciprocity. Wealth can also be communicated through a devotion of excess resources to create effect. Wealthy diners enjoyed dishes that took many demanding steps to prepare. Sauces, according to Fernández-Armesto, are "the essence and evidence of elaborate preparation," requiring the time-consuming reduction of stock, careful combinations of aromatics, and "practice and informed judgment."[163]

Voluntary Austerity

In something of an irony, austerity and self-denial have also characterized elite diets. By the late nineteenth century, tastemakers disdained abundance, deciding that "overindulgence was too cheap and easy to obtain."[164] Once the poor and middling could indulge in excess, it no longer served to differentiate. The elite reacted by declaring parsimonious eating fashionable. For example, when refined white flour was rare and expensive, white breads were seen to "embody refinement" as the "product of a longer process, a more intense use of labor, a greater degree of waste and a demand for subtler flavor."[165] Once technological advances made white flour cheap, the elite developed a new interest in the brown, whole-grain bread formerly considered indigestible.

Food and Class in the Twenty-First Century

Food continues to be a class marker. Many of the survival and distinction strategies of the past are seen today. The expansion of choice for the lower and middle classes is probably the most significant change; despite rising inequality, the diets of Americans at all class levels more closely resemble one another than at any previous time in history. Most Americans see the same food marketing, shop in similar large-scale grocery stores, and buy almost all foods in all seasons. In addition, most Americans have access to many more calories than they did at any previous time in history—such an abundance, in fact, that maladies of excess have increased among both the poor and the rich. At the same time, what Fernández-Armesto calls the "embourgeousiment" of food has set middle-class diets up as the norm, even for those who cannot really afford them.[166] Lower-cost and healthier diets for all classes would be more similar to those of preindustrial Americans and immigrants—fresh produce, legumes, and eggs rather than meats and cheeses, and cooking from scratch rather than buying convenience foods. But to eat so well, people need access to good sources of fresh food, equipment and fuel for cooking, know-how, and time—all in short supply among the least well off. In addition, people already enduring a great deal of privation may be understandably reluctant to give up their food aspirations. Eating like the middle class may provide emotional sustenance and the joy of celebration, even if it requires sacrifice. Meanwhile, in keeping with the reactionary principle behind elite austerity, the highest-status foods today are those raised, at greater expense, outside of the industrial food system. Grass-fed beef, cage-free eggs, free-range poultry, and wild-caught seafood command top dollar. Convinced of the superiority of organic and locally raised foods, many middle-class and lower-income consumers, too, stretch their budget to purchase these foods, claiming elements of the lifestyle of the well-off for themselves.

Food stories, sensory and immediate, lead to insights about hardship and survival, creativity and challenge, individual choice, and the American urge toward economic self-determination and financial security. Historian Megan Elias advocates for interpreting hunger and hardship, noting that it

> presents an opportunity to introduce drama and action into the public history site, because periods of food scarcity involve the compelling themes of tradition, loss, hunger, and ingenuity.

Because periods of food scarcity recur throughout history, most historic houses would lend themselves well to a discussion of "food when there was none," and the general public, perhaps particularly during the current recession, are interested in how to make do with less. Talking about food scarcity also allows us to use food to talk about class, race, gender roles, and municipal politics, topics which are essential to our understanding of the American past and increasingly engaged by public history sites.[167]

Recent USDA reports identify nearly 15 percent of American households as food insecure.[168] More than twenty-two million American households are eligible to receive support from the Supplemental Nutrition Assistance Program (SNAP), a successor to food stamp relief programs of the past. Hunger and hardship have yet to be eradicated in America, and food—both access to it and expressions using it—remains an important component of class identity.

Best Practices: Interpreting Economic Position

- Follow the food to reveal the labor involved in its production. Delve into occupational and community sources as needed to reveal more than a single phase of food sourcing and preparation. Link consumption to agriculture, fishing, manufacturing, transportation, and retail; many individuals had several concurrent involvements in the business of food. Discuss both the pride and the backbreaking work that produces food, including hours, wages, disputes and negotiations, entrepreneurship, and profiteering—all are part of the story of food and labor.
- Be clear about class. Make clear distinctions about economic resources available to interpretive characters. Be direct enough to deter inaccurate assumptions about relative prosperity based on modern understandings of material wealth. Historically, many museums have encouraged visitors to imagine themselves in the role of a successful economic protagonist, such as an elite homeowner or mistress. It is statistically much likelier for a person to have been in the role of servant or laborer. Critics have noted that house museums in particular often "do not say who belonged to the middle class or how it was located within a larger class structure."[169] Identification only with the elite can occlude a full understanding of social organization.
- Don't overstock kitchen exhibits. Use inventories and comparables to determine what a household at this economic level would likely have had. Avoid choosing "one of each" from the reproduction catalog or making kitchen exhibits home to an overabundance of collection items derived from many different households.
- Depict both hardship and celebration, not solely one or the other. Interpret hunger and seasonal scarcity as well as abundance.
- Use active rather than passive voice to describe the food activities of workers, servants, indentured, and enslaved people—for example, "the village's children and women laid the codfish out to dry" rather than "the codfish were laid out to dry."
- Use individuals' names whenever known—for example, "Nancy Flanagan" rather than "the cook."

- Specify the job titles as well as the legal and economic status of enslaved people and household workers.
- Don't rely on cookbooks and magazine articles to craft interpretive menus. Everyday food, especially for the poor, was rarely written about. Look for personal narratives and the writings of observers, such as social workers and reporters.
- Open and interpret servants' rooms, work areas, pantries, basements, outbuildings and other less glamorous sites, where food laborers lived and food production took place. Depict the processes of food preparation and preservation, including multistep ones that occur over a longer term and disrupt normal household function.
- Discuss dining rooms and the food served there as emblems of aspiration and status, and etiquette as an important behavior in establishing and maintaining economic position, employment, and personal relationships—not just as a set of archaic, silly rules.

Discussion Starter: Linking Food Interpretation to Identity

One way to reveal the multiple connections between food and identity is to explore its complexity first from a personal perspective. Foodways, says folklorist Millie Rahn, "are usually the cultural elements that people hold on to longest in their personal archaeology."[170] Use this discussion activity to generate new ideas for ways to reveal identity through food using the settings, artifacts, and material culture, and live interpretation at your site.

1. Choose a simple food familiar to most interpreters: perhaps popped popcorn, an Oreo cookie, or pickles. Bring in samples of the food—enough for each person to have a taste or a small portion.
2. Round One: Reveal the food item and allow people to look at it, but not yet eat it. Let them know you'll be doing three rounds of writing based on experience with this food. Invite participants to spend two to three minutes jotting down personal memories and associations based only on the sight of the food. This can be in the form of a list, a narrative, or even cartoons.
3. Round Two: Invite participants to smell the food, but not yet taste it. Spend another two minutes jotting down associations with the scent.
4. Round Three: Invite everyone to taste the food. In the final few minutes, write a few notes about the taste, and any associations it conjures.
5. Go around the group and ask people to share some of the content from Rounds One, Two, and Three. After everyone has had an opportunity to share, discuss questions like the following:
   - *How did experiences with this food link to ethnic and racial identity?* Was it more familiar in some cultural groups than in others? Was it especially loved or reviled by anyone? What individuals, events, or cultural practices was it associated with?

- *How did experiences with this food link to gender identity?* Was the food associated more with consumption by one gender or another? Whose job was it to purchase or prepare this food?
- *How did experiences with this food link to economic identity?* Was this food aspirational, a rare and special treat? Or was it an everyday item? Were there times it was wanted but unavailable? Were there times when there was too much of it? What kinds of resources—monetary and physical—were needed to prepare and serve it?

To transition this personal experience into interpretive contexts, ask interpreters to try a similar sensory food experience from the point of view of a character interpreted at your site or in your project. Determine as closely as possible the individual identity of this character—their age and level of education, access to food resources, health condition, racial or cultural background, and region. Identify a food item likely to have been common in that person's life, and ask the interpreters to write, from the point of view of their character, as many questions, ideas, and associations related to that food item as they can. Consider questions such as:

- Where did the food come from? Where did each of the individual ingredients come from? Were they raised, borrowed, or purchased? Who harvested or sold them? What constraints were there on their selection or purpose?
- Who prepared the food? How did the preparation fit into their social role and its responsibilities?
- Who taught the preparer to make it? Does your interpretive character know how to make it, or any part of it?
- Does your interpretive character have special knowledge about the cultivation or use of this food? Do they feel any responsibility to transfer this knowledge?
- Does your character love, hate, or tolerate this food—or are they indifferent to it?
- Is this food nutritious? Is it abundant enough? Is the character satisfied, or still hungry, after eating?
- Does anything about the food represent cultural continuity? Does anything about it represent changes to an earlier diet?

Fresh Ideas: Michael Twitty on Museums and Culinary Justice

Michael W. Twitty is a culinary historian, food writer, and historical interpreter personally charged with preparing, preserving and promoting African American foodways and parent traditions in Africa and the African diaspora, and their legacies in the food culture of the American South. He chronicles his work on his blog *Afroculinaria* and in his forthcoming book, *The Cooking Gene*.

You have been developing the idea of "culinary justice," a principle advocating ways to reveal and honor the complex intercultural roots of America's cuisines and the cooks whose labor and ingenuity created them. Do museums and historic sites have a special responsibility to advance culinary justice through interpretation?

We have a responsibility to engage with the surviving community, if there is one. A lot of museums and historic sites don't engage with the local community, the descendants of the former enslaved people, or working-class white people whom they interpret. I want museums to end this sort of elitist caretaker position when they deal with culture and place. I've been invited to places where they don't give a damn about anything but the architectural merits. You don't have all the facts if you just go by the book; there are so many details to be filled in. Engagement between the community and the interpretive site or museum must be sacrosanct, a continuous process of operation.

Another thing we need to address is the idea that—especially in the South and on the East Coast, where you find the most living history sites and house museums—they're already incorporating food. They are, but they're not doing it in a meaningful way. Lots of places do events with "food and jazz," or spirituals. It was black folks' condition that cemented those traditions. They were the ones who cooked the food, and there were also layers of Native American and multiclass European and Hispanic and Latino people woven into the narrative. And yet how often do you see a "Southern food weekend" with no black chefs, no black history with the food? These events just congratulate other elites about the high price point, as if the narrative of why the food's important has nothing to do with the social consequences that brought that food to the table. We have a serious problem there. The food is being created and marketed, but with no sense of culinary justice or environmental justice. That robs local communities of another opportunity to grow, enrich, and empower themselves. Those events are doing nothing to incorporate the culture, values, or material life of local black communities whose ancestors built that. Then history becomes a cultural deficit instead of a cultural advantage.

What first steps would you identify to improve culinary justice in food interpretation?

Integrating the elders and employing them—but also getting young people into junior interpreter programming, especially for minority communities. It's really important for local Native, African American, and Latino young people to be engaged in junior interpretation or a similar program, because they can get insights into what it means to be a cook, a scientist, an archaeologist, an ethnobotanist, to work in architectural preservation and artifact conservation—the myriad jobs that are incorporated into museum work. These are lily-white industries, because nobody thinks to ask black and brown kids to come into them. It's really important to find people like myself and other independent researchers and interpreters to come in and be the specialist, to help things along.

Sometimes people brush up against attitudes that are painful. Wealthy, powerful descendants' and daughters' associations don't want certain stories told. That is a huge barrier to progress in this field. Somebody needs to shake up how the systemic process in museum interpretation works, because as long as we put all the power in the hands of people who have romantic and comforting views of the past, we won't have discourse on ethnic, racial, and gender histories—they don't want to tell those stories. People are not coming in because they are not represented. They see that big house and say, "I am not that. That is not me. This has nothing to do with my identity." The absence of women is one example; I don't think there's a single domestic space that is historically interpreted that should not be filled with mothers, daughters, and women of all kinds. Those spaces were given their life's breath by those women for centuries. How many museums really emphasize the role of the women— and not just the typical domestic, stereotypical roles but also their roles as the builder, the designer, the architect, the manager of these spaces? Women ran these places by themselves for years at a time. One place that does this well is the Lower East Side Tenement museum, who are frank about a man who left for nowhere, never to be found again. Women survive this type of circumstance.

How can museums and historic sites support the goal of the "reconstruction and revival of traditional African American foodways"?

When museums open their doors, and their collections and their labs, to people like myself, it really helps refine the narrative, the story, the lesson. I can't do without them. The books I've read, the oral history interviews I've conducted, the elders that I've talked to can only take me so far, but when I go to a museum and they show me an artifact that doesn't get much circulation, I can discover a story to tell. For example, I did a teacher training about slavery and food in the Chesapeake, and I was fascinated with some museum spaces where they were finding artifacts that indicated a completely different narrative than what we have been told. There were elements of African American folk religion with tinges of African diaspora spiritual knowledge that continued into the twentieth century—someone had found a yellow pine phallus sculpture and pierced coins at the cardinal directions in a black-owned cabin in Montgomery County. That stuff was happening here, right up until World War I, World War II; that's spectacular. Archaeological collections, libraries, rare books—museums have these resources, and they should be explored.

In terms of food, museums sometimes have the wrong attitude: "We'll just go based on what we find here, and stop the narrative there." I believe we need a global and regional perspective. Your little museum space can be an amazing window on the Atlantic and global story, if you allow those "small things forgotten" to tell wider stories. Plant samples—my God! Think about what it took to get that sweet potato or that cowpea to a plantation. Think about the journey of that one seed, and how it had to bounce ship to ship, place to place, all the way from the middle of West Africa to Virginia. How did that happen? Who is bringing that seed? It didn't mail itself. It's a human story.

Museums can also create spaces where people can come in and hone their craft. Whenever I get the opportunity to do a presentation at a living history site, I give myself a mandate to make something new. That's because I'm not independently wealthy yet, where I can have a model cabin kitchen where I can play and experiment. Living history sites and museums should really think about opening up their facilities and their grounds to the cooks and materials specialists that you find in the interpretive community. Those are the laboratories. And by that experimentation we're mastering the new, doing new things, so we also further the goals and missions and the knowledge of those institutions. We wonder about all these details that come down to the material, traditional, spiritual, political, and social, things we claim are mysteries that are really solvable; they're really just begging for a detective.

How do you begin identifying the important food stories at a new interpretive site?

I always walk the land. That's true whether I'm in a house or plantation museum. I look around for what's growing. What animals do I see? I ask questions about what fish are in the water, what birds are in the trees, what wildlife makes itself known. I want to understand the terroir and merroir of the place. Even though ecological conditions do change, a lot of things will be the same and can be read on the land. That's how I create the texture. When I go into a living history space and try to bring it to life, especially one aligned with African American history or slavery, when visitors come in from the area I can have a conversation about a chinquapin or an heirloom vegetable, and their eyes light up, because they have something of value to share. Museums need to understand that when locals are engaged, people testify and share narratives. Someone needs to be right there, on hand with the tape recorder or the cell phone to record those memories, so they can become part of the growing body of knowledge in that place.

Notes

1. Megan Elias, "Summoning the Food Ghosts: Food History as Public History," *The Public Historian* 34, no. 2 (2012): 13.
2. Reay Tannahill, *Food in History* (New York: Three Rivers Press, 1989), 252.
3. For discussion of the terms *creole* and *creolization* as applied to history and culture, see Robin Cohen, "Creolization and Cultural Globalization: The Soft Sounds of Fugitive Power," *Globalizations* 4, no. 3 (2007): 369–84. There, Cohen explains the concept of creolization as one that "centers on the cross-fertilization between different cultures as they interact. When creolization occurs, participants select particular elements from incoming or inherited cultures, endow these with meanings different from those they possessed in the original cultures and then creatively merge these to create new varieties that supersede the prior forms."
4. Knut Oyangen, "The Gastrodynamics of Displacement: Place-Making and Gustatory Identity in the Immigrants' Midwest," *Journal of Interdisciplinary History* 39, no. 3 (2009): 326.

5. Lawrence A. Clayton, Vernon James Knight Jr., and Edward C. Moore, eds., *The De Soto Chronicles: The Expedition of Hernando de Soto to North America in 1539–1543, Vol. 1* (Tuscaloosa, AL: University of Alabama Press, 1993; first paperback edition, 1995), 194. Citations are to first paperback edition.

6. A widely known example is maize. Developed from a wild grass in what is now Mexico, maize traveled first to the American Southwest and then through the Mississippi River and its tributaries to spread over the continent. Maize and beans spread rapidly in the Northeast around 1250, likely due to the awareness that coplanting them improved yield. In his 1643 *A Key into the Language of America*, Roger Williams notes that native people did not view crows as pests because "they have a tradition, that the Crow brought them at first an *Indian* Graine of Corne in one Eare, and an *Indian* or a *French* Beane in another," which were planted together. Here, oral history, the documentary record, and archaeological findings combine to shed light on foodways dating to before contact. Roger Williams, *A Key into the Language of America*, edited by Howard M. Chapin (Bedford, MA: Applewood Books, 1997), reprint of the fifth edition of 1936. Originally published in 1643.

7. C. Margaret Scarry and Elizabeth J. Reitz, "Changes in Foodways at the Parkin Site, Arkansas," *Southeastern Archaeology* 24, no. 2 (2005): 116–18.

8. Tannahill, *Food in History*, 203.

9. Alfred W. Crosby, *The Columbian Exchange: Biological and Cultural Consequences of 1492* (Westport, CT: Greenwood Press, 1972).

10. Alfred Crosby, "The Columbian Exchange," *History Now* 12 (Summer 2007), Gilder Lehrman Institute of American History, accessed April 26, 2015, http://www.gilderlehrman.org/history-by-era/american-indians/essays/columbian-exchange; Brian Cowan, "New Worlds, New Tastes," in *Food: The History of Taste*, ed. Paul Freedman (Berkeley and Los Angeles: University of California Press, 2007), 213–14.

11. Jennifer Jensen Wallach, *How America Eats: A Social History of U.S. Food and Culture* (Lanham, MD: Rowman & Littlefield, 2013), 20.

12. Wallach, *How America Eats*, 1–6, 17–18.

13. "Berry Berry American Cranberry," in *Renewing American's Food Traditions: Saving and Savoring the World's Most Endangered Foods*, ed. Gary Paul Nabhan (White River Junction, VT: Chelsea Green Publishing Company, 2008), 111.

14. Wallach, *How America Eats*, 37.

15. Michael Twitty, "Terroir Noire: The Historic Chesapeake and Tidewater: Foodscapes of Slavery," *Afroculinaria* (blog), February 4, 2011, http://afroculinaria.com/2011/02/04/terroir-noire-the-historic-chesapeake-and-tidewater/.

16. Wallach, *How America Eats*, 42–45.

17. William Pierson, *Black Legacy: America's Hidden Heritage* (Amherst: University of Massachusetts Press, 1993), 111.

18. Cowan, "New Worlds, New Tastes," 223

19. William Hugh Grove, "Virginia in 1732: The Travel Journal of William Hugh Grove," ed. Gregory A. Stiverson and Patrick H. Butler III, *The Virginia Magazine of History and Biography* 85, no. 1 (1977): 29–30; Cowan, "New Worlds, New Tastes," 223.

20. Cowan, "New Worlds, New Tastes," 223–24. Coffee and tea, inextricably linked to the social and intellectual culture of the Enlightenment era, were rarely offered without slave-produced Caribbean sugar.

21. Wallach, *How America Eats*, 35.

22. Thomas Anburey, "Travels Through America During the War," quoted in "Travelers' Impressions of Slavery in America from 1750 to 1800," ed. Andrew Burnaby et al., *The Journal of Negro History* 1, no. 4 (1916): 407.

23. Wallach, *How America Eats*, 40.

24. Wallach, *How America Eats*, 41. Care should be taken in interpreting gardens tended by enslaved people; they are sometimes interpreted as evidence of owners' generosity, but the availability of gardens was also used to justify leaner rations.

25. Michael Twitty, "The Unbearable Taste: Early African American Foodways," *Commonplace* 11, no. 3 (2011), accessed April 26, 2015, http://www.common-place.org/vol-11/no-03/twitty/.

26. Wallach, *How America Eats*, 60.

27. Wallach, *How America Eats*, 66. The very name of this dish of rice, meat, and spices is polygot: as Wallach relates, "there is some disagreement about exactly which influences it pays tribute to. 'Jam' is a diminutive for the French word for ham, *jambon*, and 'ya-ya' is derived from a West African word for rice. Others have suggested that the name of the dish is combination of the words *jambon* and *paella* or a melding of *jambon* with the Choctaw word *falaya*, which means 'long' and could refer to a meal designed to feed many people."

28. Wallach, *How America Eats*, 71.

29. David Lowenthal, "Pioneer Museums," in *History Museums in the United States: A Critical Assessment*, ed. Warren Leon and Roy Rosenzweig (Urbana: University of Illinois Press, 1989), 120.

30. Nabhan, *Renewing America's Food Traditions*, 50–52.

31. Wallach, *How America Eats*, 59.

32. Joel Denker, *The World on a Plate: A Tour through the History of America's Ethnic Cuisine* (Boulder, CO: Westview Press, 2003), 138–41.

33. Department of Health and Human Services, Indian Health Service Division of Diabetes Health Treatment and Prevention, "Diabetes in American Indians and Alaska Natives: Facts-at-a-Glance," Department of Health and Human Services, 2012, online document accessed April 26, 2015, https://www.ihs.gov/MedicalPrograms/Diabetes/HomeDocs/Resources/FactSheets/2012/Fact_sheet_AIAN_508c.pdf.

34. Pat Willard, *America Eats!: On the Road with the WPA: The Fish Fries, Box Supper Socials, and Chitlin Feasts that Define Real American Food* (New York: Bloomsbury, 2008), 183–84.

35. Jillian Jimenez, "The History of Grandmothers in the African American Community," *Social Service Review* 76, no. 4 (2002): 526–27.

36. Robert T. Dirks and Nancy Duran, "African American Dietary Patterns at the Beginning of the Twentieth Century," *Journal of Nutrition* 131, no. 7 (2001): 1883.

37. Joe William Trotter Jr., "African Americans and the Industrial Revolution," *OAH Magazine of History* 15, no. 1 (2000): 21.

38. Paul R. Mullins, "Race and the Genteel Consumer: Class and African-American Consumption, 1850–1930," *Historical Archaeology* 33, no. 1 (1999): 33–34.

39. Barbara Burlison Mooney, "The Comfortable Tasty Framed Cottage: An African American Architectural Iconography," *Journal of the Society of Architectural Historians* 61, no. 1 (2002): 55.

40. Jimenez, "The History of Grandmothers in the African American Community," 528.

41. Mooney, "The Comfortable Tasty Framed Cottage," 64.

42. Wallach, *How America Eats*, 188.

43. William Woys Weaver, "The Dark Side of Culinary Ephemera: The Portrayal of African Americans," *Gastronomica: The Journal of Critical Food Studies* 6, no. 3 (2006): 76.

44. Weaver, "The Dark Side of Culinary Ephemera," 78.

45. Darlene Clark Hine, *Black Women in America: A Historical Encyclopedia, Vol. 1* (Brooklyn, NY: Carlson Publishing, 1993), 53.

46. Weaver, "The Dark Side of Culinary Ephemera," 81. For more detailed discussion and imagery of African Americans in food advertising, see "The Jim Crow Museum of Racist Memorabilia," an online resource hosted by Ferris State University in Big Rapids, Michigan: http://www.ferris.edu/jimcrow/.

47. Roberto A. Ferdman, "The Disturbing Ways That Fast Food Chains Disproportionately Target Black Kids," *Washington Post* (Washington, DC), November 12, 2014.

48. Dirks and Duran, "African American Dietary Patterns at the Beginning of the Twentieth Century," 1889.

49. Dirks and Duran, "African American Dietary Patterns at the Beginning of the Twentieth Century," 1887.

50. Charles L. Lumpkins, "Soul Food," *Encyclopedia of African-American History, Vol. 4* (New York: Oxford University Press, 2009), 338–40.

51. Connie Geer and Matthew Shepherd, *The Negro Travelers' Green Book* digital collection, South Carolina Digital Academy and University of South Carolina, 2011, http://library.sc.edu/digital/collections/greenbook.html.

52. Wallach, *How America Eats*, 76.

53. Wallach, *How America Eats*, 59.

54. Israel Zangwill, *The Melting-Pot* (Baltimore: The Lord Baltimore Press, 1921), from Internet Archive, http://archive.org/stream/themeltingpot23893gut/23893.txt.

55. "'Melting Pot' America," BBC News website, May 12, 2006, accessed April 26, 2015, http://news.bbc.co.uk/2/hi/americas/4931534.stm.

56. Shannon Lee Dawdy, "'A Wild Taste': Food and Colonialism in Eighteenth-Century Louisiana," *Ethnohistory* 57, no. 3 (2010): 395.

57. Wallach, *How America Eats*, 86.

58. Laura Schenone, *The Lost Ravioli Recipes of Hoboken: A Search for Food and Family* (New York: Norton, 2008).

59. Denker, *The World on a Plate*, 81–83.

60. Jane Ziegelman, *97 Orchard: An Edible History of Five Families in One New York Tenement* (New York: Smithsonian Books/HarperCollins, 2010), 24.

61. Ziegelman, *97 Orchard*, 113.

62. Ziegelman, *97 Orchard*, 216.

63. Ziegelman, *97 Orchard*, 144.

64. Ziegelman, *97 Orchard*, 213.

65. Denker, *The World on a Plate*, 19–20.

66. Denker, *The World on a Plate*, 20–26.

67. Ziegelman, *97 Orchard*, 29–31.

68. Denker, *The World on a Plate*, 68.

69. Denker, *The World on a Plate*, 7–8.

70. Ziegelman, *97 Orchard*, 216.

71. Denker, *The World on a Plate*, 89–92.

72. Denker, *The World on a Plate*, 98.

73. Ziegelman, *97 Orchard*, 222.

74. Oyangen, "The Gastrodynamics of Displacement," 324.

75. Mark Kurlansky, *The Food of a Younger Land* (New York: Riverhead Books, 2009), 52–54.

76. Denker, *The World on a Plate*, 121–25.

77. Ziegelman, *97 Orchard*, 201–4. Contamination fears related to immigrants are a continuing motif in American history; for a discussion of this topic, see Howard Markel and Alexandra Minna Stern, "The Foreignness of Germs: The Persistent Association of Immigrants and Disease in American Society," *Millbank Quarterly* 80, no. 4 (2002): 757–88, doi:10.1111/1468-0009.00030.

78. Oyangen, "The Gastrodynamics of Displacement," 338–39.

79. The song is found in many variants using similar-sounding names: Dunderbeck, Johnnie Rubek, and others.

80. Zeigelman, *97 Orchard*, 126–30.

81. Oyangen, "The Gastrodynamics of Displacement," 347–48.

82. Wallach, *How America Eats*, 86.

83. Ziegelman, *97 Orchard*, 215.

84. Ziegelman, *97 Orchard*, 160–62.

85. Wallach, *How America Eats*, 78–79.

86. Oyangen, "The Gastrodynamics of Displacement," 340–48.

87. Wallach, *How America Eats*, 77.

88. Ziegelman, *97 Orchard*, 196.

89. Evan D. G. Fraser and Andrew Rimas, *Empires of Food: Feast, Famine, and the Rise and Fall of Civilizations* (New York: Free Press, 2010), 212–14.

90. Ziegelman, *97 Orchard*, 56–57.

91. Fraser and Rimas, *Empires of Food*, 214.

92. Ziegelman, *97 Orchard*, 59.

93. Ziegelman, *97 Orchard*, 54.

94. Ziegelman, *97 Orchard*, 55–56.

95. Ziegelman, *97 Orchard*, 155.

96. Zeigelman, *97 Orchard*, 22.

97. Wallach describes how a similar process eroded differences in the diets of Jewish immigrants from different food cultures across Central and Eastern Europe, who created a "multiethnic Jewish cuisine" in America. Regardless of origin, Jewish immigrants "became enthusiastic consumers of German delicatessen foods such as corned beef and salami, which were previously unfamiliar to them," along with bagels, knishes, rugelach, and other intermingled European foods. Wallach, *How America Eats*, 83.

98. Ziegelman, *97 Orchard*, 223.

99. Willard, *America Eats!* 284; Wallach, *How America Eats*, 87.

100. Nicole M. Waguespack, "The Organization of Male and Female Labor in Foraging Societies: Implications for Early Paleoindian Archaeology," *American Anthropologist* 107, no. 4 (2005). Waguespeck theorizes that when hunting was good, there was less pressure to supplement the diet with plant foods, making food gatherers more selective. When hunting was poor, women foraged more heavily, drawing on less-valued food sources to make up the needed calories. Some of these might require more time-consuming processing, such as shelling nuts or seeds, or force them travel farther to find hard-to-reach plant species they might pass over in fatter times. "As meat contributes less to the diet," she summarizes, "women work

increasingly longer hours." If hunting was more productive, women's time was freed up to engage in "nonsubsistence tasks," which might have included the production of technology: making stone tools, building houses, working leather, and carrying equipment.

101. Barbara Roth and Andrea Freeman, "The Middle Archaic Period and the Transition to Agriculture in the Sonoran Desert of Southern Arizona," *Kiva* 73, no. 3 (2008): 524.

102. Wallach, *How America Eats*, 111.

103. Jane C. Nylander, *Our Own Snug Fireside: Images of the New England Home, 1760–1860* (paperback edition New Haven: Yale University Press, 1994; originally published New York: Knopf, 1993), all citations from paperback edition, 61–62.

104. Jack Larkin, *The Reshaping of Everyday Life, 1790–1840* (New York: Harper & Row, 1988, paperback edition), 29–30.

105. Susan Strasser, *Never Done: A History of American Housework* (New York: Pantheon, 1982), 180–82.

106. Jane Adams, "Resistance to 'Modernity': Southern Illinois Farm Women and the Cult of Domesticity." *American Ethnologist* 20, no. 1 (1993): 91.

107. Susan Williams, *Savory Suppers and Fashionable Feasts: Dining in Victorian America* (New York: Pantheon Books in Association with the Margaret Woodbury Strong Museum, 1985), 2.

108. Williams, *Savory Suppers and Fashionable Feasts*, 144.

109. Williams, *Savory Suppers and Fashionable Feasts*, 145. The word *lunch* originally referred to a midmorning snack; Noah Webster defined it as "a slight repast between breakfast and dinner, eaten in company."

110. Tamara K. Hareven, "The Home and the Family in Historical Perspective," *Social Research* 58, no. 1 (1991): 277.

111. Elizabeth Drury and Philippa Lewis, *Kitchen Memories: Food and Kitchen Life 1837–1939* (London: National Trust Books, 2007), 7.

112. Strasser, *Never Done*, 178.

113. Sheila Phipps, "Kitchen Cache: The Hidden Meaning of Gender and Cooking in Twentieth-Century American Kitchens," master's thesis, Appalachian State University, 34–35.

114. Samantha Barbas, "Just Like Home: 'Home Cooking' and the Domestication of the American Restaurant," *Gastronomica: The Journal of Food and Culture* 2, no. 4 (2002): 43.

115. Barbas, "Just Like Home," 45.

116. Barbas, "Just Like Home," 51.

117. Barbas, "Just Like Home," 46.

118. Elaine F. Weiss, "Before Rosie the Riveter, Farmerettes Went to Work," *Smithsonian Magazine*, May 28, 2009.

119. Judy Barrett Litoff and David C. Smith, "To the Rescue of the Crops: The Women's Land Army during World War II," *Prologue* (magazine of the National Archives and Records Administration) 25, no. 4 (1993).

120. Wallach, *How America Eats*, 159.

121. Wallach, *How America Eats*, 162.

122. Wallach, *How America Eats*, 135.

123. Wallach, *How America Eats*, 136.

124. Wallach, *How America Eats*, 135–36.

125. Wallach, *How America Eats*, 139.

126. Phipps, "Kitchen Cache," 36.

127. Phipps, "Kitchen Cache," 4.

128. Laurie K. Mercier and Glen Montgomery, "Montana Episodes at Work: Montanans Camp Cooks in Montana," *Montana: The Magazine of Western History* 39, no. 3 (1989): 72.

129. William C. Davis, *A Taste for War: The Culinary History of the Blue and Gray* (Mechanicsburg, PA: Stackpole Books, 2003), 1–2.

130. Davis, *A Taste for War*, 8–9.

131. Davis, *A Taste for War*, 10.

132. Davis, *A Taste for War*, 13.

133. Thomas A. Adler, "Pancakes on Sunday: The Male Cook in Family Tradition," *Western Folklore* 40, no. 1 (1981): 51.

134. Phipps, "Kitchen Cache," 37.

135. Phipps, "Kitchen Cache," 5.

136. Phipps, "Kitchen Cache," 65.

137. Ryan Sutton, "Women Everywhere in Food Empires But No Head Chefs," *Bloomberg Business* website, March 6, 2014, accessed April 26, 2015.

138. "American Time Use Survey Summary—2013 Results," Bureau of Labor Statistics website, June 18, 2014, accessed April 26, 2015, http://www.bls.gov/news.release/atus.nr0.htm.

139. Felipe Fernández-Armesto, *Near a Thousand Tables: A History of Food* (New York: Free Press, 2002), 101.

140. "The Gray Cat on the Tennesee Farm," Max Hunter Folksong Collection, Cat. #1588 (MFH #1041), Missouri State Library digital collection, accessed April 26, 2015, http://maxhunter. missouristate.edu/songinformation.aspx?id=1588.

141. Hans J. Teuteberg, "The Birth of the Modern Consumer Age," in Freedman, *Food: The History of Taste*, 235.

142. Strasser, *Never Done*, 26.

143. Teuteberg, "The Birth of the Modern Consumer Age," 235.

144. Strasser, *Never Done*, 16; Ziegelman, *97 Orchard*, 19.

145. Ziegelman, *97 Orchard*, 70.

146. A good resource for personal remembrances of simple, cheap cooking during the Great Depression is the web video series "Great Depression Cooking with Clara," http://www. greatdepressioncooking.com/Welcome.html.

147. Ziegelman, *97 Orchard*, 190.

148. Ziegelman, *97 Orchard*, 191.

149. Ziegelman, *97 Orchard*, 143.

150. Hareven, "The Home and the Family in Historical Perspective," 274.

151. Ziegelman, *97 Orchard*, 70.

152. Supplemental Nutrition Assistance Program, "A Short History of SNAP," United States Department of Agriculture Food and Nutrition Service website, November 20, 2014, accessed April 26, 2015, http://www.fns.usda.gov/snap/short-history-snap.

153. Marion Nestle, *Eat Drink Vote: An Illustrated Guide to Food Politics* (New York: Rodale Books, 2013), 20–24.

154. Shannon Palus, "Nine Out of Ten Americans Consider Themselves Middle Class," Smithsonian.com website, April 13, 2015, accessed April 26, 2015, http://www. smithsonianmag.com/smart-news/nine-out-10-americans-consider-themselves-middle-class-180954970/.

155. Dennis Gilbert, *The American Class Structure in an Age of Growing Inequality* (Thousand Oaks, CA: Pine Forge Press, 2008), 46.

156. Tannahill, *Food in History*, 295–96.
157. Robert K. Fitts, "The Archaeology of Middle-Class Domesticity and Gentility in Victorian Brooklyn," *Historical Archaeology* 33, no. 1 (1999): 54.
158. Fitts, "The Archaeology of Middle-Class Domesticity and Gentility in Victorian Brooklyn," 54.
159. Fitts, "The Archaeology of Middle-Class Domesticity and Gentility in Victorian Brooklyn," 53.
160. Fernández-Armesto, *Near a Thousand Tables*, 124.
161. "French Cuisine in a Virginia Kitchen," Monticello website, http://www.monticello.org/site/plantation-and-slavery/french-cuisine-virginia-kitchen, accessed April 26, 2015.
162. William Hageman, "America's First Foodie," *Chicago Tribune*, October 3, 2012.
163. Fernández-Armesto, *Near a Thousand Tables*, 115.
164. Fernández-Armesto, *Near a Thousand Tables*, 107.
165. Fernández-Armesto, *Near a Thousand Tables*, 126.
166. Fernández-Armesto, *Near a Thousand Tables*, 202.
167. Elias, "Summoning the Food Ghosts," 14–15.
168. Alisha Coleman-Jensen, Christian Gregory, and Anita Singh, "Household Food Security in the United States in 2013," United States Department of Agriculture Economic Research Service website, September 4, 2014, accessed April 26, 2015, http://www.ers.usda.gov/publications/err-economic-research-report/err173.aspx.
169. Barbara Melosh, "Speaking of Women: Museums' Representations of Women's History," in *History Museums in the United States: A Critical Assessment*, ed. Warren Leon and Roy Rosenzweig (Urbana: University of Illinois Press, 1989), 200.
170. Millie Rahn, "Laying a Place at the Table: Creating Public Foodways Models from Scratch," *Journal of American Folklore* 119, no. 471 (2006): 33.

CHAPTER 3

It's Good for You! Interpreting Food and Health

"EAT IT! It's good for you!"

It's an exhortation many American children have heard. The idea that food choices have utilitarian benefit is deeply embedded. Throughout history, Americans have chosen things to eat—or avoid—to optimize health, prevent disease, and even forestall moral decay. Personally and publicly, Americans have evaluated food for qualities it was thought to produce in the body, the soul, and the nation itself. This chapter focuses on interpretive themes that foreground the physical, moral, and spiritual aspects of cooking and eating, highlighting potential ideas to explore.

Key Interpretive Concepts

1. *Individual food decisions are often supported by food ideologies.* Beliefs and values about food, whether scientific, religious, or ethical, linked eating with worldview.
2. *The state of scientific food knowledge has always been evolving, never complete.* Examining past practices can encourage deeper thinking about present-day bases for food decisions. How do we know what we know about food and health? How do we reconcile religious or moral beliefs and dietary choices?
3. *Beliefs about food and health are powered as much by social factors as by scientific discovery.* Fashion and personality, among other things, have influenced food behavior even when results were not demonstrable.

An Apple a Day Keeps the Doctor Away: Food and Bodily Health

Though the saying originated in England, the principle behind "an apple a day" has a history as American as, well, apple pie. Colonists arrived in the New World carrying ideas about dietary medicine. Native communities had their own sets of health guidelines and edible remedies. Fernández-Armesto sees in these prescientific systems as "a kind of transformative magic" in which people take on the qualities of the food they eat—"a 'hot' temper, a 'cool disposition.'"[1] At the same time, a "commonsense assumption" links food and health. We know when we're thriving and feeling energized, when we're sluggish and weak. As Fernández-Armesto says, "Much of the history of food and of medicine could be written in terms of the search for a more exact tabulation of the correspondences between particular foods and particular physical conditions."[2] European ideas about eating were often built upon humoral theories, derived from the physiologies of ancient Greek and Roman thinkers, particularly Hippocrates and Galen.[3] Galen's second-century thinking influenced eating for more than a millennium. Galen popularized the theory that bodily systems were made of up of "basic fluids or 'humors': blood, phlegm, black bile and yellow bile or choler, each of which possessed two basic properties, being either hot or cold and either wet or dry."[4] The mix of fluids in a person's body determined his or her temperament. Foods bore matching characteristics. Galenic dietetics sought to counterbalance excesses or deficiencies in the body by introducing foods of the opposite characteristic.[5] Humoral theory governed food combinations as well as individual foods. Those who enjoyed melons, which were cool and wet, could prevent too much dampness by preparing them with hot and dry ingredients—marinating them in wine or tossing them with onions. Indigestion could be caused by an increase in phlegm; a hot, dry remedy like wine mixed with black pepper might restore equilibrium.[6] The basic principles of Galen's system remained current through the Renaissance and, in some circles, long after. At Plimoth Plantation, first-person interpreters playing English colonists are trained in humoral dietary theory, as this interaction with a visitor shows:

> "We eat a great deal of fish," said Sarah Godbertson, standing in the kitchen garden behind her home. "Fish being, by its nature, cool and wet, that breeds too much phlegm. We cook it with onions, garlic, fennel, that are dry and hot."
>
> It was a woman's job to keep her family healthy. A good cook, said Godbertson, is half a physician.
>
> "This is a medicine chest for your home," she said, nodding to her garden.[7]

This holistic interpretation of the link between food and health—encompassing a food demonstration, re-created garden and house, conversation and role playing, and strong interpretive messages—is an effective way to communicate the tight connection between the Puritan worldview and food.

The link between food and bodily health has been made, explicitly and subtly, in different ways throughout American history. The next few sections discuss some commonly recurring ideas about eating for health that have influenced people and events.

Take Your Vitamins

After a millennium dominated by the doctrine of humors, the eighteenth century brought a rational and investigative approach built on physical evidence. The first major breakthrough was the work of French chemist Antoine Lavoisier, who "succeeded in proving that humans and animals were heat engines fueled by food."[8] In the 1830s, Baron Justus von Liebig, a German chemist, identified components in foods that seemed to be used by the body: proteins, fats, and carbohydrates. For some time, people were convinced that fats, carbohydrates, and proteins were the only important compounds in the diet, but this hypothesis was challenged by the Industrial Revolution. Mechanized roller milling sapped the nutritional power of wheat flour, eliminating the nutrient-dense wheat germ in the quest for bright white flour. This "gorgeous white powder was nutritionally worthless,"[9] and children began showing signs of illness. Wherever refined grains dominated the diet, deficiency diseases followed. A team of scientists investigating the causes of an 1890s epidemic of beri-beri in Dutch Indonesian colonies established the existence of "accessory food factors," previously unknown compounds eventually named "vitamins."[10] Christiaan Eijkman, credited with the discovery, witnessed the power of unseen compounds as he watched hens feed. Those who ate white rice developed beri-beri, but when they ate brown rice, symptoms disappeared. His discovery of what would later be known as Vitamin B1, or thiamine, was the first milestone in an enumeration of vital food compounds that would stretch over several more decades.[11]

Elmer McCollum, a scientist who restricted the diets of rats to detect components that weakened or strengthened them, discovered vitamins A and B and identified the link between vitamin D and rickets. Research accelerated during World War I. The government found that large percentages of recruits, "theoretically in their physical prime and from all classes of society," were too undernourished for service.[12] Upon entering World War II, America again found undernourished recruits. The U.S. government called on nutritionists to advise on rationing systems to prevent any slip in health gains.[13] Thiamine was dubbed the "morale vitamin," and the U.S. Food Agency trumpeted that "vitamins will win the war."[14]

By the 1950s, scientists had established minimum vitamin intakes for stable health. The nutrition-obsessed continue to develop ever more optimized vitamin cocktails—in 2014, an online entrepreneur began selling "Soylent," a food product designed to replace the known nutritional components in a complete diet.[15] Meanwhile, contradictory and inconclusive information is everywhere. As Tannahill cautions, though, "some experts talk as if today's knowledge is as absolute and unquestionable as revealed truth, the more responsible members of the profession acknowledge that many mysteries remain."[16]

Gurus of Grub

From Dr. Kellogg to Dr. Oz, Americans have turned to health experts—ersatz or genuine—for dietary recommendations. Every era has its authorities, advisers, and charismatic leaders. In women's magazines and newspaper columns, in lecture halls and on the Internet, America's dietary experts have been locked in a centuries-long struggle to control the direction of the public discourse on food—while the rest of us struggle to parse confusing and conflicting research to develop a useful understanding of how food interacts with health. Beginning in the early nineteenth century, America developed a number of food celebrities who became household names for their pronouncements on healthy eating. Some of the most influential are described below.

Sylvester Graham (1794–1851)

A Presbyterian minister, Graham was involved in the fight for temperance, urging Americans to resist alcohol, when he homed in on gluttony as a cause of drunkenness. He crafted a theory that the source of most illness was "gastrointestinal distress," and he determined that "the best way to soothe the American stomach was to avoid 'stimulating' foods," which he believed contributed to sexual excitement, in turn damaging health. His forbidden foods included alcohol, tea, coffee, pepper, ginger, mustard, cinnamon, horseradish, and meat, especially pork, all of which "created an excess of digestive activity, causing sexual arousal that could only sap vitality and well-being."[17] Graham advocated fresh, raw fruits and vegetables, a radical notion for many Americans who had been taught that uncooked produce carried disease. Drawing on eighteenth-century philosophers who advocated a return to nature, Graham recommended whole grain breads, which seemed closer to their natural state.[18] Over the course of the nineteenth century, Americans gradually adopted many of his foundational principles, eating more fresh produce and whole-wheat products, including the digestive biscuit we know today as the "Graham cracker."

Catherine Beecher (1800–1878)

Daughter of a Presbyterian minister, Catherine Beecher used her platform as a leading women's educator to claim authority over all things related to home and family, and, indirectly, the larger society.[19] In Beecher's 1856 *Letters to the People on Health and Happiness*, she offers "Rules for Selecting Food." Stimulating items like meat, she cautioned, "make the heart beat quicker, and all the organs of the body work faster," and they should be eaten sparingly. Vegetable foods fostered calm and focus. Beecher advocated portion control, saying that "men have so abused Nature that appetite has ceased to be a guide to most persons of the amount of food needed."[20] Beecher and her peers worried about the health of the women of their generation, believing them less "robust" than their foremothers. This concern lent urgency to her campaigns—if women were too weak to tend to their own families, the moral and physical health of the entire society would go into decline. Beecher established a logic model that became deeply embedded in writing about food, cooking, and family for decades, perhaps centuries, to come: proper eating produced good health and a good society, and mothers and wives—not medical professionals—were to take primary responsibility for ensuring it.[21]

James H. Salisbury (1823–1905)

James Salisbury, in his "Relation of Alimentation and Disease," describes how he determined the relative value of foods by testing "the effects of living exclusively upon one food at a time."[22] He began with baked beans, making extensive notes on the flatulence and constipation they caused. Progressing through dozens of foodstuffs, he used his observations to build a diet plan that maintained the "nerve force." The body was a machine, he asserted, that needed to be kept "sweet and in good running order."[23] Bucking the trend set by those who came before him, Salisbury promoted a high-protein diet, heavy on meat. Vegetables seemed to be the most frequent cause of digestive difficulties for humans, who by nature's design were "about two-thirds carnivorous." Encouraging people to avoid diabetes-causing starches, he developed a recipe for the "steak" that would bear his name in TV dinners and school lunches ever after: "Eat the muscle pulp of lean beef . . . when cooked, put it on a hot plate, and season to taste with butter, pepper, and salt. Either Worcestershire, Halford, or chutney sauce may be used on meats if desired."[24]

Horace Fletcher (1849–1919)

Like Graham, Horace Fletcher advocated low-protein diets, but, instead of religious purity, he preached the secular gospel of bodily wellness. He focused less on food itself, and more on the meeting of the fork and the mouth. Converted by his own experience of weight loss and improved vitality, Fletcher rallied doctors and chemists to his idea that eaters should "masticate" food until it lost all taste and texture, predigesting it in the mouth until it "swallows itself."[25] Claiming to survive on an extremely low protein intake, he impressed followers by pitting himself in fitness tests against Yale University athletes, including one in which he "doubled the world's record" in weighted leg lifting (350 pounds) and pulling stunts like bicycling two hundred miles on his fiftieth birthday. "Was I stiff the next day? Not at all, and I rode fifty miles before breakfast the next morning."[26] When followers asked what they should eat, he responded, "I eat anything that my appetite calls for; I eat it only when it does call for it; and I eat until my appetite is satisfied and cries 'Enough!'"[27]

John Harvey Kellogg (1852–1943)

The man who created cornflakes was fired by religious fervor. A Seventh-Day Adventist, John Harvey Kellogg's medical degree was funded by fellow adherents who hoped his gravitas would be used to promote a vegetarian diet divinely revealed to an Adventist prophet. Kellogg dutifully sought scientific justification for vegetarianism; positing that meat eating caused a bloom of harmful bacteria in the colon, he recommended "exterminating them with yogurt or expelling them with roughage."[28] Kellogg's Battle Creek Sanitarium in Michigan soon drew patients "with more secular intent," including celebrities such as President William Howard Taft, Thomas Edison, and Henry Ford. These spa-goers "cheerfully paid for the privilege of following a regimented schedule that included cold baths and workouts in the gymnasium and meals that consisted of items such as yogurt, stewed prunes, and unseasoned grains."[29] Kellogg wanted his patients to eat whole-grain crackers, but many patients' teeth were too sensitive. Kellogg experimented with making grain mush into paste, feeding it through rollers, and then drying it and breaking it into "flakes." Though he originally intended his cornflakes to be eaten out of hand, followers enjoyed soaking them in milk and sprinkling them with sugar. Kellogg's brother William, seeing dollar signs as the idea went mainstream, launched the Kellogg Company to market cornflakes commercially. William Kellogg "convinced many Americans . . . that a bowl of cereal was a more healthful and appealing breakfast than a plate full of greasy meat products, potatoes, syrup, and bread."[30]

Charles Post (1854–1914)

Charles Post, once a patient at the Battle Creek Sanitarium, "claimed that his stay there did not improve his health." Post was unimpressed by the quality and taste of the health foods, especially a coffee substitute made from "bran, molasses and burned bread crusts." Post concocted his own version, Postum, and launched a health food business, complete with a competing sanatorium and cereal factory in Battle Creek. There he turned out Grape-Nuts, a cereal that contained neither grapes nor nuts but sounded natural and wholesome, and a flake cereal initially titled "Elijah's Manna" until religious leaders pushed him to rename it "Post Toasties."[31] At its peak, the Battle Creek cereal industry produced 107 brands of breakfast cereal. The advertising and marketing flair of businessmen like William Kellogg and Post had turned "obscure health food" into a profitable, mainstream product enjoyed by a wide swath of Americans. By the twentieth century, more than eighty million Americans were eating breakfast cereal daily.[32]

Sarah Tyson Rorer (1849–1937)

A middle-class housewife whose claim to expertise in nutrition science initially derived from having a chemist father, Sallie Rorer was a sought-after cooking teacher and eventually head of the Philadelphia School of Cooking. A leading figure in the domestic science and home economy movements, she endorsed the view that social ills were caused by "unscientific feeding" and were curable through "educated cooking."[33] Claiming to have cured herself of chronic indigestion—a frequent ailment of diet gurus—she advocated "modest rates of consumption" and "salad every day." Rorer was frequently quoted in women's magazines and newspaper columns, spoke before audiences, gave product endorsements, and in the 1920s appeared on radio shows. However, the gap between her confident assertions and her scientific knowledge yawned wider as time went on and professional dietary science advanced.[34] By the time of her death in 1937, dietetics had professionalized, and university-trained women had taken the lead in making dietary prescriptions.[35]

Betty Crocker (1921–)

Dietary gurus didn't even have to be real. Betty Crocker, a fictional character representing the collective wisdom of hundreds of marketers and food scientists, was born of consumer confusion. In 1921, the Washburn-Crosby Flour Company offered a prize for solving a puzzle in one of their ads. Along with nearly thirty thousand answer submissions came notes with cooking questions like "How long should I knead bread?" Advertising head Samuel Gale, believing that "women did not want advice from a man, who presumably did not know his way around the kitchen," normally sent consumer questions to the all-female staff of domestic scientists in the Gold Medal Home Service Department. Gale saw a public relations opportunity in the incredible volume of correspondence, and, with his advertising team, he developed the persona of Betty Crocker to dispense advice on behalf of the brand. The concept was part of a push to "feminize product presentation" in light of the dawning awareness that women controlled more than four-fifths of consumer spending. Responses from Betty Crocker were individualized and cordial, creating confidence and trust. The Crocker character eased women over the threshold of modernization, helping them adapt to the isolating twentieth-century kitchen.[36] Crocker was not the only "corporate character" who stood in in for the anonymous domestic scientists who were the source of her authority: Ann Pillsbury for General Mills, Kay Kellogg for Kellogg, Mary Alden for Quaker Flour, Mary Lynn Woods for Fleischmann's Yeast, and Carolyn Campbell for Campbell's Soup were just a few of the personas developed by public relations departments to influence consumers' relationships with national brands.

The Ann Pillsburys and Betty Crockers of the mid-twentieth century ushered in a permanent change in the nature of the food guru. Yes, extreme diets and pseudoscience were here to stay. But after the First World War and decades of investment in university science departments, professional science succeeded in winning ultimate authority over diet and health. Doctors, professors, and laboratory researchers now put the imprimatur of their institutions and professional journals on dietary recommendations. But there was still a market for guidance in eating and cooking, and a new, less nutrient-focused kind of food celebrity emerged. These new gurus focused on acquiring fancy cooking skills, expanding the repertoire, and entertaining rather than on health. Crocker's successors, including the likes of Julia Child and Martha Stewart, moved health down the list of food priorities. Despite an ongoing obsession with calorie control and weight, food in the twentieth century became more emotional and social and less instrumental, and Americans' new food gurus reflected that shift.

Too Fat, Too Thin: Nutrition and the Ideal Physique

Nineteenth-century concerns about restrictions on the diet were mostly moral or physiological. Then as now, America was "a land of overeaters," but Graham and his ilk condemned gluttony because it reflected moral corruption, not a sweet tooth.[37] But as science built an understanding of vitamins and calories, it seemed possible to use this information to perfect the operations of the body, as if it were any other machine. Americans began a conversation about the ideal physique. The size of a person was newly linked to the health of the nation. "Whether through claims that morbid obesity impacted on the health of the mother and child and thus weakened the state or whether the fat man and the thin man could not fulfill their civic and military duty and became a drain on the state," people whose bodies did not conform to the standard were "seen as a danger to themselves as well as to others."[38]

Sarah Tyson Rorer connected light eating to "daintiness." Consuming three meals a day was "unrefined."[39] Shapiro documents the "culinary idealism" of home economics experts who tried to reframe eating as a necessary evil. Nutritionally optimized concoctions were unappetizing, so new importance was placed on "dressing up" food. Surveying decades of cooking and eating advice, Shapiro concludes that people have often found "something unsettling, something very dimly fearsome, about the sight of a woman putting food of any substantial bulk into her mouth."[40] Hearkening back to Graham's fears, appetite for food might have been associated with undisciplined sexual appetite, a sign of a gross physicality the guardians of propriety felt must be suppressed.

During World War I, the Depression, and World War II, some Americans felt conflicted about their ability to buy food when so many were going hungry, manifesting their discomfort in elimination diets that helped them dispense with guilt; they, too, could suffer the loss of beloved foods. This represented an opportunity for what Fernández-Armesto describes as "a new brand of grand-scale snake-oil hucksters," most famously Gaylord Hauser.[41] Special diets including the "zigzag diet," "cosmetic diet," "transition diet," "vitality diet," and "mending diet" poured from his imaginative pen. Hauser counted Cary Grant, Mae West, and Greta Garbo among his followers. Comedians mocked him on the vaudeville stage: Jimmy Durante cracked that Hauser's diets didn't really make a person live longer—it just seemed like it.[42]

By the 1950s, intensifying expectations for women produced an obsession with dieting. Most diets at midcentury worked by declaring normal foods and meals off limits. "At last it was possible," Shapiro wryly observes, "to believe that women had no right to food."[43] Fad diets came and went: "Appropriate industries proselytized for the coffee-and-donuts diet; a crash diet of raw fruit and vegetables was promoted by Californian fruit interests; the United Fruit Company backed the 'bananas and skim milk' diet."[44] Others were circulated in bestselling books, like Adelle Davis's *Let's Eat Right to Keep Fit* (1954) and *Let's Get Well* (1965). Magazines and television also promoted diet news and spread images of a new physical ideal. As Tannahill relates, "The slim, leggy teenage look was in and . . . [e]very woman who was not a slim, leggy teenager either embarked on, or contemplated embarking on, a craze for dieting that has scarcely faltered since."[45] The continuous focus on weight evaded criticism until the 1978 publication of psychotherapist Susie Orbach's *Fat Is a Feminist Issue*. Orbach framed the diet industry as a patriarchal project commodifying women, and she suggested that overweight could be a legitimate lifestyle choice—a rejection of gender stereotypes and an expression of self-determination.

Fear of Fat

In the 1970s and 1980s, the medical community targeted dietary fat as the enemy, implicated in weight gain, high cholesterol, and increased risk of heart attack. "Fat-free" products popped onto shelves, but obesity rates only climbed over the next two decades. Confusion followed—perhaps it was really replacing fat with carbohydrates that caused weight gain. Or perhaps it was the increase in sugar—now in everything from soup to tomato sauce—or the nature of the sugar, high-fructose corn syrup being suspect number one.

Americans also struggled to navigate between the Scylla and Charybdis of overweight and anorexia. Though these conditions have different causal factors, they are characterized by a fear of body fat and a struggle to be rid of a real, or imagined, excess. Anorexia has existed since antiquity, most frequently as a symptom of another illness. After World War II, increasing incidence of anorexia nervosa—the term designating psychological origin—prompted public attention. Often mistakenly imagined as a diet "gone too far," anorexia is distinct from dieting in that an individual with the disorder typically "undergoes a radical change in lifestyle . . . due to the controlling nature of the illness."[46] By the 1980s, the disorder was commonly discussed in popular media, almost "glamorized" in the eyes of some observers. Now classed as a mental illness (along with other "eating disorders," such as bulimia, first described in 1979), anorexia brought attention to social factors that may contribute to disordered thinking, particularly the ideal of thinness, the equation of dieting and self-control, and abuse. In recent and extreme versions of this thinking, some anorexics have created a sense of belonging around anorexia as a lifestyle choice, calling themselves "pro-ana."

At the other end of the physical spectrum, the categories of "overweight" and "obesity" are defined not as a set of symptoms but as a purely physical measure, the quantification of body mass in relation to height and build. Americans, on average, have been growing in size for at least a hundred years, but since 1980 the incidence of obesity has accelerated, affecting more than a third of adults and 17 percent of children, and putting them at greater risk of heart disease, cancer, and type 2 diabetes.[47] Most often suggested as the causes of this rise are changes in the food industry (increase in processed food, added sweeteners, larger portion sizes, etc.) and a reduction in physical activity. Scientists are also exploring other possible factors, such as ecological change, epigenetics, economic position, and even the long-term effects of seemingly unrelated behavioral changes such as the dramatic reduction in smoking.

The diet industry continues to reap billions in profits each year. Many critics consider the industry as being interested mainly in its own self-perpetuation: "Its greatest failure would be the elimination of actual or perceived unhappiness with weight, for with this success would come an end to the dieting industry."[48] Food has never been more ubiquitous, at least for the well-off; yet individual people do seek, and often gain, control over their own eating patterns and body size. The problem of convincing the broader population to adopt their behaviors, though, continues to plague policymakers and health professionals alike.[49]

From Nutrition to Nutritionism

In his book *In Defense of Food*, Michael Pollan recognized "something peculiar going on. The food was gradually disappearing from supermarket shelves." He didn't mean the shelves were empty, but that whole foods were being shouldered out by packaged "edible foodlike substances" packed with "nutrients."[50] Instead of food, shoppers choose labels—"low fat," "high fiber," "probiotic," "gluten-free." This total acceptance of scientific nutrition as the best guide to eating, Pollan suspects, may be—counterintuitively—destructive to health. In thinking of foods as nothing more than nutrient cocktails, people have rejected millennia of traditional dietary knowledge. No wonder Americans, according to Pollan, are in a state of "nutritional confusion and anxiety."[51] Pollan uses the term *nutritionism*, coined by sociologist of science Gyorgy Scrinis, for the ideology that "nutritional and chemical constituents and requirements" in food are "all we need to understand."

The U.S. government has been one of nutritionism's major proponents. As soon as the field of nutrition science developed, the Department of Agriculture began publishing pamphlets such as "How to Select Foods" (1916), "Choose Your Food Wisely" (1917), and "Foods for Young Children" (1916). In 1943, the USDA issued a one-page infographic of

Figure 3.1. The USDA began promoting dietary guidelines during World War II to combat wartime malnutrition. This version of the "Basic Seven" dates to 1946. (National Archives and Records Administration)

the "Basic Seven" foods, which set a pattern for the graphic presentation of nutrition guidelines to the present day.[52] People complained the structure was too complicated, so in the 1950s the groups were boiled down to the "Basic Four"—bread and cereals, milk and cheese, fruits and vegetables, and meats, fish, and beans. In 1979, a new "Hassle Free Food Guide" added a "fats and sweets" group for the purpose of slapping a "caution" sign on it. The next decades saw an increasingly politicized struggle over representation. The 1984 Food Wheel and 1992 Food Guide Pyramid attempted, for the first time, to convey recommended portion sizes for each food group. Food industries sparred with health officials over the size and shape of their chunk, forcing redesigns. The new MyPyramid was difficult to understand, lasting only six years before MyPlate was introduced. A spare image of a plate with colored fields for each group, it was by far the simplest of all.

The struggle over MyPyramid is part of a cultural tug-of-war. The messages of government public health agencies and private food industries compete with or even contradict one another, and marketers exploit the resulting anxiety by promoting the health promises of their products. Pollan nicknames the network of businesses, agencies, and advertisers a "Nutritional Industrial Complex" consisting of "well-meaning, if error-prone, scientists and food marketers only too eager to explore every shift in the nutritional consensus." Americans may have forgotten that food has more than instrumental value. We don't eat just to promote health and avoid disease but to connect with other people, to express identity, to enjoy ourselves, and to celebrate rituals.[53] After a solid century of nutritionism, Pollan and others are advocating that Americans restore those cultural and interpersonal values to the act of eating.

Angel Food, Devil's Food: Spiritual Dimensions of Eating

Eating nourishes the soul. In many religious traditions, food connects humans to the divine—an offering, a sacrifice, a communion. Even in secular realms, food stands for abstract ideas and values. During America's second Great Awakening, religious communities developed guidelines for eating. The Shakers, a Christian sect strongest in the early nineteenth century, grew their own vegetables and herbs, made bread, and raised livestock. At first, "there were few rules beyond the expectation that the brothers and sisters graciously and unselfishly eat the food that the community cooks prepared." But many adherents were swayed by Graham's arguments against eating animal flesh, while others refused to abandon meat. The two factions were pitted against each other when, in 1841, the ministry declared that a divine edict now required followers to give up meat, coffee, and tea. In 1855, permission was restored—perhaps, Wallach speculates, due to declining membership.[54]

The practices of abstinence (avoiding specific foods for a given time) and fasting (avoiding all food for a period of time) appear across religious traditions. Abstinence in Christian traditions most often meant going without meat during periods of observance such as Lent and Advent, though it was usually acceptable to replace meat with fish or other proteins. Abstinence from all ritually impure foods has long been part of the dietary discipline of Jews and Muslims. Prescribed fast days occur in Jewish traditions as well as Islamic, Hindu, and many indigenous religions.[55] Though these traditions became more difficult to maintain in the polyglot twentieth century, for many people, religious strictures on eating remain an element of spiritual practice.

Many traditions include premeal ceremonies, such as offering an expression of gratitude or consecrating food to a deity. In middle-class Victorian families, the ritual of saying "grace," a short prayer before meals, became popular—though hosts were counseled not to offer grace when guests were present, "lest he or she run the risk of offending those of a different religious inclination."[56] Even when not directly connected to divine edict, food brought religious communities together. The *America Eats* project documented eating events that marked part of a church's liturgical year, allowed communal grieving, or noted important life events. Among them are church suppers, Passover seders, a Cherokee funeral feast, and weddings as occasions on which food, spirituality, and community were tightly intertwined.

Best Practices: Interpreting Food and Health

- Use contextual information to consider how prevailing ideas of diet and health likely impacted people in your interpretive scope. A socially prominent man in the late nineteenth century, for instance, especially one in the enervating business world, could be expected to at least have an opinion on the Graham diet and the Kellogg cures. Was medicinal gardening or eating for the four humors important in your scope of interpretation? Can you discover records or material culture related to patent medicines, influential leaders, or cooking demonstrations at which messages about food and health were communicated?
- Display the material culture of "good for you" food. This might include:
  ○ printed texts, propaganda, and advertisements with health messages
  ○ religious artifacts, such as dishes dedicated to eating ritually purified food
  ○ sickroom diets that sometimes required special servingware, such as enamel dishes and funnels for feeding
- Interpret intersections of food and religion. Jewish and Catholic immigrants worked hard to secure appropriate foods to keep up their observances—or deal with internal struggles about compromising those standards.
- Interpret intersections of health recommendations and individual identity. Many dietary gurus recommended special diets for different groups of people and stages of life. Anyone following their dictates would plan meals differently for infants, young children, people in the prime of life, manual laborers, "brain workers," the ill, and the elderly.
- Explore the ethics and moral philosophy of eating in your interpreted period or scope, perhaps inviting philosophy faculty or students from a local university to lead a discussion on ethical eating and vegetarianism in the past and today.
- Connect with religious communities observing contemporary dietary practices and invite them to compare/contrast present-day methods with past ones visible at your site, serving as resources for interpretive development. Invite the celebration of sacred meals and feasts in your museum spaces.

- Explore potential relationships with hospitals, medical management programs, nursing associations, and others concerned with food and health. Offer professional development programs, outreach tables, and mutual information exchanges sharing perspectives on food, health, and diet.
- Identify locavore groups and other organizations interested in developing a morally responsible approach to eating in the present day, and plan programming with them that helps put their contemporary strategies into a historical genealogy.
- Present historical gardening and cooking as more than just culinary skills but examples of the application of knowledge about medicinal properties, theories of health, and individual health needs.

Discussion Starter: Food Rules

In 2009, science writer Michael Pollan asked his readers to submit their personal dietary guidelines—inherited or original ideas about how to regulate health using food. He received hundreds of responses, and he published many of them in his 2009 book *Food Rules: An Eater's Manual*. The collected rules encompass folk wisdom, traditional cultural practice, lived experience, and medical advice. Ranging from reminders to eat slowly and savor because "the banquet is in the first bite" to "shop the peripheries of the supermarket" to ensure more whole foods than processed, the cumulative advice is a snapshot of how Americans are thinking about food and health.

Inspired by these "food rules," start a discussion on food rules your own group of interpreters can think of. To start, gather some markers and sticky notes. Take five to ten quiet minutes for each person to jot down rules they try to live by, one rule to each sticky. Then post the stickies on a wall. See if you can group the rules into groups or quadrants, such as religious, moral/ethical, physical, and traditional (or any other category that seems relevant to you). Using the posted material, discuss the diversity of beliefs and influences on your own food thinking today. Finally, think about how your discoveries apply within your interpretive scope. What sources of advice and information were guiding their food choices? Where do you need more evidence to support your interpretations? Could an experience like this help visitors understand more about your interpreted messages?

Fresh Ideas: John Forti on Museums, Health, and Historic Gardens

John Forti is director of horticulture and education at the Massachusetts Horticultural Society, the oldest institution of its kind in the United States. During his career as a historic gardener, horticultural curator, and landscape educator in history museums and botanical gardens, John has introduced the powerful allure of gardening to thousands of people through lively, interactive, and personal explorations of historic gardens. Here, he discusses how a historic garden—however small and simple—can be a powerful tool to reveal past thinking about how food is related to health.

Figure 3.2. John Forti leading a program on heirlooms and native plants at the Polly Hill Arboretum, West Tisbury, Massachusetts. (Courtesy of John Forti)

Many people think of gardens as a purely decorative component of a historic site. How can a period garden help visitors understand deeper ideas about health and well-being in the past?

Gardens are decorative—the very act of appreciating color, aroma, and growth can improve well-being—but they're educational as well. The tasks of historic gardening offer opportunities to introduce physical activity—for instance, having visitors assist in carrying water, digging, lifting, weeding, and harvesting. Gardens illustrate some of the most basic interpretive points about health; access to fresh, whole foods; and the place-based eating traditions that connect us to season, climate, culture, and flavor.

What ideas from the past about gardens as influences on health are still relevant today?

What we think of today as "nutrition science" is really an overlap between food and medicine often expressed in the past through culture, worldview, and plant selection. In historic gardens, audiences rediscover the foundations of medicine. Much as with ayurvedic and

Chinese herbal medicine, the "doctrine of humors" offers lessons in how flavor profiles and traditionally paired seasonal foods can guide us toward more balanced diets. New studies are helping us to understand that fresh, sun-ripened, and organically raised local foods offer greater nutritional value than those grown conventionally, harvested unripe, and kept in long storage. Small to midsized local farms and backyard gardens—whether in the past or in our current renaissance—remind us of the environmentally friendly and sustainable practices possible in agriculture. We see how the quality of air, water, and soils is improved through careful choices. Ultimately, these factors can have the greatest impact on our quality of life and the health of our habitats and families.

How have your garden programs touched on the topics of health, nutrition, and wellness?

At Plimoth Plantation, we shared the seventeenth-century understanding that "the cook was half a physician." In the 1627 Pilgrim Village, interpreters presented the idea that "you are what you eat," preparing historic recipes for food and medicine made with over 150 plant varieties introduced by colonists and recorded in primary sources. The Gardens at the Massachusetts Horticultural Society's Elm Bank site give families and home gardeners the opportunity to learn best practices for organic growing, plant selection, and nutrition. Our Garden to Table garden organizes produce associated with many cultures, which visitors explore through tours, exhibit panels, and daily conversations with master gardeners. We use the vegetables we harvest in educational programming, and we also contribute more than four thousand pounds of produce to local food banks each year, reaching a wider audience over the sharing of fresh, local food with a historical tradition. In the Children's Garden, family-friendly themed beds invite learning about native, heirloom, and cultivated food plants. The Herb Society of America's Herb Garden helps home gardeners learn about herb varieties as well as herbal foods and beverages. Partnerships with master gardeners, Tufts University's Food Policy and Applied Nutrition Program, and Slow Food Boston help deliver classes, events, and prominent speakers that help participants reconsider the link between plants, landscape, and health.

How might a historic site link gardens with interpretation and programming inside the buildings?

Museums with gardens are pushed by nature to research and prepare seasonal foods in order to use produce and create realistic depictions of past lifeways. That constraint can help forward educational goals, opening up opportunities to learn about how people before us ensured adequate nutrition over the course of a year. Seasonal changes also build curiosity and repeat visitation; people want to understand the full arc of the garden and kitchen year. Partnerships with chefs, brewers, farmers, artisanal food producers, and farmers' markets can also make powerful contributions to special event programing. These talented professionals can use and celebrate products from our gardens in hip, fun, intergenerational events. Their enthusiasm helps audiences embrace regional foods—heirloom plants, native plants, rare breed animals—building a local market that helps to continue preserving these important products.

Notes

1. Felipe Fernández-Armesto, *Near a Thousand Tables: A History of Food* (New York: Free Press, 2002), 35.
2. Fernández-Armesto, *Near a Thousand Tables*, 35.
3. Francesco Perono Cacciafoco, "Food as Therapy: Elements of the History of Nutrition in Ancient Greece and Rome" (master's thesis, University of Gastronomic Sciences, Bra, Italy, 2012), 45.
4. Hans J. Teuteberg, "The Birth of the Modern Consumer Age," in *Food: The History of Taste*, edited by Paul Freedman (Berkeley: University of California Press, 2007), 202.
5. Teuteberg, "The Birth of the Modern Consumer Age," 202.
6. Cacciofoco, "Food as Therapy," 48.
7. Doug Fraser, "Life Before Medicine at Plimoth Plantation," *South Coast Today* newspaper website, November 26, 2009, accessed April 26, 2015, http://www.southcoasttoday.com/article/20091126/News/911260332.
8. Reay Tannahill, *Food in History* (New York: Three Rivers Press, 1989), 333.
9. Michael Pollan, *In Defense of Food: An Eater's Manifesto* (New York: Penguin Group, 2008), 108.
10. Tannahill, *Food in History*, 333. The term at first was *vitamine*, based on the Latin *vita*, for "life," and *amine*, a chemical term denoting the presence of nitrogen. Later discoveries showed that not all of these compounds contained nitrogen, so the final *e* was eventually dropped.
11. Tannahill, *Food in History*, 333.
12. Tannahill, *Food in History*, 334.
13. Tannahill, *Food in History*, 335.
14. Fernández-Armesto, *Near a Thousand Tables*, 50.
15. The product name references the food supply in the 1973 dystopian movie *Soylent Green*.
16. Tannahill, *Food in History*, 335.
17. Barbara Haber, *From Hardtack to Home Fries: An Uncommon History of American Cooks and Meals* (New York: Free Press, 2002), 64.
18. Susan Williams, *Savory Suppers and Fashionable Feasts: Dining in Victorian America* (New York: Pantheon Books, 1985), 94; Jennifer Jensen Wallach, *How America Eats: A Social History of U.S. Food and Culture* (Lanham, MD: Rowman & Littlefield, 2013), 148.
19. Williams, *Savory Suppers and Fashionable Feasts*, 94.
20. Catherine E. Beecher, *Letters to the People on Health and Happiness* (New York: Harper and Brothers, 1855), 69.
21. Williams, *Savory Suppers and Fashionable Feasts*, 94.
22. James H. Salisbury, *The Relation of Alimentation and Diseases* (New York: J. H. Vail and Company, 1888), v.
23. Salisbury, *The Relation of Alimentation and Diseases*, 46.
24. Salisbury, *The Relation of Alimentation and Diseases*, 127; Fernández-Armesto, *Near a Thousand Tables*, 47–48.
25. Horace Fletcher, *Fletcherism: What It Is, or How I Became Young at Sixty* (New York: Frederick A. Stokes, 1913), in Internet Archive, accessed April 26, 2015, 10.
26. Fletcher, *Fletcherism*, 24.
27. Fletcher, *Fletcherism*, 32.

28. Fernández-Armesto, *Near a Thousand Tables*, 44.
29. Wallach, *How America Eats*, 154.
30. Wallach, *How America Eats*, 154.
31. Joy Santlofer, "Cereal, Cold," in *The Oxford Companion to American Food and Drink*, ed. Andrew Smith (New York: Oxford University Press, 2007), 102.
32. Santlofer, "Cereal, Cold," 101–2.
33. Fernández-Armesto, *Near a Thousand Tables*, 44–45.
34. As an example, Rorer counseled against including salt and vinegar in one's diet, because they were corrosive to pots and pans. Fernández-Armesto quoted one of her scaremongering questions as follows: "If salt and vinegar will eat away copper, what will it do to the lining of the stomach?" (*Near a Thousand Tables*, 45).
35. Laura Shapiro, *Perfection Salad: Women and Cooking at the Turn of the Century* (New York: Farrar, Straus, and Giroux, 1986), 192–94.
36. Susan Marks, *Finding Betty Crocker: The Secret Life of America's First Lady of Food* (New York: Simon and Schuster, 2005), 14–20.
37. Fernández-Armesto, *Near a Thousand Tables*, 43–44.
38. Sander L. Gilman, *Diets and Dieting: A Cultural Encyclopedia* (New York: Routledge, 2008), x.
39. Fernández-Armesto, *Near a Thousand Tables*, 45.
40. Shapiro, *Perfection Salad*, 233.
41. Fernández-Armesto, *Near a Thousand Tables*, 49.
42. Gilman, *Diets and Dieting*, 127.
43. Shapiro, *Perfection Salad*, 220.
44. Fernández-Armesto, *Near a Thousand Tables*, 48–49.
45. Tannahill, *Food in History*, 347.
46. Gilman, *Diets and Dieting*, 7–11.
47. "Overweight and Obesity: Facts," Division of Nutrition, Physical Activity, and Obesity, National Center for Chronic Disease Prevention and Health Promotion, Centers for Disease Control website, accessed April 26, 2015, http://www.cdc.gov/obesity/data/facts.html.
48. Gilman, *Diets and Dieting*, xi.
49. Fernández-Armesto, *Near a Thousand Tables*, 53–54.
50. Pollan, *In Defense of Food*, 1.
51. Pollan, *In Defense of Food*, 6.
52. "A Brief History of USDA Food Guides," Center for Nutrition Policy and Promotion, United States Department of Agriculture, USDA website, June 2011, accessed April 26, 2015, http://www.choosemyplate.gov/food-groups/downloads/MyPlate/ABriefHistoryOfUSDAFoodGuides.pdf.
53. Pollan, *In Defense of Food*, 8–9.
54. Wallach, *How America Eats*, 149–50.
55. Alan Davidson, *The Oxford Companion to Food*, 3rd edition (New York: Oxford University Press, 2014), 297.
56. Williams, *Savory Suppers and Fashionable Feasts*, 28.

Local Flavor: Interpreting Food and Place

I N THE NOVEL *Moby-Dick*, Herman Melville's Ishmael is introduced to the island of
Nantucket, center of Yankee whaling, through a local inn's chowder. Guests at the Try
Pots eat "chowder for breakfast, and chowder for dinner, and chowder for supper, till you
began to look for fish-bones coming through your clothes."[1] In 1851, Melville was already
attuned to the ways in which foods defined American places and regions.

American landscapes are patterned over with variations in climate, architecture, speech,
and, of course, food. Travelers trade information about regions they've visited, publishing
accounts and, more recently, sharing photos, videos, and online reviews. Travel magazines,
movies and television, and the tourism industry generate and reinforce expectations of place.
But sometimes, Americans have leaned away from regional identities and more toward pan-
Americanism and homogeneity. Celebrated during the 1930s, regionalism was out of fashion
in the 1950s and 1960s. Regional sensibilities have waxed and waned throughout American
history in what historian Edward Ayers calls "a cyclical process of forgetfulness and rediscovery." Recently, regionalism has been rising again in the form of an "impassioned localism"
seeking to revitalize communities and strengthen links between people, land, and culture.[2]

History museums and historic sites are inherently place-based. Many history institutions
are already linking food and place in interpretation as they explore the environmental and
social conditions that give rise to regionally specific food resources and traditions, revealing thick interconnections between natural and cultural heritage. As exciting as that is,
museums also have a responsibility to resist celebratory oversimplifications. Food historian
Sandy Oliver cautions that regional food history is both "terrifically underexplored and over-
romanticized," reminding interpreters to challenge themselves with questions like:

> When do distinctive regional foodways appear? How long do they last? How self-conscious
> are they? What does economic condition have to do with it? Did not the northern and south-
> ern elite eat more similarly to one another than to the lesser classes in either region? How
> many regional foods reflect climate and local species, and how many are based on introduced

foods? Which resulted from the predominant ethnic group? And which resulted from market conditions? Are there, in fact, parts of the country with no distinctive regional foodway?[3]

Teasing apart inherited place-based food stories from concrete evidence about food production and dissemination can be tough. Cultural imperialism and similarities in climate, Oliver says, may have caused "greater similarities across the country even before the homogenizing effects of industrial food production and nationwide transport occurred." Colonial and early Anglo-American eating habits, no matter the region, seem to have been more alike than not. According to historian Susan Strasser, for most of written history, American meals were fairly homogenous:

> Salted meat and cornmeal, which could be kept all year, dominated winter diets; summer brought milk and fresh produce, but milk spoiled . . . butter and cheese prevailed among dairy products because they kept better. Leafy vegetables also spoiled, and many farmers did not plant them because of the need for constant care, limiting their diets to wild greens or vegetables that could be stored or preserved, such as turnips, pumpkins, and beans. They raised orchard fruits more for cider and brandy than for eating, and picked and ate wild berries (rarely preserved because of the high cost of sugar) . . . a steady fare of bread, butter, coffee, and bacon, appears accurate for farmers everywhere before the middle of the nineteenth century.[4]

Unique regional foodways may have been the exception, not the rule, for most of American history. Even in our own time, separating truth from hype can be challenging. Oliver cautious museums to avoid "bland assertions" like "New England's regional foodways are characterized by potato eating." As she wryly notes, "If you know anything at all about other regions you might rightfully say, 'So what?' We may discover that some of the differences among regions may in fact be merely a result of shaded emphasis, of frequency, not of pure distinction."[5] Still, there are powerful emotional and conceptual attachments between food and place. The first thing many people do on returning to a former hometown is to seek out that local barbecue, bagel, tamale, or doughnut made only that way, in that place, and emblematic of the entire experience of being there. Museums can help visitors understand how such characteristic foodways result from the complex interactions of historical forces.

Key Interpretive Concepts

1. *Place is defined by specifics.* It is the unique *terroir* and *merrior* of a region that define it as special and different.
2. *Regional food identity has complex and sometimes surprising roots.* Underlying popular narratives may be even more fascinating stories of food origins and connections between people and place.
3. *Food moves.* Foodways from all regions follow human tradition bearers on their own travels. Follow food from your own region as it finds a place in national and world cuisine, as well as tracking the introduction of new foodways to your area.

Creating American Flavor

America's first regional cuisines were indigenous. Despite the spread of corn culture and the wide range of foodstuffs like deer and fowl, regional foods were tied to varying soil composition, plant communities, and animal populations. Fisheries and wild plant foods on the West Coast differed from those on the East. Even where individual foods—such as squash or beans—were widespread, literally thousands of specialized local varieties were developed over centuries through breeding. Native people managed the environment to expand the range of desired foods and increase the number of options in a given place.

English settlement melded English foodways and indigenous resources. The colonists' goal was to replicate a middle-class European diet in the New World, not to enjoy a new culinary sense of place. In his discussion of food in colonial and early American literature, Mark McWilliams calls it "not surprising" that British colonists tried to stick to familiar foodways, because they "had resisted gastronomic change at home as well. Food historians have noted that, as continental cuisines underwent dramatic change from the fifteenth to seventeenth centuries, English cookery remained relatively static. . . . This resistance to change in the food habits that the colonists brought to the New World helped establish British cookery as the unshakable foundation of American foodways."[6] By the eighteenth century, tastes were changing. Colonists, burdened by British policies, lost enthusiasm for all things British. No longer granting England cultural superiority by default, they latched onto humble American foods like corn, pork, and squash as symbols of self-sufficiency, simplicity, and honesty. American foods were wholesome and democratic; English foods were decadent, "tainted by association with monarchy." The food on a well-to-do colonist's plate did reflect place, but more strongly, political loyalties.

Formerly despised, corn took on new layers of meaning. The British "loathing" for corn spurred Americans to reclaim it with a prideful defensiveness. This combative impulse even underlies the typical menu of today's Thanksgiving dinner. When the Old Colony Club of Plymouth, Massachusetts, launched their annual Thanksgiving celebration in 1769, they deliberately chose local fare: "1, a large baked Indian whortleberry pudding; 2, a dish of sauquetash; 3, a dish of clams; 4, a dish of oysters and a dish of codfish; 5, a haunch of venison, roasted by the first Jack brought to the colony; 6, a dish of seafowl; 7, a dish of frost fish and eels; 8, an apple pie; 9, a course of cranberry tarts, and cheese made in the Old Colony." Every dish was indigenous to North America and "dressed in the plainest manner (all appearance of luxury and extravagance being avoided, in imitation of our ancestors, whose memory we shall ever respect)."[7] These emphatic food statements "reflect the translation of necessity into virtue central to republican simplicity."[8]

The first cookbook written in the United States, Amelia Simmons's *American Cookery*, also promoted Americanness through native foods. Simmons modified British recipes to incorporate cornmeal, molasses, squash, and berries. She also recommended the use of pearl ash, a product developed in 1790s America as a leavening and soon exported to England. It was no small point of pride that American ingenuity was now changing British cuisine.[9]

Americans needed to experience regional differences before they could conceptualize regional foodways. After a century of relative unity focused on separating American colonies from their mother countries, American nationals in the nineteenth century began to notice variations between regional cuisines and to celebrate culinary variety as expressive of Republican ideals. Food was one of the ways that Georgians and Virginians differed from Pennsylvanians and New Yorkers, and the differences were remarked on by travelers as a pleasing curiosity, and proof of unity in diversity.

At first, opportunities for travel were rare. Tannahill estimates that until the rail network linked the nation in the mid-nineteenth century, about 90 percent of people never traveled more than five to ten miles from their homes, and had "no direct experience of any style or quality of cooking other than their own, and therefore no standards of comparison."[10] Most travel centered on relocation, trade, or attending to the sick.[11] As few as 1 percent of Americans traveled for pleasure in early America, and those were mostly to elite destinations like spas and mineral springs.[12] Cuisine was not an enticement for wealthy travelers, but a hazard of travel, an uncontrollable and unpredictable element. To travel was to run the risk of being served off-puttingly strange food. In 1870, Samuel Clemens (under his pen name, Mark Twain) published *Roughing It*, a semiautobiographical account of his travels in western territories during the 1860s and 1870s. Clemens recalled his meals at stagecoach stations with exaggerated disgust:

> The station-keeper upended a disk of last week's bread, of the shape and size of an old-time cheese, and carved some slabs from it which were as good as Nicholson pavement, and tenderer. He sliced off a piece of bacon for each man, but only the experienced old hands made out to eat it, for it was condemned army bacon which the United States would not feed to its soldiers in the forts, and the stage company had bought it cheap for the sustenance of their passengers and employees. . . . Then he poured for us a beverage which he called "Slum gullion," and it is hard to think he was not inspired when he named it. It really pretended to be tea, but there was too much dish-rag, and sand, and old bacon-rind in it to deceive the intelligent traveler. . . . Our breakfast was before us, but our teeth were idle.[13]

Later, a breakfast of "hot biscuits, fresh antelope steaks, and coffee" was for Clemens "the only decent meal we tasted between the United States and Great Salt Lake City, and the only one we were ever really thankful for," standing out from the "monotonous execrableness of the thirty that went before it."[14] Versions of Clemens's critique are echoed in travel narratives throughout the nineteenth century.

Travelers to America rarely singled out regional differences. Early nineteenth-century British traveler John Melish noted many differences between regions, but cuisine was not a significant one. Exports, industries, architecture, and the presence or absence of slavery were, for him, more salient characteristics of place. When he did mention food, his focus was on a consistent abundance found everywhere. Melish was startled to find even working-class Americans eating meat and dairy at all three meals, and pouring coffee and tea by the gallon. At a breakfast in Ohio, Melish's modest expectations clashed with definitions of American hospitality:

> I was anxious to be gone as soon as possible, and urged the landlady to make all the haste as she could. She said she would have the breakfast ready in a minute; but the first indication I saw of despatch was a preparation to twist the necks of two chickens. I told her to stop, and she gave me a look of astonishment. "Have you any eggs?" said I. "Yes, plenty," replied she, still keeping in a stooping posture, with the chicken in her hand. "Well," said I, "just boil an

egg, and let me have it, with a little bread and tea, and that will save you and I a great deal of trouble." She seemed quite embarrassed, and said she never could set down a breakfast to me like that. I assured her I would take nothing else. "Shall I fry some ham for you along with the eggs?" said she. "No," said I, "not a bit." "Well, will you take a little stewed pork?" "No," said I. "Shall I make some fritters for you?" "No." "Preserve me, what will you take then?" "A little bread, and tea, and an egg." "Well, you're the most extraordinary man that I ever saw; but I can't set down a table that way." I saw that I was only to lose time by contesting the matter further, so I allowed her to follow her own plan as to the cooking, assuring her that I would take mine as to eating. She detained me about half an hour, and at last placed upon the table a profusion of ham, eggs, fritters, bread, butter, and some excellent tea.[15]

American meals were not "local" but either civilized or rude, abundant or paltry. Before the Civil War, the middle class traveled to auctions, seats of government, relatives' homes, and camp meetings, but rarely did these trips take them more than a day's journey away. Not until the transportation advances of the mid-nineteenth century did the number of travelers begin to expand, and not until then were there many appealing places to go. The profit to be made in packing trains and steamers with leisure passengers spurred the development of what are now known as "destinations." Oceanside and mountain resorts beckoned the affluent. Railroad lines built hotels in major cities, linking destinations to one another. The travel industry powered a commodification of place that still fuels modern tourism.[16] City and state governments, real estate industries, railroad and steamship companies, and hotels invested in self-representation, turning local foods into icons and essential experiences. Travelers picked up on and shared these conceptualizations. In anecdotes and travelogues, postcards and photographs, their food experiences contributed to ideas of regional character in the American mind.

One example is the iconic seafood Maine lobster. Though Maine is home to many food traditions shared with New England and Eastern Canada—baked beans, brown bread, clambakes, codfish, boiled dinners, blueberries—and though the same species of lobster is found in coastal waters from North Carolina to Labrador, the association between Maine and lobster draws millions of tourists each summer to tear into the crustacean on outdoor decks and to purchase its likeness on T-shirts, key chains, and mugs. As author Colin Woodard describes, the process by which this simple food came to dominate Maine's food identity mirrors that of the development of many regional cuisines. Until the railroad era, Maine's coast was in decline as the age of sailing declined and left shipbuilders idle and wharves empty. Railroads gradually brought the state's coastal towns within a few hours' reach of Boston, at a time when urban Americans of means wanted to escape the sooty air of industrial cities. Undeveloped seasides were havens of fresh air, ease of living, and outdoor exercise. Mainers took up a trade in hosting "summer people." Maine fed its tourists what it had—seafood—giving inshore fisheries such as shellfishing and lobstering a "critical boost."[17] Rusticators were eager to try local specialties as a marker of status. "Fishermen found they could sell every lobster they pulled out of their traps in the 1880s . . . the number of lobstermen exploded, from a few dozen in the late 1840s to 1,843 in 1880."[18] Lobsters, once shrugged at, took on the cachet of their buyers. To eat lobster was to have the free time and money to visit Maine. By 1920, tourism was the state's largest revenue source. As Maine struggled to maintain its fishing industry, tourists invested in shined-up villages stripped of

Figure 4.1. Not just a food, Maine's iconic lobster has become a place-defining icon. In this photograph, Ruth and Wimpy's lobster stand in Hancock, Maine, promises the complete local experience. (Library of Congress/Carol Highsmith, photographer)

signs of poverty and labor. In the former fishing town of Boothbay Harbor, commercial fishing wharves became parking lots, and hotels replaced fish processing plants. In the process of commodifying Maine for tourism, its food industries were pushed aside to make way for signs and symbols of themselves, re-presented for tourist consumption.

By the twentieth century, the cost of transportation had fallen so low that the middle and working classes could explore the country. Many more Americans than ever before experienced differences in culture and cuisine within their own nation.[19] As in the nineteenth century, the unpredictable nature of travel made stopping for lunch or dinner a gamble. One was as likely to end up in a greasy spoon as to find delicious regional dishes. Fast food chains arose to take the element of chance out of travel dining, offering the promise of consistency to travelers with nothing to go on but a brand name.

Travelers' tastes exerted opposing forces on American cuisine. Seeking out foods like Maine lobster, Louisiana crawfish, or southern fried chicken, travelers contributed to the celebration and commodification of regional foodways. At the same time, they exerted a homogenizing force, rewarding businesses that provided familiar foods. In the late nineteenth and early twentieth centuries, local boosterism, expressed through fairs and community cookbooks, helped enshrine local food traditions.

Food at the Fairs

Nineteenth-century travelers, xenophobic when traveling independently, flocked to the new industrial and agricultural fairs. As discussed in chapter 1, these exhibitions were part economic and part educational, heavily flavored with regional boosterism. Regions themselves, and the foods they grew, were the products. Fairs drew agricultural community members from a wide geographic area, giving them a place to do business—negotiate sales, arrange livestock breeding, purchase equipment, or discover new technologies. Pat Willard describes fairs as "the center of the universe for rural people: they were the place to show off the fruits of your labor; to buy and trade livestock; to find or court a sweetheart; to lighten, for a moment, the struggles of a hardscrabble working life."[20] Agricultural fairs were established by the early 1800s and proliferated throughout the nineteenth century; by 1900, there were more than two thousand annually.

As fairs added more amusements, agriculture and food exhibitors found imaginative ways to grab attention and promote a region's products. Some were dignified, some intentionally ridiculous, and some a bit of both. Between 1880 and 1930, more than thirty-four "grain palaces" were built at fairs, showcasing the quality of Midwestern corn and wheat. At the 1893 Chicago fair, visitors marveled at Wisconsin's enormous Christopher Columbus made of chocolate. California's Liberty Bell was built from oranges, lemons, and grapefruit, and its prunes were unforgettable after the sight of Sir Preserved Prunes, an all-prune armored knight on horseback.[21] Fairs offered juried competitions for the largest and best examples of produce and livestock breeds, shining an approving light even on the baked goods and preserves made by farm families. Stunt contests, like Iowa's cornhusking competition or Oklahoma's jalapeño-eating contests, reinforced certain foodways as emblems of identity and belonging. Fair activities supported regional self-definition, communicating among participants an understanding that they shared a food culture; that the success of these products was necessary to the success and prosperity of the entire community; and that local products were deserving of dignified display, public notice, press, and applause. The "world's" fairs further cemented these notions. The physical separation of state halls and pavilions supported a psychological separation of regions into distinct places with unique agricultural and food traditions. Fairgoers experienced "travel" in microcosm, forming perceptions of state and regional foodways in planned exhibits.

Though agricultural fairs were about food's future, they were also places where food heritage was remembered and displayed, venues for the self-aware presentation of regional and local pasts. In 1929, organizers of the Tunbridge World's Fair in rural Vermont built a mock village called "Antique Hill," complete with schoolhouse, sawyer, printing press, and other booths exhibiting industries of Vermont's past. Antique Hill continues today, presenting a nostalgic and antiquarian vision of regional agricultural life. In a long shed housing vignettes of homes and businesses, women in an early American-style kitchen prepare stew over a hearth fire, dishing up steaming bowls for volunteers as visitors watch enviously. At a "general store," a waistcoat-wearing "storekeeper" sells Vermont cheddar and hard maple candies. One local editorialist critiqued the presentation, charging Antique Hill with "false nostalgia" and reminding readers that historically, life in rural Vermont "was hard and miserable. Unremitting toil, rampant disease, and isolation were the norms."[22] Antique Hill shares interpretive agendas and tactics with many colonial revival museum villages and historic houses founded in the 1920s, including their rosy view of the past. But despite the sentimental aura, the displays of kitchen gadgets and agricultural implements, the flavors of the Vermont-made foods, and the sights and smells of hearth cooking spur conversation and the sharing of memories among fairgoers. Today's Vermonters use this display to celebrate, remember, and reexperience the history of the local agricultural economy.

Agricultural fairs are still very well attended. The Eastern States Exposition (or "The Big E"), for instance, draws more than a million visitors during its annual run. Though midway attractions and vendors now seem much the same place to place, at the heart of most agricultural fairs one can still find growers' associations, garden clubs, and 4-H groups displaying produce, preserves, and baked goods. Fairs remain economically significant to farmers, enhancing the reputations of their operations, products, and breeding stock. Fairs are still important sites of defining, presenting, policing, and indulging in local and regional foodways.

Community Cookbooks

Community cookbooks were a second way of corralling and codifying local food practice. The first fund-raising cookbook in the United States was published to fund Civil War Sanitary Fairs. Maria Moss's *A Poetical Cook-Book*, published for the 1864 Philadelphia fair, combined recipes with snippets of verse and a few original poems. Moss had invented a new publishing model: compiling recipes from many sources and printing and selling the collection to raise money for charity. The easily replicable idea appealed to women's groups. Between 1864 and 1922, churches and religious organizations, women's clubs, social groups, and reform organizations sold more than three thousand community cookbooks. The idea continues today; thousands of new titles are printed each year.[23]

The cookbooks shared the boosterish spirit of agricultural fairs, taking on the character of their collective authors' social and geographical worlds, but also "demonstrat[ing] the participation of the women who wrote them in the creation of that society."[24] Alison P. Kelly, as a Library of Congress reference specialist, has studied how cookbook writers constructed the character of place with descriptive text like that found in the 1874 *Housekeeping in the Blue Grass*: "The Blue Grass region of Kentucky, as is well known, is considered the garden-spot of the State. It is celebrated for the fertility of its soil, the beauty of its pastures, its flocks and blooded stock, and last, but not least, for the hospitality of its people and their table luxuries."[25] Some books sought to uplift marginalized communities, while others, such as those by local chapters of the Daughters of the Confederacy, used their assertions of culinary culture to uphold ideals of white supremacy.[26] Authors in recently built frontier communities and railroad towns, Kelly notes, were "literally, as well as figuratively, creating the place where they lived." Their cookbooks pooled personal tastes and culinary histories into a cohesive food community, making their books "an affirmation that this particular place is a civilized society."[27] A survey of community cookbooks indicates the awareness of regional foodways—"quahogs and cranberries in Massachusetts, Olympic clams in Oregon, gopher turtles in Alabama, scrapple in Pennsylvania, peanuts and opossum in Georgia, and okra all over the South"—but Kelly cautions that recipes "don't often stay in their place."

Authors took their foodways with them as they moved around the country, so "a recipe for Boston baked beans may turn up in a book from Seattle, or one for jambalaya in a book from Illinois."[28] The appearance of an out-of-context dish can sometimes be combined with other sources to reveal how foodways leaped social or cultural boundaries.

Community cookbooks testify to the presence of foodstuffs in a given place, and they often give some depth of understanding to the role they played on the table and in the imagination. At the same time, they can mislead. Compiled to sell, they often contain groups' "best" recipes, the most special and most praised, rather than telling what was eaten at everyday meals. Holiday treats, party foods, desserts, and fancy luncheon dishes play a larger role in these cookbooks than they do in life. But as rare period documents conceptualized, written, and edited by women, the recipes and accompanying texts reveal details of memory, family history, friendships and rituals, customs and traditions, political thought, and beliefs about obligation and social organization. Historians reconstructing past social relationships may find they are able to use local fund-raising cookbooks to "tease out intersections of personal, community, and national history."[29]

Redefining Region in the New Deal

The next great boost to American regionalism came from the relief programs of the New Deal. Writers and photographers employed by federal agencies roamed the country, documenting thousands of meals. Their explorations of American food took on a new tone: curious, not wary, and celebratory, not snooty. They identified local flavors, and then packaged them for outsiders, developing ideas of regional identity still with us today.

Images by photographers from the Farm Security Administration (FSA) were among the first to establish a strong sense of regional difference—something they were intended to do. Created in 1935 within the USDA, the FSA's charter was to improve the condition of struggling farmers, helping them to resettle after the Dust Bowl, offering farm improvement loans, and building clean water and sewer infrastructure. The agency's "History Unit" was asked to document the need for this assistance by recording images of rural poverty and creating a record of the federal response. The History Unit's eleven photographers chronicled everyday life, capturing racial and ethnic populations, clothing, homes, work, transportation, and food rarely seen in the mainstream press. In the words of Roy Stryker, supervisor of the History Unit, the FSA photographs "introduced America to Americans."[30] FSA photos documented harvest and hunger. The iconic Dorothea Lange portrait of Florence Owens Thompson, a migrant worker with her young children, showed Thompson in a farmworkers' camp. Lange remembered Thompson saying that "they had been living on frozen vegetables from the surrounding fields, and birds that the children killed. She had just sold the tires from her car to buy food."[31] Imagery like this revealed realities of agricultural labor to the nonfarm public. The FSA documented grapefruit canners sorting and sectioning in California, sugarcane harvesters in Puerto Rico, and children under ten harvesting potatoes in northern Maine.

But if the FSA photos revealed hardships, they also offered heartening, even optimistic depictions of loving families, strong communities, and unique traditions. For the first time, many Americans saw a church "fried supper" in Bardstown, Kentucky; a picnic of pinto beans and barbecue in Pie Town, New Mexico; a roadside stand offering catfish, trout, perch, drum, eel, and giant watermelons in Birmingham, Alabama. The images gave such a clear sense of place that "no one would confuse an Oklahoma dust bowl migrant with an Alabama sharecropper or a New York City slum resident with a Miami socialite."[32] "Local color excited outsiders at a time when mass consumer culture was smoothing them over with sameness." The FSA photography introduced images of regional culture that would strengthen in the projects of the Works Progress Administration (WPA).

The WPA, a large-scale set of relief programs designed to employ out-of-work Americans, set up several programs in which writers, artists, and other creative professionals contributed to projects benefiting the nation as a whole. The WPA Federal Writers' Project (FWP) presented local texture in a book series known as the *American Guides*, published between 1935 and 1943. This series for motorists was the first set of guides to America written by Americans.[33] The FWP divided the nation into bureaus, assigning writers familiar with each area to write contextual essays including snapshots of local color, which often meant food culture. A guide to Portland, Oregon, includes a survey of local foodstuffs in a chapter titled "Huckleberry Cakes and Venison," giving descriptions of fern pie, meat pancakes, huckleberry griddle cakes, apple McGinties, sourdough biscuits, salted salmon, and Tillamook cheese.[34] In Guilford, Connecticut, drivers were invited to stop at "rustic stands" advertising Guilford clams, where "cheery, suntanned fisherfolk cater to the passing trade and wrap up a purchase in yesterday's newspaper."[35] Travelers to Miami and Dade County, Florida, could use the *Guides* to find markets selling "odd fruits such as the brown sapodilla, guava, mango, scarlet surinam cherry, golden tangelo and kumquat."[36] In treating each region as a subject of open-minded inquiry, the *Guides* helped define regional character in the American consciousness.

Once all forty-eight states, Alaska, and Puerto Rico had been covered by *American Guides*, series editor Katherine Kellock turned the focus to food. Kellock sensed that regional foodways were passing out of existence, and she planned a book to capture them. To be titled *America Eats*, it would describe American foodways with "a strong social and anthropological component" that would "show varying ethnic traditions as well as the regional and local customs." Five regional sections would cover the Northeast, South, Midwest, Far West, and Southwest. FWP writers were asked to submit pieces that would describe "group meals that preserve not only traditional dishes but also traditional attitudes and customs," taking care to avoid "tea shoppe" prose.[37] Their reports reflected the writers' progressive political bent, as they described Americans "drawn together out of necessity and loneliness . . . conceiving a common table."[38]

Writers built up a picture of incredibly diverse foodways, captured at a time of great transition. As Pat Willard says in her study of the archive, the work is an invaluable record because

> in the 1930s, people were still alive who, as pioneers and immigrants, crossed the Great Plains in wagons or worked their way as miners, loggers, and saloon keepers. There were Native Americans whose memories held faint traces of daily lives and rituals before their tribes were shattered. There were cowboys and chuck wagon cooks who once roamed along the cattle

trails. In the 1930s, the family farm was still producing much of what the country ate, and, although grocery shelves held some processed and engineered foodstuff, it was hardly what it would be even five years later . . . the dishes set on many of the nation's tables could be traced back in ingredients and structures from our forebears.[39]

America Eats was never completed. The deadline for submissions was Thanksgiving 1941. As Kurlansky relates, "On December 3 a gentle reminder that the deadline had passed was sent out. Four days later the Japanese attacked Pearl Harbor."[40] Writers were told to pack up their files in whatever state they existed and forward them to Washington, where they were archived. The FWP transitioned into a War Services group, writing training manuals and other war-related material.[41] The *America Eats* archive—far more material than would have fit into any one book—remains at the Library of Congress and is still used by researchers.[42]

Road to Nowhere: A Homogenized Nation

After World War II, Americans started to complain about the loss of a sense of place. Populations had shuffled as the Depression, war effort, and Great Migration diffused food-ways from their origins and reformed them in new geographies. The Interstate Highway System, begun in 1956, created high-speed roads across the country that allowed travelers to bypass downtowns and farmstands in favor of chain restaurants and gas stations. Federally subsidized school lunch programs standardized youth diets. National brands and fast food chains expanded. Grocery store chains carried the same inventory from coast to coast, and national advertising on television and radio reached everyone from Honolulu to Bangor with messages about what Americans should buy and eat. The nation's cuisine became less intensely regional, but more varied everywhere. Looking back on the road trips of his childhood in the 1950s and 1960s, Mark Kurlansky remembers pronounced regional distinctions in food culture:

> I was struck by the differences in how people ate in other parts of the country—how break-fasts got bigger as you traveled west and hamburgers became increasingly adorned until by California they were virtually a salad sandwich. In New England you ate corn relish or cottage cheese, each served in little metal cups before the meal in better restaurants, where popovers were often dispensed from a deep tin box, big enough to be an oven and strapped to the server's shoulders. You had to find a Jewish bakery to get a respectable rye bread. Crusty bread came from Italian bakeries. . . . As you left the Northeast you said good-bye to almost all traces of Jewish food, including bagels, until you reached California. I remember being struck by the fried food and the powdered sugar in the South. In Seattle we ate aplets and cotlets, the little apricot or apple sugar-dusted fruit bars of Washington State. In Albuquerque I thrilled to my first taste of Mexican food and in Pismo Beach, California, I got to eat for the first time wonderful crunchy sandwiches called tacos.[43]

By the 1980s, the foods Kurlansky was "struck" by were consumed everywhere. Freed from dependence on only local sources of food, Americans indulged a yen for novelty that had probably always existed but was well suited to mass consumer culture. Food discourse began to identify homogenization as a problem. Local food culture and history were being lost as

Americans heated up frozen pizzas, rolled into drive-ins, and dined at restaurant chains. Seasonality, also tightly connected to place, was under threat. Because fresh produce of almost any kind could now be had throughout the year, festivals formerly connected with agricultural traditions became more symbols than true reflections of the annual round; apple cidering, for instance, was a less meaningful celebration once Americans could buy cider any time.

Food writing and activism took a defensive stance. Local and regional foods were disappearing, and only obsessive documentation could preserve them for all time. Food writers Jane and Michael Stern launched their first collecting project in 1984, traveling the United States looking for recipes and restaurants still maintaining their traditions. The Sterns prioritized rural and small-town locations, often romanticizing the folksy feel of their finds, which they described in the 1985 book *Square Meals* and many subsequent works. Their enthusiasm, like that of many of their peers in food journalism, was built on what Ayers calls "a persistent set of assumptions" about regional culture, particularly the idea that "regional identity is, at heart, an inheritance from the past, a moral and intellectual 'heritage' that, if it is to endure, must be preserved from the ravages of modern life." Cultural critic Greil Marcus had coined the term *old, weird America* to describe historical conditions that had produced unaccountably unique variations in folk music before the commercial homogenization of radio airways. Pursuing a culinary version of old, weird America, the Sterns and other authors chronicled aging regional culture as if in fear of the total loss of variation from the American landscape. On television, journalist Charles Kuralt's CBS News *On the Road* series focused national news cameras on local food culture like a hot pepper–eating contest in Louisiana and a maple-sugaring operation in Vermont. Curated lists of "authentic" eateries "discovered" by popularizers in the media sent foodies off in search of the perfect slice of Michigan cherry pie or the only place still making old-fashioned beef pasties, re-creating a sense of regionality by self-consciously eating foods canonized by journalists.

Recovering Regionality

The concern about disappearing foodways may be unwarranted. Ayers notes that despite the fact that Americans tend to "speak of region only to speak of loss, regions do not seem to be disappearing."[44] Regional behaviors and tastes are on the rise. Ayers speculates that "Americans refuse to let regional identity die because it offers something that appears to be hard to find in a mass society: a form of identity that promises to transcend ethnic boundaries, to unite people across generations."[45] Instead of being static and codified, regional cuisines exist in dynamic evolution with one another, and the people continue to experiment with and reinterpret them. Ayers urges Americans who promote regionalism to "see regions more expansively, to include more people as genuine participants in the creation of regional life," and use region as a way of developing belonging rather than exclusion. Fluid and flexible, porous and permeable, America's regional foodways may never have had more cultural currency than they do today. Connections between food and place imbue foodways with meaning often felt to be missing in a commodified food system that separates consumption from production—sometimes by thousands of miles. Today, Americans celebrate, reward, and romanticize regional and local foods and traditions (as long as they don't feel that they must also turn down all the choices offered by the globalized food industry).

The combined agendas of activists and scientists are restoring food regionality. Environmental scientists and botanists are concerned with the narrowing of genetic diversity that comes with increasing dependence on the few crops selected for industrial production. The United Nation's Food and Agriculture Organization reported in 2004 that 75 percent of the world's food is derived from only twelve plants and five livestock animals.[46] Over the past century, cultivation of locally and regionally specific plants and animals declined. During the 1800s, thousands of unique varieties of apples were cultivated in America's orchards—some ideal for cider making, others for storage, and others for cooking. In a typical supermarket today, there are perhaps five apple choices, the same varieties all over the nation. Pressures from industrial buyers inadvertently eliminate foods from the growing cycle; for instance, if breweries or mills demand a single wheat variety, grain growers are likely to stop cultivating other varieties.[47]

In the past two decades, organized efforts have developed to shore up regional food production. The Renewing America's Food Traditions (RAFT) coalition united seven groups to promote and preserve plant and animal foods tied to regional history and culture.[48] Dividing the U.S. map into seven food "nations," RAFT compiled regional inventories of historical "place-based food traditions" deemed "at risk of being lost, either ecologically or culturally."[49] Theirs was the first such listing of foods unique to the North American continent, and RAFT found that more than a thousand of those varieties were "threatened, endangered, or functionally extinct."[50] The coalition recognizes that "not everyone will take up the challenge to cook traditional recipes like Crow bison cattail stew, blue crab and Choppee okra stew, or carpetbag steak stuffed with Apalachicola oysters," but believes that preserving foodstuffs themselves will be a useless exercise if the cultural traditions that sustained them are not also maintained.[51] Members insist that foods and foodways be considered together, as expressions of culture in living relationships with people, not just genetic formulas. Foods at risk, they believe, should not be perceived as "quaint oddities"; rather, they should be relinked to the "health, wealth, gustatory pleasure, and spiritual well-being of America's diverse communities." Historic foods and foodways should reconnect to a living "cultural fabric," with museums among the cultural organizations helping to sustain, or revive, dormant traditions.[52]

The market for travel continues to encourage regional self-definition. Food traditions and new food industries can reinforce collective imagery or lend new food identity, which can then become a central point of appeal to travelers and a new source of pride for locals. Sometimes tourism can help small-scale industries survive in the face of competition from cheaper industrial food sources. Each year in late winter, small sugarhouses in Vermont welcome visitors to watch gallons of maple sap boil into syrup and crystallize into maple sugar. Guests walk through sugarbushes, learn about traditional sugaring, and purchase products in owner-operated stores. Vermont produces only 5.5 percent of the world's maple products; the province of Quebec contributes more than ten times that amount. But maple sugar and syrup are iconic Vermont foods, linked to the region's ways of life, seasonal round, culinary traditions, and need for value-added products when fields are fallow. Sugaring creates an experience of belonging for Vermonters and a sense of place for travelers. Its symbols and imagery have cultural and economic impact far beyond the scale of its output, helping to define Vermont in the American mind.

Museums and historic sites are involved in these tourism processes. Often, museums develop and reinforce narratives of food and place through activities such as cooking demonstrations using local ingredients, talks about local food history, demonstrations of skilled processing work, or an exhibition on local products, communities, or celebrations. Many museums also go beyond their own boundaries to share cultural and historical links to the regional food scene. For example, Memphis's Stax Museum of Soul Music offers a list of neighborhood restaurants, with the recommendation that "when you come to Memphis to visit the world's only full-fledged soul music museum, you should really get in the groove and have some Memphis soul food!"[53] In New York City, the Lower East Side Tenement Museum offers neighborhood walking tours, including one on which tourgoers "taste dumplings, fried plantains, cream puffs and more while exploring the immigrant experience and some of the ways immigrant foods have shaped American food."[54]

Opportunities to center interpretation on food and place will continue to grow. Museum thinker Hal Skramstad observes that as tourism—already one of the world's largest industries—continues to expand, "there will be an increased interest in what is unique and special about each tourist destination. Museums will be extremely important organizations in defining the specialness of a place, the 'there' of a specific locale."[55] Museums interpreting food have the responsibility to support their statements with careful research. Information should come from contextualized readings in period sources, but also from critical secondary studies, archeology, material culture, oral history, and the sciences of landscape, including soil science, botany, wildlife biology, and climatology. Cross-disciplinary understandings of interactions between geographical place and human activity will result in richer, more exciting, and more deeply meaningful interpretation.

Best Practices: Interpreting Food and Place

- Trace change over time in favorite local products and specialties.
- Consider participating in festivals and food events to connect your historical understandings with contemporary food culture.
- Add a historical perspective to discussions of regional food and farm policy by writing op-eds, providing speakers to civic panels and other programs, and offering tours and discussions.
- Invite visitors to participate in local food traditions, including preparing and tasting the foods.
- Contribute research and recipes from your museum to the local and regional food press.
- Explore connections between dominant food industries and resources in your region and the foodways associated with them.
- Invite local food producers or practitioners of a local food tradition to train staff and/ or present to the public.

- Rather than create a petri dish to preserve foodways, use museum resources to sustain the foodways as local living traditions.
- Use regionally specific resources, like seed catalogs, community cookbooks, advertising, oral histories, corporate and government archives, and landscape histories to craft interpretation.
- Consult contemporary references for ideas about food resources your museum or historic site might feature—for instance, Slow Food's Ark of Taste listing of endangered American food varieties.

Discussion Starter: Mapping Your Foodshed

In 2005, Canadian writers Alisa Smith and James Bernard MacKinnon decided to try living for a year on foods originally sourced from within one hundred miles of their home. This challenging, and sometimes comic, project resulted in their best-selling book *The 100-Mile Diet: A Year of Local Eating*. Smith and MacKinnon loved learning about wild plants, making their own sea salt, and sampling local meats after years of vegetarianism. They were not as enthused about having no sources for wheat flour or oil at first. Their challenges revealed a great deal about contemporary dependence on food shipping, and their book spawned eating clubs and one-hundred-mile dinners in America, turning attention to hyperlocal sources of food and sparking a rediscovery of native and traditional foods in the locavore community.

Take inspiration from this idea to get a clearer picture of your museum's own foodshed and the interpretive possibilities it contains. Print out a large map of your region and pinpoint the location of your museum or site. Then use a compass to draw a circle at a one-hundred-mile radius from your museum. Considering this your regional "foodshed," select a time period to begin reconstructing the products available. Museums and historic sites that interpret a specific time period may want to focus on reconstructing the local foodshed of that moment in time, using documentary and archaeological evidence. Other museums may want to focus on the contemporary foodshed—what is available today? What foods have become iconic emblems of your region? The farmer's market can be helpful, but don't overlook wild plant foods and game, fish, preservation traditions, and unique animal breeds linked to your place.

Fresh Ideas: Elizabeth Williams on Interpreting Regional Foodways

The Southern Food and Beverage Museum, founded in 2008, presents the cultural history of the American South through food exhibits and programs. President and director Elizabeth Williams is a lawyer who writes about the legal aspects of food, reflecting culture, policy, and economics. Here, Williams talks about SoFaB's approach to collecting, exhibiting, and interpreting regional food.

Your museum may be one of the first developed to interpret a regional cuisine. Why did Southern food need a museum?

Establishing a collection is an important way to preserve artifacts that get lost. The material culture of Southern food was disappearing. So many things people do with food, especially the nonpretty things, are trashed. People throw them away. We are trying to be the intersection of culture and food, and in that intersection, the artifacts tell more of the story than just food could. They tell how food supported your identity, how you celebrated and commiserated, in community as well as individually. We knew that somebody needed to preserve them. We think they're worthy of maintaining. For example, there's a thing in New Orleans called the St. Joseph's altar. It celebrates people's religion through the use of food; on the altar is a St. Joseph statue, food, flowers, a big bowl of lemons. There's a belief that if a single woman steals a lemon that she'll be married in the following year, so there are always lemons there for her. That represents so much more than the food itself. Another example of an object that illustrates the centrality of food comes from the Shrimp and Petroleum Festival. The scepter of the queen of the festival has a big shrimp on it, and the shrimp is holding an oil derrick. It's one of those artifacts that indicate that food and the culture are intertwined.

What are the understandings about Southern foodways you want visitors to take away?

We want them to realize that food affects their lives. The most important thing is for them to realize "I have a food identity. It interacts with my life, and the way I interact with it is part of my culture too." That is something that affects us all. Everyone eats, and everyone has a cultural identity. In addition, it's important for people to know that food is not monolithic. Southern food isn't only one thing; it's not all fried chicken and watermelon. There are some givens—corn is everywhere, a lot of people use cast iron pots—and there are some unifying themes, but it is not monolithic. Also, food is very much shaped by geography. On the coast, you're going to eat seafood. In more mountainous regions or more agricultural regions, you're going to eat things that are grown in that climate. That doesn't mean that there isn't creep. Traditions spread, and in the contemporary economy there are certain universals—for example, everyone today is eating hamburgers. But from a cultural standpoint, people still eat food that is cultural, especially for holidays, birthdays, and celebrations.

Food and drink are by nature ephemeral. How do you bring your subject to life in exhibits and programs?

We use the tools—we grow the food, make the food, serve the food. Our restaurant and bar is attached to the museum. We make sure people can buy samples of food and drink, and we allow them to walk around with food and drink. We decided we couldn't forbid that. I think people are more respectful than we give them credit for. And our collection may be a little safer—it's hard to hurt a cast iron pot. At the same time, we need to think about how to

Figure 4.2. Liz Williams among some of the exhibits at the Southern Food and Beverage Museum. (Courtesy of the Southern Food and Beverage Museum)

preserve the things that are very precious. Ultimately, you need to make the commitment. As far as I'm concerned, when people talk about interactives, they always talk about touch screens and things like that. Being able to consume the material that is the subject of the exhibit is the ultimate interactivity. It adds all the dimensions of the senses.

Notes

1. Herman Melville, *Moby-Dick* (1851; Project Gutenberg, 2013), chap. 15, https://www.gutenberg.org/files/2701/2701-h/2701-h.htm#link2HCH0015.
2. Edward Ayers, "Introduction," in *All Over the Map: Rethinking American Regionalism*, edited by Edward Ayers, Patricia Nelson Limerick, Stephen Nissembaum, and Peter Onuf (Baltimore: Johns Hopkins University Press, 1996), 2.
3. Sandy Oliver, "Ruminations on the State of American Food History," *Gastronomica* 6, no. 4 (2006): 98.
4. Susan Strasser, *Never Done: A History of American Housework* (New York: Pantheon, 1982), 14.
5. Oliver, "Ruminations on the State of American Food History," 98.
6. Mark McWilliams, "Distant Tables: Food and the Novel in Early America," *Early American Literature* 38, no. 3 (2003): 366.
7. Old Colony Club, "The History of the Old Colony Club 1769–Today," Old Colony Club website 2004, chap. 1, accessed April 26, 2015, http://oldcolonyclub.org/ClubHistory/occhist1.htm.
8. McWilliams, "Distant Tables," 373.
9. McWilliams, "Distant Tables," 374.

10. Reay Tannahill, *Food in History* (New York: Three Rivers Press, 1989), 326.

11. Susan Claire Imbarrato, *Traveling Women: Narrative Visions of Early America* (Athens: Ohio University Press, 2006), 30.

12. Thomas Weiss, "Tourism in America before World War II," *Journal of Economic History* 64, no. 2 (2004): 291.

13. Mark Twain [Samuel Clemens], *Roughing It*, chap. IV, Project Gutenberg, released August 18, 2006, accessed April 26, 2015.

14. Twain, *Roughing It*, chap. XII.

15. John Melish, *Travels Through the United States of America in the Years 1806, 1807, and 1809, 1810, and 1811* (London: George Cowie and Co., 1818), 442.

16. Celia K. Corkery and Adrian J. Bailey, "Lobster Is Big in Boston: Postcards, Place Commodification, and Tourism," *GeoJournal* 34, no. 4 (1994): 491–92.

17. Colin Woodard, *The Lobster Coast: Rebels, Rusticators, and the Struggle for a Forgotten Frontier* (New York: Penguin Books, 2004), 195–99.

18. Woodard, *The Lobster Coast*, 213.

19. Weiss, "Tourism in America before World War II," 291.

20. Pat Willard, *America Eats! On the Road with the WPA* (New York: Bloomsbury, 2008), 56.

21. Francine Kirsch, "Eat Me at the Fair," *Gastronomica: The Journal of Critical Food Studies* 11, no. 3 (2011): 82–83.

22. Don Kreis, "Personal Essay: A Contrarian View of the Tunbridge World's Fair," Vermont Digger website, September 24, 2010, accessed April 26, 2015, http://vtdigger.org/2010/09/24/personal-essay-a-contrarian-view-of-the-tunbridge-world%E2%80%99s-fair/.

23. Jan Longone, "Introduction," *Feeding America: The Historic American Cookbook Project*, Feeding America digital collection, Michigan State University Museum, accessed April 26, 2015, http://digital.lib.msu.edu/projects/cookbooks/html/intro_essay.html#6.

24. Alison P. Kelly, "Choice Receipts from American Housekeepers: A Collection of Digitized Community Cookbooks from the Library of Congress," *The Public Historian* 34, no. 2 (2012): 36.

25. Kelly, "Choice Receipts from American Housekeepers."

26. Kennan Ferguson, "Intensifying Taste, Intensifying Identity: Connectivity through Community Cookbooks," *Signs* 37, no. 3 (2012): 704.

27. Kelly, "Choice Receipts from American Housekeepers," 38.

28. Kelly, "Choice Receipts from American Housekeepers," 46.

29. Kelly, "Choice Receipts from American Housekeepers," 41.

30. Pat Brady, "Out of One, Many: Regionalism in FSA Photography," online archive of the American Studies Group at the University of Virginia, accessed April 26, 2015, http://xroads.virginia.edu/~ug99/brady/intro.html.

31. Prints & Photographs Division Staff, "Dorothea Lange's *Migrant Mother*: Photographs in the Farm Security Administration Collection, an Overview," Prints & Photographs Division, Library of Congress website, 1998, accessed April 26, 2015, http://www.loc.gov/rr/print/list/128_migm.html.

32. Pat Brady, "Local vs. National Culture," online archive of the American Studies Group at the University of Virginia, accessed April 26, 2015, http://xroads.virginia.edu/~ug99/brady/region.html.

33. Mark Kurlansky, *The Food of a Younger Land* (New York: Riverhead Books, 2009), 15.

34. Workers of the Writers' Program of the Works Progress Administration in the State of Oregon, *Oregon, End of the Trail* (Portland, OR: Metropolitan Press, 1940), 87–90, on the

Internet Archive, accessed April 26, 2015, https://archive.org/stream/oregonendoftrail00writ rich#page/90/mode/1up. Apple McGinties are a kind of bar cookie.

35. Members of the Federal Writers' Project of the Works Progress Administration in the New England States, *Here's New England! A Guide to Vacationland* (Cambridge: Riverside Press, 1939), 7, on the Internet Archive, accessed April 26, 2015, https://archive.org/stream/heresn ewenglandg00federich#page/7/mode/1up.

36. Workers of the Writers' Project of the Works Project Administration in the State of Florida, *A Guide to Miami and Dade County* (Northport, NY: Bacon, Percy, and Daggett, 1941, 130), on the Internet Archive, https://archive.org/stream/miamianddade00editmiss#page/129/mode/1up.

37. Kurlansky, *The Food of a Younger Land*, 14–15.

38. Willard, *America Eats!* 7–8.

39. Willard, *America Eats!* 4–5.

40. Kurlansky, *The Food of a Younger Land*, 18.

41. Kurlansky, *The Food of a Younger Land*, 19.

42. Willard, *America Eats!* 4.

43. Kurlansky, *The Food of a Younger Land*, 3.

44. Ayers, "Introduction," in Ayers et al., *All Over the Map*, 3.

45. Edward Ayers, "Introduction," *American Regionalism*, manuscript on http://xroads.virginia. edu/~drbr/ayers_in.html, posted September 15, 1995, accessed April 26, 2015.

46. Economic and Social Development Department, Food and Agriculture Organization of the United Nations, "What Is Happening to Agrobiodiversity?" UNFAO website, accessed April 26, 2015, http://www.fao.org/docrep/007/y5609e/y5609e02.htm.

47. Gary Paul Nabhan, ed., *Renewing American's Food Traditions: Saving and Savoring the Continent's Most Endangered Foods* (White River Junction, VT: Chelsea Green, 2008), 11.

48. These included the American Livestock Breeds Conservancy, the Center for Sustainable Environments, Chefs Collaborative, Cultural Conservancy, Native Seeds/SEARCH, Seed Savers Exchange, and Slow Food USA.

49. Nabhan, *Renewing American's Food Traditions*, 4. Nabhan explains, "The term place-based food traditions suggests a cohesive set of time-tried relationships among plants and animals, their favored habitats, and their attendant cultures, as well as their most creative, dedicated stewards . . . such relationships must have some modicum of continuity through time and must be rooted in particular places and particular cultural values. Implicit in the use of terms such as heirloom vegetable and heritage breed is the notion that these plants and animals have been part of certain cultural communities for generation after generation."

50. Nabhan, *Renewing American's Food Traditions*, 3.

51. Nabhan, *Renewing American's Food Traditions*, xiii.

52. Nabhan, *Renewing American's Food Traditions*, 3.

53. Stax Museum of American Soul Music website, accessed April 26, 2015, http://www.staxmu-seum.com/visit/soul-food/.

54. The Lower East Side Tenement Museum website, accessed April 26, 2015, http://www.tenement.org/tours.php.

55. Harold Skramstad, "An Agenda for Museums in the Twenty-First Century," in *Reinventing the Museum: Historical and Contemporary Perspectives on the Paradigm Shift*, ed. Gail Anderson (Lanham, MD: AltaMira Press, 2004), 128.

CHAPTER 5

Food—New and Improved! Interpreting Food Technology and Fashion

FOOD CHANGES. The futuristic technologies promising (threatening?) to bring us lab-grown meat, 3D-printed food, and edible packaging are just the latest of the industrial innovations that continuously reshape the food supply. Fashions change, too—whether it's the cronut, bone broth, or fermentation, people have always responded to novelty. Take the simple act of making supper: almost no two generations of homemakers did it the same way. Great-grandparents may have slaughtered their own chickens; grandparents might have bought a chicken live and had a butcher behead it; parents may remember grocery-store butchers cutting already dressed chicken into parts; and children may not recall a time when chickens did not come as nuggets. The sections that follow highlight topics a museum or historic site might explore using content specific to their own scope. Helping visitors see how food change characterized the past can help them bring perspective to their own constant adaptations to new landscapes in food.

Key Interpretive Concepts

1. *Food technology never stands still.* At every period in history, people have tinkered and invented, attempting to expand or improve the food system at home and in industrial settings.
2. *Food fads, fashions, and trends accompany changes in technology and trade.* As the food system changes, it prompts continual shifts in tastes and behavior.
3. *Points of decision in the past resulted in gains, losses, and trade-offs in the food system.* Conditions that we often take as inevitable developments arose through conscious

decision-making processes responding to past conditions. Interpretations that acknowledge the mixed successes and difficulties of America's food culture help prepare audiences to act as citizens in influencing America's food future.

Food Technology

In 2011, food fans gushed over the publication of a five-volume, forty-three-pound cookbook titled *Modernist Cuisine*. Part manifesto, part how-to, it detailed cooking methods usually grouped under the name *molecular gastronomy*. Disciples of the genre upend expectations of food with tools and techniques more commonly found in laboratories than kitchens. With siphons, syringes, and centrifuges, these chefs aim to create new techniques and, ultimately, to redefine cooking itself. Imagination and innovation combine in poetic, technically demanding dishes such as "faux caviar"—apple juice solidified into tiny spheres in a calcium chloride solution—or "hot ice cream" made with a "thermo-reversible gelling agent."[1] Home cooks can now buy molecular gastronomy kits, although it's unlikely that most Americans will whip up foams, gels, and flavored airs very often. At the same time, the movement isn't a break with American food tradition but a continuation of it, celebrating science's place in culinary artistry much as previous generations have.

If You Can't Take the Heat . . . Fireplaces and Stoves

In most homes, the central piece of cooking technology is the heat source. For millennia, food was heated directly over a flame, on a hot rock, or in a vessel of skin or clay; cooking fires were in the ground or the center of dwellings. In Middle Age Europe, the fireplace and hearth developed, and European colonists brought the technology to America. Most contained a pole or swinging crane, allowing cooks to suspend pots with hooks and to control heat by raising or lowering them. Affluent homes might amass additional equipment—boiling pots, bake-kettles with fitted lids, skillets, and gridirons. The less wealthy might make do with "only a small kettle, a spider, and a long-handled spoon."[2] Kitchen equipment proliferated in early America, but it didn't change much in function or style.

A major eighteenth-century innovation centered on the fireplace, which was never truly efficient. A design developed and promoted in the 1790s by Benjamin Thompson, Count Rumford, concentrated heat better and prevented drafts. Rumford applied his knowledge of physics to other kitchen projects, like the Rumford Roaster and the Rumford Range, significant transitional technologies.[3] The advent (about 1815) and rapid spread of the cast-iron cookstove bumped Rumford's inventions out of the dream kitchen. Cookstoves were more fuel efficient, cleaner, and more comfortable to use than a hearth. On the other hand, cookstove wood had to be split smaller, and stoves "needed much more tending than an open fireplace."[4] Cooks had to brush out ash and soot, disassemble and clean the stovepipe a few times a year, and blacken the metal against rust. With a hearth fire no longer burning around the clock, kitchen use changed. In larger homes, the locus of family life moved to parlors or sitting rooms; people no longer needed to huddle by the hearth for warmth.[5]

The stove has endured, despite its inefficiency.[6] It takes about the same amount of time to make biscuits, pancakes, or a roast with a modern stove as it did with a hearth fire or a wood or coal stove. Improvements in stove technology peaked in the mid-twentieth century, when industrial manufacturers moved from war production to making consumer goods. The General Motors 1956 "Kitchen of the Future" featured a rotating convection oven under a clear plastic dome; the Philco-Ford Corporation's 1967 film *1999 A.D.* depicted a computer-controlled freezer that dispensed individually portioned foods and automatically fed them into a microwave oven.[7] Outside of promotional films, microwaves have been a mixed success. Standard in middle-class kitchens, they are only a supplement to the range and oven. But the dream of effortless cooking survives. Companies still imagine kitchens of the future, now with touchscreen cooktops to guide cooks through recipes.[8] Ironically, the less people cook at home, the more cooking technology proliferates, as if it were only for a lack of the right gadget that Americans eat at home less often that at any time in history. Six- and eight-burner ranges, meant for institutional kitchens, are a status symbol, as are "outdoor kitchens" with gas grills and pizza ovens. Americans with means invest in kitchens that, most days, see only the simplest food preparation. The hearth's old associations with emotional sustenance endure.

Preservation, Processing, and Convenience

"Processed food" gets a bad rap these days, but for most of American history, processing promised to rid food and cooking of truly bothersome problems. Convenience foods let cooks sidestep some of the labor-intensive, unpleasant early stages of food production— slaughtering and dressing animals, boiling bones for stock, grinding grains, rendering lard. Processed food manufacturing grew hand in hand with every mechanical breakthrough in industrial production, and Americans adopted these foods gradually and with some skepticism. Historians Gerard Fitzgerald and Gabriella Petrick have studied the acceptance of industrial foods, finding that

> because of technological constraints, industrial food never tasted as good as freshly made food to many consumers. Given the tension between technology and palatability, producers continually sought to make foods that tasted good enough for consumers to purchase again and again and again. For their part, consumers were willing to accept food that may not have tasted like homemade, but there were certainly limits to what consumers thought palatable. While canned corn, peas, tomatoes, and peaches sold well, no one has ever heard of canned lettuce because it just does not taste right to Americans.[9]

Food manufacturers honed products and perfected marketing. National brands developed catchy names and appealing packaging. Convincing customers to switch to mass-manufactured food was tough. Companies tried increasing confidence with "satisfaction guarantees, advertising, elaborate in-store displays, and factory tours."[10] Aunt Jemima and the Campbell's Kids reassured homemakers with glowing sincerity. In a single century, Americans made an enormous shift, from producing most of their food themselves to acquiring much of it from retailers in processed form. Food transformations were a kind of practical magic that Fernández-Armesto says posed enticing challenges to food chemists, especially when they turned to the problem of "prettifying" meat. At the turn of the twentieth century, most Americans had witnessed or participated in the butchering of food animals. Food scientists and manufacturers wanted a cleaner, simpler way of selling meat. The meatpacking industry developed approaches still in effect today (in intensified form): concentrating live animals in stockyards and turning them into meat products in a fully mechanized system that kills, dresses, and packages them. Henry Ford was so impressed by the Armour Company's meat production system that he instituted similar assembly-line techniques at his own plants.[11] Recent innovations have put butchers out of business. Meat products today reach stores cut and sealed, with no trace of blood or visual connection with an animal. As Fernández-Armesto observes, where once "the beauty of butchered carcasses was apparent to still-life painters," today's preference is buying meat "in an emotionally sanitized form."[12]

Twentieth-century processing took more food preparation out of home kitchens. Frozen vegetables led to frozen meals. Potatoes are now available in shreds, slices, wedges, hashbrowns, "tots," shoestring fries, waffle fries, and premashed, in a variety of seasoning blends.[13] The 1937 opening of the first McDonald's drive-in seemed to drive the final nail into the coffin. Consumers had become cogs in a large-scale corporate system. Fernández-Armesto calls it "food-Fordism." A decade after opening, McDonald's stopped serving food with plates and cutlery, completing a "reversal of one of the long-sought, hard-won achievements of civilization." As convenience eating continues its rise, Americans' cooking skills are in decline. Along with scratch cooking goes the ability to customize, judge ingredient quality, and have authority over ethics and safety. Busy cooks welcome processed food, but it raises concerns like loss of togetherness, local and ethnic traditions, safety, humaneness, and health, and it creates conundrums Americans have yet to resolve.[14]

Food producers are locked in a struggle with time and distance. In the nineteenth and twentieth centuries, the distance between population centers and agricultural regions widened, raising the risk that food would go "off" during transit. Fortunes were made in the search for scientific solutions to the threat of spoilage. The very definition of freshness metamorphosized. "What exactly is fresh?" asks geographer Susanne Friedberg in *Fresh: A Perishable History*. FDA guidelines in 2000 specified that food could not be labeled "fresh" if it had been "frozen, heated, chemically treated, or 'otherwise preserved,'" but it excepted milk "because consumers expected milk to be pasteurized." Freidberg notes that the desirability of freshness also varies with the type of food, as "some foods last longer than others, and . . . a few actually improve with age."[15]

Preindustrial household managers knew how to maximize the longevity of dozens of foods, calling on a preservation repertoire including salting; drying; freeze-drying; fermentation; suspending in fat, alcohol, vinegar, or sugar; cold storage; and cellaring.[16] At the start of winter in a prosperous colonial household, dried herbs, alliums, and meats hung in the kitchen; pickles, dried beans, and potted meats packed store and closet shelves; pies and meats lined the outer walls of attics; and apple and potato barrels, squash and pumpkins, and casks of cider and beer hunkered down in the cellar. Autumn harvests brought in much of the food supply all at once, so a housewife's challenge was to transform raw goods into foods that could last into the coming months of scarcity. Losing a large piece of imperfectly salted meat or an infested sack of grain could mean the difference between hunger and satiety.

Urbanization limited household-level preservation. Homes in manufacturing cities offered less space to store food. Urban families leaned more on markets as farmland receded from city borders. Farms specialized to serve cities rather than focusing, as in former times, on local markets. Vermont, for instance, shifted pastureland from sustenance farming to intensive dairying for Boston markets, producing far more milk than could ever have been used locally.[17] Truck farms ringed metropolises; now, farmers had to not only grow food but also make sure that quality stayed high during transport. This pushed inventors toward a "massive leap forward in techniques of preserving and packing food products."[18]

The Transformative Power of Cold

For millennia, cold temperatures have been known to preserve food. Food stored in cold air, water, or ice lasted a long time, and when thawed it looked and tasted more like fresh food. But this knowledge was only helpful during part of the year. Like fire, cold offered limited usefulness until humans could bring it under control.

From prehistory well into the eighteenth century, the main source of cold was natural ice. Colonists brought ice preservation techniques from Europe, using icehouses, cellars, or springhouses to delay melting. Ice harvesting was a backbreaking process of scoring ice, sawing it into uniform chunks, and transporting it with floats, sleds, and horsepower. Price depended on the quality of the ice, something largely beyond an ice harvester's control. Air bubbles made ice cloudy. Twigs and leaf litter made it gritty.

Bostonian Frederic Tudor saw that ice commanded the highest price wherever it was rare, and in 1806 he started a business shipping ice to Martinique, Cuba, and even India. The winter ice of New England became one of America's important exports, "the first highly perishable commodity within a world market."[19] Ice was shipped in enormous quantities, including a sacrificial layer to insulate the core cargo. Over time, the domestic market for ice grew more important than the tropical trade. Tudor envisioned an ice-consuming American middle class, and by the late nineteenth century ice was an amenity Americans expected, consuming more than five million pounds per year. The icebox, an insulated cabinet with tightly sealing doors, was common in middle-class homes by the 1830s.[20] To "hook" customers, Tudor offered free ice to start, saying "a man who has drank his drinks cold at the same expense for one week can never be persuaded to drink them warm again." A doctor took out the first patent for an ice-making machine in 1844. Intending it to cool fevered patients, he saved an 1850 Bastille Day celebration in Florida by using it to chill the French ambassador's champagne. New Orleans opened the first commercial ice plant in 1865, and within a decade, many restaurants had their own compressed gas ice-making machines.[21]

Entrepreneurs soon combined ice-cooled air with long-distance shipping. In 1851, the first refrigerated rail car carried butter from New York State to Boston. The "cold chain" revolutionized the meatpacking industry. For most of history, as Fraser and Rimus put it, "the only way to move fresh meat between pasture and market was to walk it."[22] In 1879, Massachusetts butcher Gustavus Swift perfected a refrigerated rail car for meat. Customers were wary at first of buying meat that "had been slaughtered a week previously," but they gradually accepted Swift's new definition of "fresh." Meat was now "something you could

Figure 5.1. The final link in the ice distribution network was the local ice delivery business. Here, two young girls help deliver bags of ice in what is probably a family business in November 1912. (Library of Congress/Lewis Wicks Hine, photographer. National Child Labor Committee Collection)

collect and trade, a commodity."[23] Using similar technology, California produce could now reach the Midwest or East Coast, commanding premium prices. A New Yorker or Chicagoan, even in the winter, could enjoy celery, strawberries, lettuces, and peaches. Regions specialized in foods they produced best and most cheaply.[24] California left off growing wheat and shifted to more profitable table produce.

In the twentieth century, supermarkets introduced refrigeration and freezer cases. People began to buy chilled and frozen food and to store it for weeks or months[25] in home refrigerator-freezers. The concept of frozen food had occurred to inventor Clarence Birdseye after observing Inuit preservation practices. He wrapped food in cellophane and waxed cardboard that held together even when damp. The ability to pull food from the freezer and dump it into a pot of boiling water or pop it onto an oven rack changed the way Americans ate. Entire meals could be ready in minutes with little effort, in formulations designed to please a mass market—or at least not disappoint them too greatly. According to Fernández-Armesto, Birdseye had "industrialized not just production, processing and supply, but eating."[26]

We Can Because We Can

The old-timey feel of Mason jars belies the fact that canning is a relatively recent technology, not much older than frozen food. The science of canning was first mobilized in service of the military. In 1795, the French military offered a prize for inventing a long-preservation method. Distiller and chef Nicolas Appert won with his process of sealing food in an airtight container. Appert published his method, spurring others to improve the technology.[27] But home cooks were unimpressed with canning, which changed food's color and flavor. Not until the Civil War was canned food widely accepted. Gail Borden, a politician and inventor, financed the development of canned milk. Understanding that milk was 87 percent water, Borden reduced bulk by boiling it and added sugar to help prevent bacteria growth.[28] This "condensed milk" went first to Civil War units, introducing tens of thousands of Americans to the product.[29] Fisheries, with their highly perishable products, were another early adopter of canning.

Sometimes the switch to canned food had unintended consequences. Though condensed milk "was unquestionably more wholesome than the kind supplied by the old-style city cow-man," whose cows never saw a pasture, Borden's success inspired rivals to undercut him by using skimmed milk, which "lacked both fats and the as yet unrecognized vitamins A and D." Among the poor, who bought the cheaper products, the incidence of rickets and other deficiency diseases began to increase.[30] Commercial canners also relied on additives: "anti-caking agents to prevent salt, sugar, and powered milk from coagulating into lumps; emul-sifying agents, which help to homogenize, or blend, substances like fat and milk that would otherwise tend to separate, and sequestrants to stop trace minerals from turning fats and oils rancid."[31] Cereals and breads advertised that they were now "fortified" with vitamins and minerals. Some additives were dangerous. Formaldehyde and arsenic were used to preserve dairy, fish, and meat at the turn of the twentieth century. Synthetic food dyes, developed in the 1850s, added color to food dulled by preservation, but they fell under scrutiny as several compounds were shown to sicken people.[32]

Home canning lagged behind commercial canning. The vacuum seal that stopped oxi-dation was nearly impossible to create at home, using imperfect barriers like melted wax, corks, paper, or skin. In 1858, John Mason invented a system of waxed, "self-sealing" lids that used the cooling of hot preserves to create a vacuum, then locked the seal in place with a threaded lid. Several brands of glass canning jars were on the market by the 1880s, kicking off a home canning boom. Housewives and servants "put up" garden produce, summer fruit, jellies, ketchup, and pickles. The new ease of canning made it popular in frontier and rural households, but home canning was relatively short-lived. By the early twentieth century, most Americans were purchasing their canned goods at grocery stores. Canning enjoyed a resurgence during World War II when the government encouraged people to can the products of their Victory Gardens in glass, sparing tin and steel for war production.[33] Most seemed happy to abandon home canning again at war's end. Over the past decade of the twenty-first century, canning has once again become popular, hand in hand with farmers' market shopping, locavorism, and home gardening.

Transportation Technology

Today, people talk about "food miles"—the distance food products have traveled from farm to plate. But food has been globetrotting for centuries. In preindustrial America, maritime trade brought expensive luxuries to the colonies—spices, citrus, cane sugar, tea, coffee, chocolate, and European wines and brandies. During the Industrial Era, growing factory towns, which "cannot feed themselves," pushed out local farms, inviting entrepreneurs to step into the "food gap."[34] Itinerant peddlers sold food in the street. Lobstermen expanded their market with "smacks," sailboats from which a waterman could pull traps and then deliver seafood to the nearest major city.[35] Schooners ducked in and out of coastal ports, trading local surplus for products originating hundreds of miles north or south. But nothing had as transformative an effect as railways. Throughout the nineteenth century, railroad lines spread over the nation, connecting nodes in a network of trade that forever changed American eating.

Fitzpatrick and Petrick use iceberg lettuce to explore the intersections of transportation and taste. Before California farmers began growing table produce, "most Americans ate a form of butterhead lettuce (Big Boston) that was loose leafed, soft textured, and buttery in flavor."[36] California produce growers needed other qualities in their lettuces. A grower in 1953 outlined the requirements for a successful variety: one which could "withstand what we commonly call normal transportation hazards. When offered for sale it must be fresh, green, reasonably fine textured, and tender. Otherwise we can not compete." Compact, stiff, changeless, and crisp after its industrial makeover, iceberg became an American favorite. Though it was not tastier than homegrown seasonal greens, it was reliable. Without rail networks, iceberg as we know it would not have existed; plant breeders focused on perfecting it to withstand the demands of packing, shipping, and selling it days or weeks after harvest. Iceberg didn't have to be better than the best local lettuces in peak season; it just had to be better than no lettuce at all.

Best Practices: Interpreting Food and Technology

- Bring the factory to the museum through imagery, text, oral history, media, installation, museum theater, simulation, or virtual experience.
- Ask what technology falls within the scope of your interpretation. Look beyond the systems physically present in your own building or place to link to larger regional, national, and international systems—gas, water, ice, and food delivery, for instance.
- Represent differences of opinion about emerging technologies. Some early adopters loved them; some traditionalists hated them. Some could afford them; some could only wish for them. How did the characters in your interpretation react to—and interact with—available technologies?
- When developing period installations, avoid relying on the catalog of technologies currently available at the time. Instead, keep your human characters at the center and consider carefully their individual relationship to technology. Use probate inventories, oral histories, and comparable households to create contextual interpretation.
- Wherever possible, demonstrate technology in action—whether it's kitchen equipment or farm machinery. Some aspects of technology only become visible when human workers interact with them.

- Look for the ripple effects accompanying the introduction of new technology. What else had to change? Labor patterns, clothing, mealtimes? Interpret the way small changes in technology produced multiple changes in the lives of people who used them.
- Consider both the gains and the losses posed by new technologies. Though "progress" was often the ideal, be sure interpretation critically considers variations in who benefited from the progress.

Food Fashions

Each generation re-creates food culture, guaranteeing that taste will be constantly reformulated.[37] Habits, customs, and fashions in food came and went alongside styles of clothing and architecture—tastes, literally, changed. Eighteenth-century Americans taught themselves to drink tea and coffee, abandoned beer for rum, and spiced food with pepper and mace, none of which had a long history in their culture. In the nineteenth century, new product introductions sparked crazes—when bananas were first imported in the 1880s, the fruit was paired with ice cream as the banana split. Refrigeration prompted wider enjoyment of ice cream, jellies, and cold drinks. The Hawaiian Pineapple Company's early twentieth-century invention of machinery to peel, core, slice, and can pineapples dovetailed with a fad for pineapple upside-down cake.[38] Cooks remixed convenience foods into new dishes—cheese sauce with canned vegetables and pimentos, noodles with canned soup and fried onions. Some invented foods traveled like hot potatoes to everyday tables. Potato chips, invented as "Saratoga chips" in 1850s New York, were commonplace in cookbooks nationwide by 1900, soon to be joined by Waldorf salad, lobster Newburg, and Parker House rolls. By the turn of the twenty-first century, new food products were introduced at the rate of more than fifteen thousand a year, even as a backlash lured many tastemakers toward less processed foods.[39]

Many Americans can date their life stages by the food fads they've moved through—watching the tableside drama of a 1950s Caesar salad, dipping into a 1970s fondue pot, and lining up for cupcakes in the "oughts." But food fads are especially prone to apocryphal accounts that undermine the accuracy of many origin stories. It's wise to reexamine these stories using historical thinking and primary research. Stories of Ruth Wakefield's "accidental" invention of the chocolate chip cookie provide an example. In one tale, Wakefield, chef-owner of the Toll House Restaurant, ran out of walnuts for her cookie recipe and added chopped chocolate instead. In another, Wakefield planned to add melted chocolate, but she ran out of time for the melting step and mixed the bits into the dough thinking they would melt in the oven. As recent investigation reveals, it's unlikely that the development of this recipe was accidental. Wakefield had a degree in household science and years of professional cooking experience. She would have been able to predict the result of her cookie experiments. But advertisers played up a great story and played down Wakefield's professional knowledge, perpetuating certain understandings of women's scientific acumen.[40] Using evidence from biographical sources, primary sources, and critical textual analysis, interpreters of food can find tales more revealing of historical context and interpretive points.

Mavens and Moralizers

In the mid-twentieth century, a new American food movement took shape. Influenced by European ways of thinking about and preparing food, but modern in its spirit of freedom and creative reinterpretation of the past, this movement spawned dozens of food subcultures that changed American tastes.

Since the nineteenth century, overarching trends in agriculture have brought increased mechanization, larger scale, higher yield, and greater dependence upon fertilizers and pesticides. As these trends intensified, a countertrend toward small-scale farming emerged, and it continues to expand. As far back as the nineteenth century, Thoreau and others voiced antiurban, anti-industrial strains of thought. During the Great Depression, when modern society seemed to be collapsing, some urbanites began to explore the possibilities of a self-sustaining rural life. Some moved to New England looking for "bare-boned Yankee security." Dubbed "back-to-the-landers," they drew on earlier experiments by people like Ralph Borsodi, whose book *Flight from the City* chronicled his experiences in self-sufficient living. By midcentury, back-to-the-landers were represented in the public mind by Helen and Scott Nearing, left-leaning writers increasingly uncomfortable in polarized and political New York City. In 1932, the Nearings moved to Vermont to start a subsistence farm, where they "grew their own food, cut their own lumber and firewood, and tapped maple trees to make the syrup that paid their taxes and other unavoidable cash transactions." Their best-selling book, *Living the Good Life: How to Live Sanely and Simply in a Troubled World*, "inspire[d] a later generation of disaffected youth to follow in their footsteps."[41] A second wave of back-to-the-landers moved into rural areas in the 1970s, and a third wave of "off the grid" and other new agrarians is under way today. This once-niche movement is now part of the American mainstream, making celebrities of figures like poet-farmer Wendell Berry and biodynamic "grass farmer" Joel Saladin.

Culinary adventurers of the mid-twentieth century also proposed changes in food values. It may have begun with World War II. GIs in Europe and the Pacific had the chance to taste and enjoy foreign specialties, and they brought home new tastes. Americans began looking for new ideas about what to eat with an adventurous spirit matching the optimistic tenor of the times. In his history of American "foodie" culture, *The United States of Arugula*, David Kamp chronicles the birth of a new food elite.[42] Some of these tastemakers started as outsiders, discovering food careers later in life. James Beard, whose catering gigs supported dreams of acting, found his fame through food in the 1940s, appearing on television and authoring dozens of cookbooks. Former naval ensign Craig Claiborne enrolled in hotel school, then talked his way into the job of *New York Times* food editor, a role previously focused on homemaking. Claiborne used this platform to create the journalistic restaurant review and bring to food the seriousness of business and political reporting. The third figure in Kamp's trinity, Julia Child, had gone to work for the OSS, predecessor of today's CIA. Postings sent her to Ceylon and then China, where she and colleague Paul Child explored local noodle shops. Marrying after the war, the two next went to France, where Julia fell in love with French cooking. She studied at the Cordon Bleu, the only woman in her class, and after training she opened a cooking school with two friends. Child and her colleagues found that no comprehensive beginning French cookbook existed, and after years of research, they published *Mastering the Art of French Cooking*, called by Claiborne "the most comprehensive, laudable and monumental work on this subject."[43] Child went on to host a television show, becoming a household name. The French Chef encouraged the notion that excellent cooking was not that hard, her breeziness concealing the fact that she "put nineteen hours of preparation into each half-hour episode."[44]

Could American ingredients match this new sophistication? Kamp calls the foodstuffs of the time "pretty lousy."[45] Supermarkets preferred tough, bright-colored, long-lasting produce—qualities not always synonymous with flavor. In 1977, food historian Karen Hess and her husband, ex–*New York Times* food journalist John Hess, published their book *The Taste of America*, levying invective against American food quality. In an opening chapter titled "The Rape of the Plate," they fretted, "How shall we tell our fellow Americans that our palates have been ravaged, that our food is awful, and that our most respected authorities on cookery are poseurs?"[46] American eaters began to take the quality of their food more seriously.

From Markets to Supermarkets

Taste and technology also changed how Americans shopped. Two priorities are most pronounced: product choice and shopper independence. Preindustrial shopkeepers bought in bulk and sold in small quantities. Customers ordered the desired quantity, and storekeepers weighed food out. Casks held dry goods: lentils, wheat, split peas, and barley. Metal canisters, crockery, small boxes, and wooden chests held honey, butter, "portable soup" (cakes of dried bullion), tea and coffee. Most goods carried no brand name, but they were called after their place of origin: Dublin cheese, French olives. Grocers mediated the shopping, taking requests from shoppers and assembling their orders. Shoppers complained about not being able to inspect food closely, or choose for themselves, and they accused grocers of swapping cheap products for fancy ones, adulterating foods, and mismeasuring. At least some really were deceiving customers, laying the groundwork for later consumer advocacy.

Early on, much sourcing was hyperlocal. Produce, meats, and fish came from outdoor markets, supplied first by local farmers and later by truck farmers from outlying areas. Manufacturing consolidated labor, straining these local systems. Grocers and itinerant traders became "essential in spanning the spaces between marketplaces and neighborhoods,"[47] and grocers became generalists, selling dry goods and imports together with dairy and meats. Once they had mastered wholesale buying, retail pricing, advertising, and display, grocers expanded, replicating their stores in nearby towns. The first of the "chain" stores, the Great Atlantic Tea Company, a New York City retailer, was founded in 1859 and opened multiple storefronts.[48] Renaming themselves the A&P, they soon ran dozens, hundreds, then thousands of outlets. Shopping at a chain store appealed to American tastes. Independent stores varied tremendously by neighborhood and owner. Most "had a very limited selection" with "no unique products at all," says historian Mark Levinson.[49] Corner stores discouraged competition, making it easier for dishonest or dirty shops to survive. Betty Smith's 1943 semiautobiographical novel *A Tree Grows in Brooklyn* opens with preteen siblings Francie and Neeley Nolan doing their week's shopping. At a five-and-dime, their every step is followed by suspicious floorwalkers. At a candy store, a crooked game cheats kids out of their pennies. At the butcher, the children insist on watching their meat being ground to avoid getting meat made "behind closed doors and God knows what you get." At a grocery, they pick through fading produce for "an emasculated carrot, a droopy leaf of celery, a soft tomato and a fresh sprig of parsley."[50] Their experiences illustrate the hazards of shopping at a time when each business operated according to its own standards (or lack thereof). Small stores were also relatively free to practice discrimination, reducing the range of choices and insulting the dignity of many shoppers. Unlike small grocers, chains didn't extend credit, give personalized service, or offer delivery. But the chain-store model streamlined shopping in ways Americans welcomed. Larger volume allowed them to offer low, consistent pricing. Chains rarely ran out of anything, thanks to warehousing. Shoppers whose social status meant they might not have been treated fairly elsewhere favored the impersonal but equitable pricing. By 1930, A&P had become the world's largest retailer, spawning many imitators.

Tennessee-based Piggly Wiggly developed the self-service model, reinventing the act of shopping. Wholesaler Clarence Saunders hatched the idea while observing his grocer clients. According to author Mike Freeman, "Some were more saloon keepers than businessmen. . . . Even the best grocery men operated their stores as if their customers had all day to shop and gossip with them."[51] When business was slow, clerks were idle, but when it was busy, it seemed as though there was never enough help. To avoid that conundrum, Saunders launched his own store in 1916 with a cash-and-carry model. Shoppers walked up to the shelves, selected their own products, and paid at registers where clerks stood ready to ring them up. Eliminating the extra labor allowed him to underprice rivals. Saunders expanded to nine stores within a year, and he had a national network within three years. Shoppers liked choosing their own items as well as the reduced sales pressure, clearly marked prices, self-serve scales, and easy-to-read receipts. One of Piggly Wiggly's early adopters enthused in a women's magazine, "It is all so simple and easy and natural that after your first visit to a Piggly Wiggly you wonder why no one ever thought of it before. Then you wonder why anyone ever again should think of any other system."[52] Saunders never stopped experimenting with the interface between customers and groceries. He pioneered in-store bakeries and delis, and in 1936 he presented his dream store: a fully automated electronic grocery. He could never get the system to work properly, but he continued to pursue the idea until his death in 1953.[53]

The next shift in shopping was the development of the supermarket. Michael Cullen, a manager with the Kroger chain, hatched a plan to weather the Depression by replacing smaller groceries in high-rent downtowns with "monstrous" stores in outlying areas, offering free parking to create a shopping destination. The distance between home and store encouraged customers to make big shopping trips weekly instead of buying groceries every few days.[54] Cullen opened the King Cullen market in Queens, New York, in 1930 and expanded to eight stores within the second year. Imitators followed. By 1935 there were more than three hundred such "supermarket" stores in the country. Americans beat a path to supermarkets during the Depression, when price was the single most important purchase criteria.[55] Despite the rapid flow of money into supermarkets, they were (and remain to this day) a low-margin business; profits rarely exceed 1.5 percent.

In the past two decades, shopping patterns have begun to reverse. Small store formats, like the convenience store and bodega, trade expansive selection and lower prices for 24/7 access and convenient locations. Ethnic groceries, specialty food stores, and national chains such as Whole Foods and Trader Joe's cater to shoppers whose culinary interests aren't satisfied by mainstream supermarkets. Farmers' markets and CSA programs, while usually not price competitive, offer fresher produce. Discount stores such as Walmart and Target have nosed into the grocery trade, using their warehousing and supply networks to undercut prices, while BJ's and Costco offer bulk goods at low unit prices. In this fragmenting marketplace, grocery chains fight for customer loyalty, adding food courts and hosting demonstrations.[56] But the low-cost, high-volume, self-service model of the thirty-seven thousand chain stores nationwide remains the default preference for most Americans.[57] Paradoxically in this age of choice, one of the most problematic conditions in American shopping is the absence, in some neighborhoods, of places to buy food. Communities described as "food deserts" lack supermarkets, preventing residents from taking advantage of their low prices and wide selection. This lack of access to nutritious food may be a factor in health risks for low-income Americans. For people in food deserts, tastes, preferences, and changing options are less a force on their choice of food than simple access.[58]

Going Out to Eat

The amount Americans spend on food eaten away from home is at an all-time high: more than 43 percent of all food spending.[59] Though the rate is climbing fast—rising from 25.9 percent in 1970—dining out in America has a long history. In the colonial era, travelers and workers away from home needed places to eat.[60] Colonial taverns stocked larders to serve guests that might arrive unannounced at any time. Coffeehouses replenished energies with coffee and light snacks. Taverns, street vendors, and bakeries hawked ready-made snacks like roasted corn, shucked oysters, and pastries.[61] Cookshops sold take-out meals, inviting families to "send their Turine's and dishes between One and Four O'Clock" to have them filled with hot turtle soup.[62] The concept of the restaurant was imported from France, where the name *restaurant* denoted foods meant to restore physical vitality, giving the sensitive constitutions of the elite an alternative to tavern fare. A French immigrant opened the first such American restaurant, Julien's Restorator, in Boston in 1794. As cities developed a business clientele, luxury hotels opened opulent dining rooms serving an efficient buffet lunch.[63] Eateries like New York's Delmonico's, opening in 1830, served middle managers and executives. Furnished with marble, gleaming wood, and mirrored walls, these restaurants "provided a stage for the articulation of status, power, and prestige."[64] By the mid-nineteenth century, New York City boasted more than five thousand restaurants, into which various occupational groups sorted themselves at mealtime: newspapermen and firemen at one place, law clerks and scribes at another, "bachelors and sporting men" at a third.[65]

At first, dining out was a sex-segregated affair, mainly for men. "Certain locations permitted an escorted female to dine, but they were often segregated from the larger seating and lounging areas filled with robust political conversation and other public elements thought inappropriate for women."[66] Female travelers were sequestered in "ladies' ordinaries" or 'ladies' parlors."[67] Most city saloons offered a free lunch buffet, open to any (male) customer who bought a drink.[68] Women appearing in such places were assumed to be prostitutes, which kept other women away for fear of harming their reputations.[69]

In the mid-nineteenth century, tearooms began serving light, delicate, midday meals to middle-class women—"chicken, pineapple, and waffles," for instance. They closed by evening, assuming that women of good character would go home to supper with their families. Department stores lured women (and their disposable income) with elegant lunchrooms that combined the society of the public sphere with the moral safety of the home, guarding against any "threat to their bodies or reputations."[70] At the same time, men's restaurants became more self-consciously masculine, serving heartier food with fewer garnishes.[71] By the end of the nineteenth century, women joined their husbands in restaurants more often. By the 1890s, restaurants advertised an elegant atmosphere "where a respectable gentleman could take an equally respectable lady to dine of an evening."[72]

Factory shift work hit a grueling pace, fueled by round-the-clock electric power and light. In cities, newspaper staff, police officers, security guards, and delivery drivers worked through the night. A Providence press worker started a side business in 1858 selling sandwiches and coffee to night workers. Eventually, he quit the presses to buy a horse-drawn wagon, serving "night lunches" outside the *Providence Journal*.[73] Soon, night lunch wagons lined up in manufacturing neighborhoods across the Northeast. Their elegant woodwork and etched glass windows took a beating over the decades, becoming known as "greasy spoons." To fight this seedy reputation, dining car owners went back to the drawing board to design the streamlined modern diner, complete with bathrooms, tables, booths, display mechanicals, and a sparkling sheen of hygienic cleanliness.

The Automat was another effort to feed modern workers efficiently. These novelty restaurants, developed in 1902 by Joseph Horn and Frank Hardart, brought the rationality of the factory to lunchtime, creating a restaurant that mimicked a machine. Customers faced walls of small windows, each showcasing a single item—a cup of gelatin, an egg salad sandwich. Dropping a nickel into a slot opened the window, allowing the diner to take the food. The seemingly mechanized windows concealed a human-run kitchen. Still, the sleek atmosphere, total independence, and speed of Automat dining suited the times. A precursor to the fast food restaurant, the Automat held its own until the likes of McDonald's and Burger King edged out cafeteria-style food. The last Automat closed its tiny windows in 1991.[74]

After World War II, dining out became more recreational. Americans could choose from a range of restaurant types: lunch counters, delis, pubs, fine dining, home-style restaurants, diners, cafes and coffee shops, drive-ins, fast food outlets, kiosks and food stalls, ethnic and "theme" restaurants.[75] These options weren't always available to everyone. Until the 1960s, most restaurants were racially segregated; in some, blacks were discouraged by hosts' refusal to seat them, and they were seated in separate rooms or even outdoors or in the kitchen, whose cooks doused food with too much salt or pepper and wait staff delivered neglectful or insulting service and allowed unreasonable delays. It's no accident that the 1960 Greensboro Woolworth's lunch counter sit-ins, pivotal civil disobedience demonstrations of the civil rights movement, targeted food service establishments. African Americans had been protesting restaurant discrimination since at least 1890, when Charles William Anderson led a group of black diners, members of New York City's Douglass Club, to twenty restaurants in a test of the 1895 Civil Rights Act.[76] At the same time that discrimination restricted options, the "massive presence" of African Americans in cities of the North, Midwest, and West after the Great Migration created opportunity for black restaurateurs. Some, like New Orleans's Dooky Chase and Harlem's Sylvia's, became centers of black culture and politics.[77]

In the late twentieth century, young urban professionals raised the bar for food and beverage culture.[78] By the 1990s, dining out was a way to smooth out a busy day, escape the drudgery of cooking, cater to a family's varied tastes, pursue courtship, socialize with friends, celebrate special occasions, and exhibit in-the-know status. Restaurants allowed diners to experience, if temporarily, the lifestyle of the early elite and the upper-middle class of the late nineteenth century.[79] Today, even low-income Americans eat some of their meals in restaurants. Scholliers sees eating out as a training ground for the "culinary discourse" that surrounds us today in food television, magazines, and online.[80] Almost all Americans are restaurant diners and, by default, restaurant critics and food mavens. Americans' love of eating out may not be entirely positive. Restaurant cooks use more fat, sugar, and meat than home cooks, and they serve larger portions. But the proliferation of meals away from home has been a boon to working Americans, helping them sit down to an adequate, palatable meal after a busy day. The convenience restaurants provide links from contemporary food service to the communal kitchens dreamed of by nineteenth-century utopian visionaries. Perhaps it is not the American habit of eating away from home but the quality, quantity, and pricing that need to be revolutionized in order to realize the dream of freeing workers from kitchen labor.

Dining at Home

The first European settlers mostly lived in one-room houses. There was no room for separate dining areas, and no need for them—the hearth fire was the center of the home, especially in winter. As prosperity allowed for larger homes, the French-influenced fashion for a separate "dining room" took hold. Homeowners converted parlors (at least part time) into dining rooms, with a sideboard, table, sets of matching chairs, knife boxes, mirrors, and other ornaments, raising the "importance and formality" of dining.[81] Separate dining rooms remained a luxury until well into the nineteenth century. In homes with servants, the space between kitchen and dining room expanded, with swing doors concealing smells and clatter from guests.[82] Children and servants usually ate in the kitchen, a room that receded "backstage," more private, informal, and humbly furnished than the dining room.

In working-class houses, families continued cooking and eating in one room as they had for centuries. Tenement kitchens in cities were small, sometimes without windows. These hardworking rooms served as "a family workspace, a sweatshop, a laundry room, a place to wash one's body, a nursery for the babies, and a bedroom for boarders."[83] Multifamily housing units emphasized efficiency, assuming servantless households. Kitchens shrank to "galley" size, with no appliance more than a few steps from any other, and dining rooms were eliminated. The trend reversed in the post–World War II building boom, which outfitted kitchens with gleaming new appliances made in former defense plants. The standard ground floor featured a triad of living room, dining room, and kitchen. In the 1950s, architectural trends began doing away with this division. In "an orgy of wall destruction," open-plan design united kitchens and dining rooms with living areas, blurring the boundaries of daily living and further deformalizing meals.

Today, Americans' relationships with their dining rooms are conflicted. Most dining room tables are piled with homework, projects, and mail, not elegant dinnerware. The space "is usually reserved for 'ceremonial' meals," says anthropologist Robin Fox, serving more as "a shrine to ambition and hope than a functioning part of the home."[84] Americans have moved back into the kitchen as the center of daily living, counter to most of the aspirational trends of the nineteenth and twentieth centuries. In high-end home designs, architects design the "dream kitchen" with dining nooks, islands, and open bar counters that invite informal interactions. In recent decades, kitchens have spilled outside, as backyard pizza ovens, grills, and fireplaces expand the walls of the kitchen.

Etiquette and Manners

Use your napkin. Elbows off the table. Don't speak with your mouth full. The countless admonitions are just recent manifestations—some might say holdovers—of the multiple systems of eating behaviors Americans have observed over time. The specifics are mercurial, but codes appear consistently across time, place, and culture.

Why do we have table manners? The act of eating is so simple that most people can do it before they can speak. In considering the transformation of plants and animals into food, from the "raw" to the "cooked," anthropologist Claude Lévi-Strauss theorizes that eating rituals and customs are a way of resolving the psychological and spiritual conflicts involved in appropriating creatures from nature to further one's own survival.[85] The mediation of manners moves food from nature to culture. Manners also cement relationships and reinforce shared values. Scholar Margaret Visser analyzed thousands of sources in search of cross-cultural components of table manners, present and past. The attention humans devote to portioning and consuming food, Visser argues, interlocks with "kinship systems (who belongs with whom, which people eat together); language (for discussing food past, present, and future, for planning the acquisition of food, and deciding how to divide it out while preventing fights); technology (how to kill, cut, keep, and carry); and morality (what is a just slice?)."[86] Below are some elements of etiquette worth exploring in interpretation.

Giving Thanks

Lévi-Strauss finds rituals of giving thanks to deities or nature in Western as well as indigenous traditions. These rituals might happen at the time of slaughter, food preparation, consumption, or all three. Interpretive projects might explore how, when, where—and whether—thanksgiving featured in rituals govern food, and how changes in that process reflect social shifts, such as the secularization of society.

Handling Food

Though most cultures developed knives and spoons in prehistory, eating with the hands continued well into the nineteenth century (and even today, it is appropriate for certain foods like corn on the cob, sandwiches, cookies, and fruit). The first American settlers "rarely had individual cups, knives, or spoons, and they carried their own knives to the table and often used communal flatware or their fingers."[87] Fashionable diners gradually adopted the fork during the seventeenth and eighteenth centuries. For Puritans, eating with a fork was pretentiously aristocratic, but the elite took up the fork habit. As the nineteenth century went on, a proliferation of utensils—as many as eight forks, specialized spoons from soup to dessert, multiple sizes of glassware—were laid before each diner, constituting a sort of test of one's knowledge. In the twentieth century, place settings simplified, but fashions for ethnic and novelty dishes brought diversity to forms: chopsticks, skewers, fondue forks, and lobster crackers demanded new skills. Disposable plastic cutlery (including the dual-purpose "spork") and paper plates underscored a newly acceptable informality during the latter half of the twentieth century.

Eating in Company

Many Americans imagine the basic meal at home as one eaten as a nuclear family, all ages and genders together at the table. But in the past, dining was often segregated by sex, social status, or occupation. Historian Rachel Laudan describes a time in precontact Hawaii during which the punishment for women eating with men was death.[88] In Anglo-American culture, adult men and women in families ate together, sometimes with children serving them (as in Puritan households during the seventeenth century). Sometimes children and adults ate at different times (as in well-to-do Victorian households and some contemporary families).[89] Servants and slaves ate in the kitchen or in their own quarters. Workers and students, military officers and enlisted men, managers and executives ate together with others of their kind.

Dining Decorum

Not eating "properly" is the mark of a cultural outsider.[90] From at least the eighteenth century, advice books touched on table behavior. George Washington, in the "Rules of Civility" he copied out at age sixteen, listed several notes about eating: "make no Shew of taking great Delight in your Victuals, Feed not with Greediness, cut your Bread with a Knife, lean not upon the Table neither find fault with what you Eat."[91] In the next century, entire books gave detailed prescriptions for manners. A rapidly expanding middle class wanted to participate in fine dining but lacked training from birth. Into the breach came books like the 1857 *The Lady's Guide to Perfect Gentility*, the 1860 *Ladies' Book of Etiquette and Manual of Politeness*, or the 1873 *Bazar Book of Decorum: The Care of the Person, Manners, Etiquette, and Ceremonials*. Fashions in etiquette changed rapidly, creating continuous demand for new titles. Middle-class families also had to instruct their children in etiquette. Family meals were "a learning experience for children."[92] Adults bought tiny sets of teacups, teapots, and dishes in part to communicate the significance of mastering hospitality and etiquette. Advice literature was also aimed at children. Author-illustrator Gelett Burgess's 1900 children's book *Goops and How to Be Them: A Manual of Manners for Polite Infants*, told of a "Race/Void of Beauty and of Grace," whose behavior served as a cautionary tale:

The Goops they lick their fingers,
And the Goops they lick their knives;
They spill their broth
On the tablecloth—
Oh, they lead disgusting lives!
The Goops they talk while eating,
And loud and fast they chew;
And that is why I'm glad that I
Am not a Goop—are you?[93]

After World War I, table manners simplified. Emily Post established a voice of authority on modern manners. Her 1922 best-seller *Etiquette: In Society, in Business, in Politics and at Home* made her a household name. Post's book addressed a newly socially mobile audience.[94] She upheld manners even as advice columns in newspapers and magazines urged informality, warmth, and creativity as more modern aspects of hospitality. In the late 1970s, journalist Judith Martin, under the moniker "Miss Manners," staged a revival, transmuting the detailed obsession of the past into guidelines based on consideration for others. Her humorous edge camouflaged a serious interest in reinforcing polite behavior in the face of increasing incivility and hostility.

Dining continues marching toward informality. Twentieth- and twenty-first-century debates have asked whether it is appropriate to have the television on while eating or check your smartphone at the table. A 2013 poll showed that 86 percent of Americans sit down to a family dinner regularly, but only between once and four times a week.[95] Another poll found that Americans ate more than half of meals all by themselves, partly because 27 percent of households consist of a single person.[96] With fewer opportunities to practice social eating behaviors, table manners may continue to simplify and tolerance for idiosyncrasy increase.

Order of Service

The shift from *service a la Francaise* to *service a la Russe* in the mid-nineteenth century impacted the elite, but "family-style" service, combining communally shared serving dishes with individual place settings, dates as ordinary practice to the middle nineteenth century. By the mid-twentieth century, hosts wanted to demonstrate their creativity. A casual dinner party was a three-act performance beginning with cocktails and appetizers, moving on to an entree, and ending with dessert and coffee. Themed informal dining led to outdoor grilling, Swedish-style "smorgasbord" buffets, and Spanish-influenced tapas. The buffet was favored in the United States in the 1930s, when its ease matched the strained budgets of the times. The entire meal could be made ahead of time and laid out for guests to serve themselves—allowing the hosts to mingle.

Best Practices: Interpreting Food and Behavior

- Present the food mavens and moralists of your site's past. Who promoted the standards your interpretive characters followed?

- Interpret shopping and retail as connected to kitchen and table. How did your characters' food sources change over time? Where could they shop, and what did they buy?
- Display ephemera related to shopping, dining out, and food fashion.
- Confirm food origin stories with primary source research.
- Consider interpreting restaurants, vendors, and other commercial food purveyors, underrepresented at museums and historic sites.
- Connect architecture to prevailing ideas about dining and food preparation. Why is there a dining room (or not)? A swinging door between kitchen and dining room?
- Resist the urge to take a mocking tone when presenting highly prescriptive and outdated information about etiquette and manners. Though it may seem extreme to us, using approved behavior to fit in was, for many, essential to social and financial success.

Discussion Starter: Analyze a Recipe

Written recipes can be miniature time capsules reflecting period assumptions about food tastes and technology. In this discussion activity, interpreters can "unpack" a recipe to discover more about the world it came from. This discussion starter can be done individually or as a group.[97]

1. Choose a historic recipe from within the scope of your interpretation. It can be published or handwritten, or even transcribed from oral transmission.
2. Post the recipe on a large wall or whiteboard, leaving plenty of space around it to diagram discoveries.
3. Begin breaking down the information provided in the recipe, adding notes about what each of the components reveals. As you go, take a close look at:
    - *Source:* Where was this recipe found? Was it promoted in newspapers or cookbooks, handed down through the family, or developed through practice? What was the relationship between the recipe's users and its originators? Where did museum staff find this recipe?
    - *Accompanying Information:* Does the recipe include information about why it is being shared? Does it contain recommendations for eating occasions or serving styles? Does it indicate anything about fashions or tastes? Who was the expected audience that would eat the food made with this recipe?
    - *Ingredients:* Where did they come from? At the time the recipe was written, what were the likely sources of the components? Were they homegrown, or locally purchased? Does it reflect a new availability or new affordability of ingredients?
    - *Equipment:* What cooking and serving equipment does this recipe assume the cook has? How specific is it about the equipment to be used? What does the difference between "a spoonful of milk" and "3/4 teaspoon of milk" say about the recipe's context?

- *Instructions:* What degree of explanation is provided? Does the writer assume the reader already knows how to make something like this, or does it describe each step, give specific quantities and temperatures, and more? Who are the instructions directed to—professional, homemaker, and mistress?
- *Comparison:* How do the ideas revealed about this recipe compare to the way this food would be prepared today? As a next step, try creating a comparison chart contrasting the answers to each of the questions above with answers that would apply today. This can help reveal points of interpretive connection to use with visitors.

Fresh Ideas: Deb Friedman on Responding to Visitors' Changing Tastes

Deb Friedman is senior vice president for Visitor Experience, Old Sturbridge Village, the birthplace of ALHFAM and a pioneer in the immersive re-creation of farm and food history. The museum continues to commit itself to sophisticated thinking in the connection of food and farming history to contemporary ideas. In recent years, they've launched a sustainable agriculture initiative and enhanced food interpretation across the program.

What led you to embrace sustainable agriculture and food history in programs and interpretation?

We started to realize about twenty years ago that society was changing. People were not as connected to their food sources, and did not always know how to cook food from scratch. People would be shocked when a gardener pulled a carrot out of the ground, as if they didn't know that carrots grew in dirt. I was training people on hearth cooking and started having to cover basics like "this is how to use a knife to peel a potato," because people were using so much processed food they weren't accustomed to doing those steps themselves. We realized that if the staff didn't understand, our visitors wouldn't understand. So even before sustainable agriculture and local and slow foods were in the news, we decided we needed to create those experiences for visitors, so they wouldn't be lost. It's amazing what an easy fit it was. We do third-person interpretation, so it's easy for us to connect past and present. There's no such thing as a new food, just a tradition given a new twist. Every culture has similar food, whether you're talking about polenta or corn mush, or blood pudding or sausage. Let's face it—lots of visitors are fascinated by the blacksmith and the potter, but the one thing we can guarantee is that everyone can relate to food.

Is the audience receptive?

At first it was difficult. Twenty years ago, people didn't want to know where food was coming from. We had problems presenting butchering demos or talking about rennet for cheesemaking, because people didn't want to think about those aspects. Now we find that people are asking those questions, rather than us having to slip it in. We have also found that people want to learn to do it themselves. We now offer classes on cheesemaking, butchering, dressing out fowl. Twenty years ago no one would have signed up, but now there's a huge interest. As more and more people do home gardening, we can give them the opportunity to try some foods that were never available in stores. Most people have never had a spring-dug parsnip. When they come to gardening programs we recommend they try growing Student parsnips, an heirloom from our gardens. You'd be surprised how many people come back and thank the staff for suggesting it.

What are some of the new ways visitors experience food interpretation at OSV?

We added a farmers' market, running May through October, that has helped to spur connections. Seasonal scarcity is something people can understand better now. Years ago, interpreters would say, "There was a lot of food in the fall and winter, if you preserved it right, but come spring there's nothing," and people would say, "What do you mean, nothing?" Now, people who buy from a farmers' market understand that nineteenth-century way of eating, how people didn't have the expectation of having certain foods year round, but enjoyed the freshness and quality of flavor when things were in season. We've also added an observation beehive exhibit along with nineteenth-century beekeeping, and do tours on honey production that highlight the importance of bees in agriculture. This brings in colony collapse disorder, making it relevant to today. In the agricultural and horticultural programs, we're teaching seed saving, showing people the advantage of growing heirloom vegetables: they can save the seed and the vegetable itself will acclimate to their personal gardens. We also offer classes in how to have backyard chickens at home. Not everybody's looking to farm, but they want some aspect of it, something they can take home and try. In one of our newer special events, *From Field to Table*, we invite in twenty-first-century producers and purveyors to give talks, demos, and samples. People love to compare and contrast contemporary food and the nineteenth century; they see so many connections to local food movements and sustainable agriculture.

What are the next steps in the evolution of food interpretation at OSV?

In our interpretive planning, one of the things that virtually everyone says is that we need to do more with food. We know we can reach every visitor through food, and we're looking at more and more ways to expand the food experience and involve all the senses. A recent members' event was *A Taste of the Nineteenth Century*, with tastings of a whole variety of foods from our interpretation that they'd never been able to try. We took nineteenth-century recipes and prepared them in a commercial kitchen throughout the year, preserving them to eat that day. Three thousand people had tastings throughout the village. People raved—we kept getting letters and comments on the website. Because people could taste, it moved the experience to a higher level. We're trying to continue to find ways we can bridge the gap between just seeing something and being able to taste. For our Christmas program, the

Figure 5.2. Old Sturbridge Village presents techniques for food preservation and storage. Here, squash and cabbages are stored in dry, dark, cool spots. (Courtesy of Old Sturbridge Village)

staff goes into our food service facility and spends the day cooking in a certified kitchen, so we can offer tastes of gingerbread, fruitcake, and plum pudding. Tasting is a dilemma for museums because there are so many regulations from local boards of health, but it's also something that boards of health are willing to work with you on because of the educational value. You have to meet them halfway.

Is all this enthusiasm for food just a flash in the pan?

I honestly don't think so. The last fifty years was more the flash in the pan, as people became enamored with fast food, processed food, convenience food. Today, more and more people are asking about what's going into their food—what are the ingredients? Who's processing it? That allows us to continue to be relevant.

Notes

1. Grace S. Yek and Kurt Struwe, "Deconstructing Molecular Gastronomy," *Food Technology* 7, no. 11 (2008): 39.
2. Jane Nylander, *Our Own Snug Fireside: Images of the New England Home, 1760–1860* (New Haven, CT: Yale University Press, 1994), 187.
3. Nylander, *Our Own Snug Fireside*, 218. The roaster was "a cast-iron cylinder with a firebox below," built into a fireplace wall and connected to the chimney with ventilating tools; the range was a set of burner holes in a counter-level surface set above a firebox, venting to the

chimney by means of a hood above. Lovers of innovation experimented with Rumford's new technologies; though they were expensive, more than five hundred were installed in New England by the 1820s.

4. Nylander, *Our Own Snug Fireside*, 214.

5. Nylander, *Our Own Snug Fireside*, 219–20.

6. For a discussion of stove inefficiency and the quest to perfect a low-energy-demand stove for the developing world, see Burkhard Bilger, "Hearth Surgery," *New Yorker* website, December 21, 2009, accessed April 26, 2015, http://www.newyorker.com/magazine/2009/12/21/hearth-surgery.

7. MPO Productions, *Design for Dreaming* (1956), sponsored by General Motors Corporation, on the Internet Archive, accessed April 26, 2015, https://archive.org/details/Designfo1956; *1999 A.D.*, sponsored by Philco-Ford Corporation, on the Internet Archive, accessed April 26, 2015, https://archive.org/details/Year1999Ad.

8. The Whirlpool Company debuted its interactive touchscreen cooktop at the 2014 Consumer Electronics Show.

9. Gerard J. Fitzgerald and Gabriella M. Petrick, "In Good Taste: Rethinking American History with Our Palates," *Journal of American History* 95, no. 2 (2008): 399.

10. Fitzgerald and Petrick, "In Good Taste."

11. Philip Ackerman-Leist, *Rebuilding the Foodshed: How to Create Local, Sustainable, Secure Food Systems* (White River Junction, VT: Chelsea Green Publishing, 2013), xvi–xvii.

12. Felipe Fernández-Armesto, *Near a Thousand Tables: A History of Food* (New York: Free Press, 2002), 199–200.

13. Hans J. Teuteberg, "The Birth of the Modern Consumer Age," in *Food: The History of Taste*, edited by Paul Freedman (Berkeley: University of California Press, 2007), 260.

14. Fernández-Armesto, *Near a Thousand Tables*, 220–21.

15. Susanne Freidberg, *Fresh: A Perishable History* (Cambridge, MA: Harvard University Press, 2009), 4.

16. Fernández-Armesto, *Near a Thousand Tables*, 211–12.

17. Woodsmoke Productions and Vermont Historical Society, "The Co-Op Movement," *The Green Mountain Chronicles*, Vermont Historical Society 1988–1989, accessed April 26, 2015, http://vermonthistory.org/research/research-resources-online/green-mountain-chronicles/the-co-op-movement-1919.

18. Teuteberg, "The Birth of the Modern Consumer Age," 240–41.

19. Jonathan Rees, *Refrigeration Nation: A History of Ice, Appliances, and Enterprise in America* (Baltimore: Johns Hopkins University Press, 2013), 4.

20. John F. Mariani, *The Encyclopedia of American Food and Drink* (New York: Lebhar-Freeman Books, 1999), 162.

21. Mariani, *The Encyclopedia of American Food and Drink*, 162.

22. Evan D. G. Fraser and Andrew Rimus, *Empires of Food: Feast, Famine, and the Rise and Fall of Civilizations* (New York: Free Press, 2010), 148.

23. Fraser and Rimus, *Empires of Food*, 149–50.

24. Fraser and Rimus, *Empires of Food*, 151–52.

25. Teuteberg, "The Birth of the Modern Consumer Age," 258–59.

26. Fernández-Armesto, *Near a Thousand Tables*, 215.

27. Fernández-Armesto, *Near a Thousand Tables*, 213.

28. Reay Tannahill, *Food in History* (New York: Three Rivers Press, 1989), 332.

29. "Borden's Milk Factory," Southeast Museum website, accessed April 26, 2015, http://www.southeastmuseum.org/html/borden_s_milk.html.

30. Tannahill, *Food in History*, 332.

31. Tannahill, *Food in History*, 330–31.

32. Adam Burrows, "Palette of Our Palates: A Brief History of Food Coloring and Its Regulation," *Comprehensive Reviews in Food Science and Food Safety* 8, no 4 (2009): 395–96; Julie N. Barrows, Arthur L. Lipman, and Catherine J. Bailey, "Color Additives: FDA's Regulatory Process and Historical Perspectives," *Food Safety Magazine*, October/November 2003, accessed on FDA.gov website, April 26, 2015, http://www.fda.gov/ForIndustry/ColorAdditives/RegulatoryProcessHistoricalPerspectives/.

33. Hilary Greenbaum and Dana Rubinstein, "Who Made That Mason Jar?" *New York Times Magazine* website, April 27, 2012, accessed April 26, 2015, http://www.nytimes.com/2012/04/29/magazine/who-made-that-mason-jar.html?_r=0.

34. Fernández-Armesto, *Near a Thousand Tables*, 190.

35. Colin Woodard, *The Lobster Coast: Rebels, Rusticators, and the Struggle for a Forgotten Frontier* (New York: Penguin, 2004), 171.

36. Fitzgerald and Petrick, "In Good Taste," 399.

37. Teuteberg, "The Birth of the Modern Consumer Age," 261.

38. Lynne Olver, "Pineapple Upside Down Cake," on the Food Timeline, January 23, 2015, accessed April 26, 2015, http://www.foodtimeline.org/foodcakes.html#pineapple.

39. United States Department of Agriculture Economic Research Service, "New Product Introductions of Consumer Packaged Goods, 1992–2010," USDA website, October 30, 2014, accessed April 26, 2015, http://www.ers.usda.gov/topics/food-markets-prices/processing-marketing/new-products.aspx.

40. Kathleen Cooper, "Toll House Cookies: A Long Secret History (with Recipes)," *The Toast* (blog), December 5, 2014, http://the-toast.net/2014/12/05/toll-house-cookies-secret-history/; John Michaud, "Sweet Morsels: A History of the Chocolate Chip Cookie," *The New Yorker* magazine website, December 19, 2013, http://www.newyorker.com/culture/culture-desk/sweet-morsels-a-history-of-the-chocolate-chip-cookie.

41. Woodard, *The Lobster Coast*, 219–21.

42. David Kamp, *The United States of Arugula: The Sun-Dried, Cold-Pressed, Dark-Roasted, Extra Virgin Story of the American Food Revolution* (New York: Broadway Books, 2006).

43. Kamp, *The United States of Arugula*, 85–88.

44. Kamp, *The United States of Arugula*, 95.

45. Kamp, *The United States of Arugula*, 115.

46. John L. Hess and Karen Hess, *The Taste of America* (Champaign: University of Illinois Press, originally published 1972, paperback edition 2000), 1.

47. Fernández-Armesto, *Near a Thousand Tables*, 195.

48. David Gwynn, "A & P History: The Early Years," Groceteria website, accessed April 26, 2015, http://www.groceteria.com/store/national-chains/ap/ap-history/.

49. Mark Levinson, "How the A&P Changed the Way We Shop," interview by Terry Gross, *Fresh Air from WHYY, National Public Radio*, August 23, 2011, http://www.npr.org/2011/08/23/139761274/how-the-a-p-changed-the-way-we-shop.

50. Betty Smith, *A Tree Grows in Brooklyn* (1943; reprint, New York: Harper Perennial Modern Classics, 2001), 48.

51. Mike Freeman, "Clarence Saunders: The Piggly Wiggly Man," *Tennessee Historical Quarterly* 51, no. 3 (1992): 162.

52. Freeman, "Clarence Saunders: The Piggly Wiggly Man," 162.

53. Freeman, "Clarence Saunders: The Piggly Wiggly Man," 168.

54. Andrew F. Smith, *Eating History: Thirty Turning Points in the Making of American Cuisine* (New York: Columbia University Press, 2009), 191.

55. Andrew Smith, ed., *Oxford Companion to American Food and Drink* (New York: Oxford University Press, 2007), 385–86.

56. Peter Scholliers, "Novelty and Tradition," in Freedman, *Food: The History of Taste*, 249.

57. Food Marketing Institute, "Supermarket Facts," *FMI: The Voice of Food Retail* website, accessed April 26, 2015, http://www.fmi.org/research-resources/supermarket-facts.

58. Anthony Troy Adams, Monika J. Ulrich, and Amanda Coleman, "Food Deserts," *Journal of Applied Social Science* 4, no 2 (2010): 104.

59. United States Department of Agriculture Economic Research Service, "Food-Away-from-Home," USDA website, October 29, 2014, accessed April 26, 2015, http://www.ers.usda.gov/topics/food-choices-health/food-consumption-demand/food-away-from-home.aspx.

60. Robin Fox, *Food and Eating: An Anthropological Perspective* (Oxford: Social Issues Research Center, n.d.), eBook, accessed April 26, 2015, http://www.sirc.org/publik/foxfood.pdf.

61. Cindy R. Lobel, "'Out to Eat': The Emergence and Evolution of the Restaurant in Nineteenth-Century New York City," *Winterthur Portfolio* 44, no. 2/3 (2010): 204.

62. Olive R. Jones, "Commercial Foods, 1740–1820," *Historical Archaeology* 27, no. 2 (1989): 37.

63. Lobel, "Out to Eat,'" 193.

64. Lobel, "Out to Eat,'" 198–203.

65. Lobel, "Out to Eat,'" 205.

66. Stella Jean Pierce, "Kitchen Cache: The Hidden Meaning of Gender and Cooking in Twentieth-Century American Kitchens" (master's thesis, Appalachian State University, 2010), 61–62.

67. Paul Freedman and James Warlick, "High-End Dining in the Nineteenth-Century United States," *Gastronomica : The Journal of Food and Culture* 11, no. 1 (2011): 48.

68. Tannahill, *Food in History*, 328–29.

69. Pierce, "Kitchen Cache," 61–62.

70. Lobel, "Out to Eat,'" 194.

71. Freedman and Warlick, "High-End Dining in the Nineteenth-Century United States," 48.

72. Tannahill, *Food in History*, 328.

73. "Diner History and Culture," American Diner Museum website, accessed April 26, 2015, http://www.americandinermuseum.org/site/history.php.

74. Carolyn Hughes Crowley, "Meet Me at the Automat," *Smithsonian Magazine*, Smithsonian.com, August 2001, accessed April 26, 2015, http://www.smithsonianmag.com/history/meet-me-at-the-automat-47804151/?no-ist.

75. Scholliers, "Novelty and Tradition," 351.

76. Carolyn Wedin, "Charles William Anderson," in *Encyclopedia of African American History, Vol. 1*, ed. Paul Finkleman (New York: Oxford University Press, 2009), 65.

77. Charles L. Lumpkins, "Soul Food," in *Encyclopedia of African American History, Vol. 4*, 340.

78. Scholliers, "Novelty and Tradition," 352.

79. Fox, *Food and Eating*.

80. Scholliers, "Novelty and Tradition," 352.

81. Nylander, *Our Own Snug Fireside*, 248–50.

82. Fox, *Food and Eating*.

83. Jane Ziegelman, *97 Orchard: An Edible History of Five Families in One New York Tenement* (New York: Smithsonian Books/HarperCollins, 2010), xii.

84. Fox, *Food and Eating.*

85. Claude Lévi-Strauss, *The Origin of Table Manners: Mythologiques, Vol. 3* (Chicago: Chicago University Press, 1990), 487.

86. Margaret Visser, *The Rituals of Dinner: The Origins, Evolution, Eccentricities, and Meaning of Table Manners* (Toronto: HarperCollins, 1992), 1–3.

87. Carol A. Greenberg, "Etiquette Books," in *The Oxford Encyclopedia of Food and Drink in America*, 2nd edition, ed. Andrew Smith (Oxford: Oxford University Press, 2013), 714.

88. Lynne Rossetto Kasper, "The Empire: The Political Unit That Shaped and Transmitted Cuisines," radio interview, transcribed on *The Splendid Table* (radio show blog), January 10, 2014, accessed April 26, 2015, http://www.splendidtable.org/story/the-empire-the-political-unit-that-shaped-and-transmitted-cuisines.

89. Sharon J. Huntington, "How Table Manners Became Polite," *Christian Science Monitor* website, November 28, 2000, accessed April 26, 2015, http://www.csmonitor.com/2000/1128/p22s1.html.

90. Fox, *Food and Eating.*

91. George Washington, *Rules of Civility & Decent Behaviour in Company and Conversation: A Book of Etiquette* (Williamsburg, VA: Beaver Press, 1971), 91.

92. Robert K. Fitts, "The Archaeology of Middle-Class Domesticity and Gentility in Victorian Brooklyn," *Historical Archaeology* 33, no. 1 (1999): 49.

93. Gelette Burgess, *Goops and How to Be Them* (New York: Frederick A. Stokes, 1900), Project Gutenberg eBook, accessed April 26, 2015, 4.

94. Greenberg, "Etiquette Books," 715.

95. Larry Shannon-Missal, "Are Americans Still Serving Up Family Dinners?" Harris Polls website, November 13, 2013, accessed April 26, 2015, http://www.harrisinteractive.com/NewsRoom/HarrisPolls/tabid/447/ctl/ReadCustom%20Default/mid/1508/ArticleId/1319/Default.aspx.

96. "Consumers Are Alone Over Half of Eating Occasions as a Result of Changing Lifestyles and More Single-Person Households, Reports NPD," NPD Group, August 6, 2014, https://www.npd.com/wps/portal/npd/us/news/press-releases/consumers-are-alone-over-half-of-eating-occasions-as-a-result-of-changing-lifestyles-and-more-single-person-households-reports-npd/.

97. Adapted from Nancy O'Brien Wagner, "Using Primary Sources in the Classroom," Minnesota Humanities Council website, October 2006, accessed April 26, 2014, http://www.minnesotahumanities.org/Resources.

CHAPTER 6

Edible Activism: Interpreting the Politics of the Plate

E DIBLES AND POLITICS have always been tightly intertwined. From early in America's history, official policies touched on food production and distribution. Citizens, for their part, have voiced concern over food issues—food safety, pricing, labor, agriculture, and the environment among them. Power struggles, protests, popular movements, and policymaking keep the American food scene in constant flux. Certain issues surface repeatedly. The next sections offer some topical areas interpreters might use when working with the theme of food and politics.

Key Interpretive Concepts

1. *Current events in food politics, such as the locavore movement or attempts to more tightly regulate food safety, are phenomena with their own histories.* It can sometimes seem as though we live in an unusually stressed and contentious age, when in fact, food issues, problems, and aspirations have rarely been far from Americans' thoughts.
2. *Because everyone has something to do with food, every citizen has a stake in food policy development and ways to take action on issues that matter to them.* From consumer activism to legislative advocacy, food issues offer many opportunities for individuals to get involved.
3. *Food takes on multiple meanings in political contexts.* It can be used to show support or opposition, and it can be an economic tool or a symbol of protest.

Safety First

Food safety is in the news regularly. As each new outbreak of listeria, salmonella, or *E. coli* is reported, Americans search their fridges for the suspect item, hoping it hasn't already been eaten. Scientific exactitude allows public health agencies to identify the specific contaminant, and manufacturing controls track the path of tainted products to the individual stores and cafeterias where it was distributed. These modern tools help limit the spread of foodborne illness, but issues of unsafe food have been present throughout American history.

In the early colonial era through the nineteenth century, anxiety focused on public markets as disease vectors. Long before germ theory, markets presented many of the signs Americans associated with illness: odor, manure, scraps left to rot, vermin, and spoiling food. Food baked in the sunshine. Customers pawed through bins with their hands and juggled meats, live fowl, and produce together in baskets. Market days left streets scattered with filth, and officials contended with drinking, fighting, and gambling. Some of the earliest laws enacted in colonial towns aimed to regulate markets. Many cities corralled vendors into public stalls, collecting rents and fees in order to hire paid managers to control the chaos. With the arrival of railroads, planners pushed century-old markets out of city centers to allow redevelopment along more seemly lines. These modern "terminal markets" were sited at rail or steamship hubs.[1] During the twentieth century, public markets fell out of favor, archaically unhygienic compared to sparkling supermarkets.

Dairies were another source of foodborne illness. Cows' milk transmitted typhoid, tuberculosis, strep, and other bacterial infections. Though the risks had long been known, epidemics rarely spread rapidly or far until people and animals became tightly packed together through urbanization. In city dairies, poor diets and crowded stalls led to "sick cows and bad milk." The "thin, blue" milk that city cows gave looked so unappetizing that some dairies doctored it with molasses for color and Plaster of Paris or starch for body. Partly due to poor or adulterated milk, in major cities at the turn of the twentieth century infant mortality measured around 9 percent, with spikes as high as 15 percent. Not until a campaign demanded that states implement pasteurization did the incidence of milk-related illness decline.[2]

Industrialization divorced people from the sources of their food, introducing more risks and fears. Wallach considers the fear reasonable, "founded at least in part by genuine fraud and unsanitary conditions on the part of unscrupulous industrial food outlets."[3] Consumers embraced convenience foods while at the same time regarding them with uncertainty. Food science, Fernández-Armesto says, grew "obsessed with purity and the course of development in food industries was directed toward products that would be uniform, predictable, and safe. . . . Hygiene was a selling point, which would enhance any brand."[4] For domestic science reformers, cleanliness—expressed as "sanitation" or "hygiene"—bordered on obsession. In their formulation, dirt caused, as well as resulted from, poverty and lack of education. If the working classes suffered from disease, slovenly housekeeping and unhygienic cooking were to blame.

The industrialization of the food supply over the twentieth century created risks related to the scale of operations and wide distribution. A panic followed the outbreak of BSE or "mad cow disease" in Britain in the late 1980s. Four BSE-positive cows were found in the United States between 2003 and 2012, fueling critical review of industrial beef processing. Following safety guidelines promulgated by government agencies, restaurant cooks now chop meats, fowl, and vegetables on separate cutting boards, while fast food workers pull on a new pair of food-safe gloves with each order. In 2010, Congress passed the Food Safety Modernization Act over the objections of food manufacturers, who argued they could voluntarily regulate themselves.[5] These measures nip some potential disease outbreaks in the bud. But Americans' preference for uncontaminated food is at odds with their embrace of large-scale industrial food manufacturing. As Fernández-Armesto observes, "When foods are mass-produced, one mistake can poison a lot of people."[6] Reluctant to give up the benefits of industrialized food, Americans seem willing to tolerate occasional, and sometimes life-threatening, outbreaks of foodborne illness.

Adulteration and Pure Food

Foodborne disease contamination was usually accidental, but Americans have also had to worry about intentional tampering. By the turn of the nineteenth century, Americans were fed up with unscrupulous merchants and manufacturers whose products were other than they claimed to be. Early brands used their marketing to establish a reputation for trustworthiness. Their promises were not always fulfilled. Food manufacturers built on shady retailers' tactics—stretching products with fillers, selling one food as another. According to Tannahill, pepper, for example, "had always been adulterated with comparatively innocuous materials like mustard husks, pea flour, juniper berries, and a commodity known as 'pepper dust,' which appears to have consisted of the sweepings of the store-room floor."[7] Consumers were used to being wary with local grocers, but the industrial food economy and its lengthening supply chains obscured food origins. Dietary guru Sylvester Graham's insistence on minimally processed bread was partly based on his belief that most manufactured flours were tainted. He was not entirely wrong. Wallach explains that "some bakers infused their loaves with fillers like alum, which disguised an inferior product and helped give the bread a whiter appearance, which consumers ironically associated with quality and purity."[8] The 1820 *Treatise on the Adulterations of Food, and Culinary Poisons* revealed some food industry secrets: "that pickles owed their appetizing green color to copper," and that the "rich orange rind of Gloucester cheese came from ordinary red lead."[9] A series of "adulteration scandals" in the late nineteenth century forced reform and increased oversight. A coalition of women's clubs, chemists, domestic scientists, and others formed the Pure Foods Movement, pushing for regulations eventually written into the 1906 Pure Food and Drug Act. Among other provisions, the act set safety standards and established government authority to inspect manufacturers. Attempts to dodge these regulations resulted in an early twentieth-century spate of deceitful practices: flour noodles wrapped in yellow cellophane to look like egg noodles, berry jam that contained no berries, false-bottomed boxes, and fool-the-eye bottles. In 1933, these and other infractions were dubbed "the American Chamber of Horrors" by reporters covering the ensuing consumer revolt.[10] Another act of Congress passed in 1938 outlawed these strategies. In 1958, legislation began requiring manufacturers to establish the safety of new products before bringing them to market, and in 1965 another law stipulated that all ingredients must be listed on labels.[11] A renewed "panic over additives" accompanied the rise of convenience foods in the 1960s. Monosodium glutamate (a flavor enhancer), nitrates and nitrites (used to preserve cured meats), food dyes and colorings, and cyclamates (zero-calorie sweeteners) were all associated—in the public mind and in some scientific investigations—with negative health impacts, from cancer to migraines.[12]

Figure 6.1. Ruth Lamb, chief of Public Relations of the FDA, demonstrating some of the exhibits in the "Chamber of Horrors" during a 1937 campaign focusing consumer attention on fraudulent product representation and product adulteration. (Library of Congress/Harris and Ewing, photographers, Harris & Ewing Collection)

In the past three decades, concern for purity has risen again, tripling the sale of organic food. In 2002, the USDA established the National Organic Program, a standards-based certification for growers. In part, the choices arise from continued concern over the safety and purity of America's food system. Some see the shift to organic sourcing as an attempt to sidestep some of the inherent risks of massively scaled production; others see consumers hearkening back to an imagined simpler time when food was pure and wholesome, always completely safe. But a look into America's food past and consistent agitation for food regulation shows that there has never been such a time. Rather than seeking shelter in the past, organic consumers are attempting to bring about a future food system that retains many of the gains of industrialization while minimizing its risks.

Voting with the Wallet: Boycotts and Buycotts

Americans discovered early on that their purchasing power had protest potential, asking one another to eat—or avoid—specific foods to advance shared political goals. In the years before the Revolutionary War, supporters of independence ostentatiously rejected British foods, responding to the Sugar Act of 1764 with a boycott on British sugar, molasses, and rum.[13] Rejecting British-imported tea—and importation taxes—colonists foraged for substitutes, brewing tea from peppermint, hyssop, bee balm, dill, fennel, thyme, and lavender.[14]

Organized boycotts inaugurated a tradition historian Lawrence Glickman calls "consumer activism."[15] In the battle over slavery, Americans revived the strategy. Inspired in part by eighteenth-century Quaker leader John Woolman, who avoided using or wearing any product of slavery, some abolitionists refused to buy slave-produced goods, like rice, cotton, and sugar. Declaring that "if there were no consumers of slave products there would be no slaves," these activists called Northerners "accessories" to slavery, keeping slavers in business through their purchasing.[16] From the 1790s, Benjamin Franklin urged abolitionists to invest in maple sugar, a morally superior sweetener; abolitionist Lydia Marie Child and her husband tried to raise sugar beets commercially in Massachusetts. Supporters of "free produce," as the movement was called, hoped to "create an alternative economy" based on free labor, expressing their values with the enthusiastic consumption of products with proper moral alignment.[17] Free-labor vendors were "moral entrepreneurs" who "argued that consumers best actualized their ethical views through the consumption of the goods they sold."[18] Free produce shops, free labor holiday fairs, and abolitionist magazines helped consumers find approved products, advertising treats like sugarless "Free Labor pineapple, strawberry and raspberry ice creams made directly from the juices."[19] The products of this movement were the first ethically labeled goods in America, introducing a retail strategy that remains with us today as we navigate labels such as free range, fair labor, cage-free, and grass fed.[20] As today, the impact of this ethical economy was limited by high product cost. Products of slavery had low production costs, so they were cheap; abolitionist substitutes were expensive. Partly for this reason, the movement mainly involved women with the means to pay a higher margin for rougher goods.[21] Ultimately, free labor was never powerful enough to threaten the vast structures of slavery, but, in tightening activist networks, it helped to strengthen the cause of abolition.

The Southern states practiced their own version of moral economics, encouraging supporters to patronize only Southern producers. Called nonintercourse, this movement "used precisely the same methods—the boycott and buycott—and very similar rhetoric for the exact opposite cause: the maintenance of a slave labor economy and the weakening of the free labor North."[22] Advocates for nonintercourse expected it to force the South to develop its food agriculture and industry. The coming of the Civil War cut the nascent movement short before it had an appreciable impact.

The Civil Rights Movement

Americans continued to adapt the late eighteenth-century strategies of boycotts and "buycotts" to the ever-changing political landscape. During the civil rights movement of the 1960s, both strategies were used to strong effect. The 1955–1956 Montgomery bus boycott, which damaged city revenues and resulted in the end of legal segregation on public transport, was funded partly by cooking. Boycotters organized carpools to get workers to their jobs, depending on the movement for help buying gas. Georgia Gilmore, a professional cafe cook, organized a group called the Club from Nowhere to raise gas money. They made cakes, pies, and dinners, selling them door-to-door. As one participant remembers, some customers "didn't want it known that they had given any money to the movement, so they wouldn't give Mrs. Gilmore and the other ladies checks that could be traced, only cash. And Mrs. Gilmore made sure they didn't tell anybody who had made the donations. That's why it was called the Club from Nowhere, so that none of the people giving the money could be in the least bit accused of supporting the movement." Donors appreciated the cover of buying a treat or a ready-made supper, allowing them to support the movement but escape censure from segregationists. Gilmore lost her cafe job when her employer learned of her project, blacklisting her from other cooking jobs. That did not stop her from continuing to lead the Club from Nowhere.[23]

The Southern Christian Leadership Conference experimented with a buycott, a "selective patronage" effort titled Operation Breadbasket. Beginning in 1962, leaders under Martin Luther King Jr. leveraged the buying power of black shoppers in Atlanta to increase the employment opportunities available to black workers. Using a data-based approach,

> the group obtained employment statistics for companies selling their products in black communities and, if these statistics demonstrated that blacks were underemployed or restricted to menial positions, ministers from Operation Breadbasket asked the company to [in King's words] 'negotiate a more equitable employment practice.' If the company refused, clergy encouraged their parishioners to boycott those products and picket businesses selling them. By 1967 Atlanta's Breadbasket had negotiated jobs bringing a total of $25 million a year in new income to the black community.

Organizers deemed Operation Breadbasket "spectacularly successful," and they began to replicate it in Chicago, where the program secured job opportunities for black workers in the dairy industry, Pepsi and Coca-Cola plants, and supermarket chains, increasing income to the black community by $15 million in its first fifteen months.[24] After King's death, differing views on the direction of the movement led to the dissolution of Operation Breadbasket.[25] Still, it had demonstrated that black purchasing power could be an economic lever for change.

United Farm Workers

In the Delano Grape Strike of 1965 to 1970, boycotting went mainstream. The strike began when a group of Filipino-American farm workers walked out on California fruit growers to protest below-minimum wages. They were joined by the Mexican Farm Workers under the leadership of Cesar Chavez, forming the United Farm Workers (UFW) labor union. Using picket lines, a three-hundred-mile march to the state capital, alliances with shippers who let grapes rot on the docks, and a twenty-five-day fast by Chavez, the workers successfully negotiated a pay raise and fairer hiring practices. Their efforts were aided by a national consumer boycott in 1967 asking all Americans to avoid buying California-grown table grapes, raisins, lettuces, and wines and liquors made by beverage companies that purchased California grapes. UFW members and supporters distributed flyers and picketed at supermarkets. Newspaper ads and posters exhorted, "There's blood on those grapes." Clergy members, union members, and pro-union Americans joined the effort, as did young activists who identified politically with the farmworkers and gave the boycott a pop-culture-friendly face with poster and T-shirt designs. This broad coalition created the nation's most effective food boycott, a relative rarity in American history.[26]

The boycott is an activist tactic renewed whenever an appropriate cause surfaces. In 1977, members of the gay and lesbian communities led a boycott of Florida orange juice after juice spokesperson Anita Bryant publicly opposed antidiscrimination efforts. The boycott backfired, but the gay rights movement counted other gains: more open conversations about sexuality and a political unification of the gay and lesbian community.[27] In 2012, antigay rhetoric prompted another boycott when Dan Cathy, the CEO of fast food chain Chick-fil-A, condemned gay marriage on a national talk show. Protests at the restaurant's outlets and on social media resulted in a backlash of counterprotests, including a "Chick-fil-A Appreciation Day" that brought record-breaking sales. These examples are a reminder that boycotts are a two-edged sword that can win support but also rouse opposition. Even worse, many boycotts do not receive enough widespread support to get noticed by food producers. Given those dilemmas, recent activist efforts have focused more on using the buycott to support favored purveyors, as many cities' "Buy Local" campaigns demonstrate.

Plow Power: Farmers' Movements

Before industrialization, farming was the bedrock layer of the American economy. Farmers participated in local, state, and national politics, but mostly as individuals, rarely coalescing into blocs. After the Civil War, that began to change. In successive movements over time, farmers defined common interests and organized to influence the political process.[28] In the late 1800s, the impetus was economic survival. With territorial expansion came rail lines located near new plots of cheap farmland. Homesteading farmers were encouraged to grow for distant urban markets and to specialize in goods railroads would happily ship—for a price. Farmers jumped aboard, planting corn, wheat, and other durable commodity crops. Some years, profits were good. In others, farmers found themselves desperately squeezed between the unpredictable hardships of farming and the pressures of the new marketplace. Railroads and middlemen charged storage, processing, and shipping fees; farmers felt gouged by vertically integrated shipping companies that looked and acted like monopolies. Combined with banking crises, exploitive loan policies, falling crop prices caused by expansion and glut, and monetary policies that seemed arbitrary and risky, farmers found themselves in an untenable situation, and they began to organize.

The first large-scale farmers' rights group, the Grange, was initially a scholarly and social society, modeled on the Masons, in which farmers could study agricultural bulletins, join collective enterprises like building grain elevators, and share mutual aid. Within a decade of its 1867 founding, the Grange took on political issues, lobbying representatives to regulate railroads and enact favorable fiscal policies. Pitted against powerful railroad companies, Grangers rarely prevailed—what "Granger Laws" were passed were later overturned. But their influence on legislation set precedents for government regulation of domestic trade and agricultural policy, and for farmers as a significant, organized voting bloc. Grange membership flared to more than 850,000 at its peak, but it declined by the end of the 1870s as the economy improved and other farmers' organizations rose to claim some of their former membership. The Grange continued as a mostly social organization, and it is still in existence today.[29]

Farmers' Alliances inherited some of the Grange's power. Comprised of two strong organizations representing North and South, the Alliances agreed on most policy initiatives but were divided on race—black farmers could join the Northern Alliance, but not the Southern. Like the Grange, the Alliances worked to influence national party politics, electing representatives in several states. But factionalism and party division diffused their power, leading to proposals for a national third party dominated by agricultural interests. In 1891, agrarian activists founded the People's Party, or Populist Party, running a candidate for president and electing several state representatives and governors. In 1896, the Democratic Party adopted the Populist platform, but their candidate, William Jennings Bryan, lost to William McKinley. Populist issues sparked fewer passions, at least for a while. The National Farmers Union, founded in 1902, campaigned for women's suffrage, fair trade, and tariff reform, but it emphasized relationships with legislators over protest actions.

World War I boosted farmer prosperity, but a decade of decline set in again when wartime price controls ended and farm production, expanded for the war effort, outstripped domestic demand. During the 1930s, "Farm Belt" activists made themselves heard in Washington. With crop prices dropping below the cost of production, National Farmers Union members in the Midwest sought guarantees that pricing would meet or exceed their investment in commodity crops. Some farmer-activists borrowed radical tactics from the manufacturing labor movement, including strikes. One movement calling itself the Farm Holiday Association (FHA) proposed a total halt to selling produce or buying equipment until their crop price demands were met. Rallies included slogans like "Stay at Home—Buy Nothing—Sell Nothing" and

> Let's call a Farmer's Holiday
> A holiday let's hold
> We'll eat our wheat and ham and eggs
> And let them eat their gold.[30]

The movement caught the attention of Franklin D. Roosevelt, then running for president, who developed proposals for farm relief programs that eventually became core to the New Deal. FHA leaders asked activists to stand down, promising that the election would bring the policy changes they wanted. Farm relief, when it came, both improved conditions for farmers and pushed the FHA into decline. Farmers receiving relief money were less inclined to take part in radical labor actions.[31]

Farmer protests quieted between the 1940s and 1960s. A World War II boom was followed by profitable decades of record yields enabled by advances in chemical cultivation. But the costs of food production remained a constant issue, especially as inputs and equipment became more expensive. The American Agricultural Movement (AAM) arose in 1977 out of frustration with the continuing discrepancy between commodity prices and the cost of growing food. Activists "went toe to toe with Big Ag" under the rallying cry "Parity Not Charity." AAM members demonstrated to end farm foreclosures and establish a living wage. Their signature tactic was the "tractor rally," in which farmers drove tractors hundreds of miles to demonstrate their numbers, power, and the significant cost of equipment and fuel. In December 1977, "tractorcades" visited nearly every state capital. The following winter, farmers marched on Washington, D.C., and met with their senators and representatives, bringing tax returns and fuel receipts to illustrate the squeeze between rising costs and falling revenues. Unsatisfied, the group returned in 1979, this time with their tractors—nine hundred of them, parked on the National Mall. Initially greeted with hostility, tractorcade drivers became local heroes after a blizzard buried the city under twenty inches of snow. Organizers recalled that "for a few days tractors were about the only vehicles that could move. Farmers worked on mercy missions around the clock, transporting doctors and nurses to hospitals, helping the fire departments, giving blood and transporting government officials. AAM women even cooked and cleaned in hospitals because the regular staff was unable to get to work." The group stayed in Washington for weeks.[32] Though its demands were not met, AAM established a permanent office, where it continues—along with the Farm Bureau, the National Farmers Union, and many other groups—to advocate for policies favoring food growers.[33]

Figure 6.2.   Tractors paraded along the National Mall during an American Agriculture Movement rally in December 1977. (Library of Congress/Thomas J. O'Halloran, photographer)

Contemporary food justice and fair trade movements direct attention to farmworker issues, highlighting the paradox that this most essential labor is the least rewarded. Farmworkers face food insecurity at much higher rates than other workers and struggle for safe working conditions, legal status, and fair wages. Despite their skills and stamina, "the life of a farmworker is far too often a case study in injustice, from multiple angles: economic insecurity, family malnutrition, racial and cultural bias, dangerous working conditions, and sexual harassment and violence."[34] The food industry has yet to solve structural labor problems that have existed since farm sizes expanded in the mid-nineteenth century.

Farmers are still political. Though they often appear in campaign rhetoric as symbols of American stability, many issues raised by Grangers, Populists, and American Agriculturists are chronically unresolved. How can we keep food prices low while ensuring farmers a living wage? How can we help farmers survive wild swings of demand and price? Today's farmers deal with these and other questions whose solutions are necessarily political, and they often look to the farm movements and farmers' organizations of the past for inspiration. In a 2014 *New York Times* op-ed, farmer Bren Smith called farming "one of the defining issues of our generation," encouraging farmers to organize in support of higher wages for everyone in the food supply chain, to take leadership in developing new food hubs and distribution networks, and to

> fight for loan forgiveness for college grads who pursue agriculture; programs to turn farmers from tenants into landowners; guaranteed affordable health care; and shifting subsidies from factory farms to family farms. . . . But none of these demands will be met until we start our own organizations—as in generations past—and shape a vision of a new food economy that ensures that growing good food also means making a good living.[35]

In the boom-and-bust roller coaster of the American economy, the need for farmers to pursue a voice in the political process will continue.

Fries with That? Nonfarm Food Labor

Farming is iconic, but interpretation should not overlook other kinds of food work. Food systems involve an astounding number of workers. Consider interpreting food labor across three broad categories: *production*, *processing*, and *distribution*. Beyond the farm, food *producers* include orchardists, fishermen, hunters, beekeepers, and foragers. Each specialty offers its own cultures and histories. Food *processors* add value to raw ingredients by translating them into more ready-to-eat forms: bakers, meat cutters, canners, cheesemakers, and others, on scales ranging from home-based to industrial. Finally, *distributors* move raw or processed food closer to the consumer: trucking, shipping, packaging, advertising, retailing, professional food preparation, catering, and food service. Each of these subsectors is a potential interpretive focus.

The home-based processing methods common before the Civil War gradually gave way to commercially available food at much later stages of processing. Commercial processors' facilities were modeled on the rationalized, mechanized, and scientifically managed factories of other industries. Employing vast swaths of the workforce (in 2011, 14 percent of

America's total manufacturing workforce and 1 percent of the total workforce, or 1.5 million workers), food-processing plants demanded concentrated labor and sometimes dominated their localities.[36] Plant workers were exposed to factory hazards: accidents, extremes of heat and cold, long hours, repetitive labor. They also enjoyed camaraderie and pride, and many found opportunity in management structures. Issues like safety and wage parity, arising by the nineteenth century, remain with us today: food-processing workers, especially in meatpacking plants, suffer a rate of illness and injury up to three times the average across all private industry. White males predominate in management, while laborers are mostly nonwhite.[37]

Today, public concern over the ethics and practices of large-scale food industries underlies newfound fascination with "artisanal" forms of production. Despite their trendy trappings, in many locations new cheesemakers, craft brewers, and bakers businesses are simply revivals of the kinds of community food processors of generations past. Shifts from small- to large-scale food businesses and back can provide fascinating interpretive material. In 2011, more than thirty thousand food-processing plants were operating across the United States. Some 66 percent had fewer than twenty employees—a numerical majority—but these accounted for only 4 percent of total food shipments. At the other end of the spectrum, large plants employing one hundred or more people shipped 77 percent of the edible goods despite representing only 12 percent of plants.[38]

Distribution grew more crucial as food production consolidated and communications infrastructure for order and delivery improved. Between 50 and 66 percent of small-farm products in 2011 were sold through distributors, not direct to consumers.[39] Distributors' histories are highly relevant to audiences—and potentially, personally familiar. Today, one out of twelve Americans in the private sector works in the restaurant industry; half of all adults have worked in a restaurant at some point in their lifetime, and almost all adults eat a meal away from home on a regular basis.[40] Food stores are another familiar distribution point. Americans patronize more than 212,000 food stores weekly and know food retailing intimately, as consumers and often as workers.[41] Labor histories in the food distribution industry entail dramatic shifts in scale, job demands, labor standards, and workforce composition.

Most discussions of food in popular culture overlook the issue of labor. In his *New York Times* op-ed, Bren Smith noted that "the food movement—led by celebrity chefs, advocacy journalists, students and NGOs—is missing, ironically, the perspective of the people doing the actual work of growing food. Their platform has been largely based on how to provide good, healthy food, while it has ignored the core economic inequities and contradictions embedded in our food system."[42] The experiences of the millions of workers in America's food industry offer powerful, relatable topics for interpretation. Labor histories open a window into the lives and skills of workers, the import of regional industries, and the roots of vexing questions.

Growing Concerns: Garden Campaigns

Michelle Obama made news headlines with her White House vegetable garden, but her public promotion of gardens fits into a long history of gardens as political project, reflecting ideals rooted deeply in the past. In the late nineteenth century, horticultural societies and garden clubs sprouted across the country, and progressive women united their interest in flowers and plants with agendas for social improvement in civic and school gardening programs. The Massachusetts Horticultural Society was first among them, and it launched an organized school gardening effort.[43] The USDA provided seeds and manuals; for a time, school gardens received government support via the Home and School Garden Division of the U.S. Bureau of Education.[44] Gardening promised to solve issues like vandalism by "idle" youth, a by-product of the shift to concentrated manufacturing. In response to this "boys in summertime problem," the National Cash Register Company of Dayton, Ohio, organized youth gardens in 1897, inviting neighborhood boys to put in two shifts a day in a highly structured program. Whatever they managed to grow was their own to eat, share, or sell. Promoters believed gardening would cultivate a complex of pro-social qualities: "The value of the moral training is beyond any concrete estimate. By impressing children with the idea that personal, sustained effort is necessary to achieve a result they are given the first great lesson in citizenship."[45]

Gardening was also enlisted as a poverty-relief strategy. When Detroit faced high unemployment in the depression of 1893, Mayor Hazen Pingree and his Agricultural Committee offered vacant lots to hungry citizens for gardening, preventing "idle lands and idle hands" without demanding public funds. Applicants entered the program "under the threat of not receiving charity relief from the city if they did not participate." On small plots dubbed "Pingree's Potato Patches," gardeners cultivated vegetables—including gourds such as pumpkins and squash, as well as cabbage and beans—to both eat and sell. Not everyone approved. Some feared "potato bugs would invade the city"; others deplored the use of lots as a "free land scheme." Despite opposition, the program inspired imitators in cities such as Buffalo, New York, and Philadelphia, establishing a precedent for gardening as a relief strategy defined by self-reliance and sweat equity rather than public aid.[46]

By World War I, gardening enjoyed such a civic glow that it was almost inevitable that it would be included in the war effort. The United States diverted much of its food supply to allies, and to combat the resulting shortages, timber magnate Charles Lathrop Pack launched a campaign for home gardening. President Woodrow Wilson embraced it as official policy, telling Americans "every one who creates or cultivates a garden helps and helps greatly, to solve the problem of the feeding of the nations." "Liberty Gardens" cut down on food buying, leaving more available to send overseas, and they saved labor and fuel that could go toward the war effort. The Commission counted three million war gardens in 1917, increasing to more than five and a quarter million in 1918.[47]

Many war gardens stayed active during the Great Depression. Some believed the depression would not last long enough to bother planting, but as the prospect of recovery receded, groups such as the Family Welfare Society and Employment Relief Commission stepped in to organize "welfare gardens." Franklin D. Roosevelt embraced garden campaigns after his election to president in 1933. Formal support for relief gardens ended in 1935 as New Deal strategy moved away from "welfare" and toward employment. "Work garden" programs paid people to grow, producing both jobs and food. World War II demanded another diversion of food. Building on the success of Liberty Gardens, government agencies developed gardening campaigns with volunteer trainers, instruction books, posters, and radio ads. The USDA,

Office of Civilian Defense, War Food Administration, and Works Project Administration, among others, included "Victory Gardens" in their plans. Schools, youth and community groups, and civilian action committees joined in. Most adhered to the tenets laid out in government publications, including the idea that eating more fresh vegetables would build a "stronger and healthier nation" and that they would "improve the morale and spiritual well-being of the individual, family, and Nation. The beautification of the home and community by gardening provides healthful physical exercise, recreation, and definite release from war stress and strain."[48] Like civic garden clubs and Pingree Potato Patches, Victory Gardens claimed spiritual and moral benefits as well as practical ones. The gardens were a staggering success. Though most Americans had little agricultural experience (one report revealed that one-third of gardeners were trying to grow vegetables for the first time), more than three-fifths of the population cultivated food, producing 40 percent of all fresh produce consumed at the program's peak in 1943.[49] But victory gardening was unevenly adopted, and more than half of gardeners reported that they grew food to survive, not to participate in a patriotic effort. Gardening's associations—outdoorsiness, health, togetherness—offered officials an "optimistic" message in a dark time. In light of this, food historian Amy Bentley says, it is "not surprising that the quantity and quality of American's gardens was exaggerated."[50] At the end of World War II, food supplies gradually rebounded. New options in the consumer marketplace lured consumers toward purchased perfection and away from dirt under the fingernails. Americans who could afford to mostly abandoned gardening.

Gardening re-reemerged during the urban crises of the 1970s. Once-thriving neighborhoods in older industrial cities became blighted due to suburbanization, disinvestment, and aging infrastructure. Activists and city planners saw gardening as a way to infuse flagging communities with energy and to strengthen social bonds. In 1973, a New York City group called the "Green Guerillas" led volunteers in clearing a trash-filled corner lot and laying topsoil. The group won a $1-a-month lease from the city to establish New York's first community garden; by the 1980s, there would be more than eight hundred such gardens in the city.[51] In 1976, the Boston Urban Gardeners promoted "good mental health and nutrition" as well as "neighborhood vitality" and "aesthetics" with support from the Boston Housing Authority and State Department of Food and Agriculture.[52] Community gardening coalesced into a nationwide movement. Gardeners shared socially progressive ideals, aiming to bridge ethnic and economic sectors, improve community resilience and self-reliance, as well as to improve access to healthy food. Many garden programs drew on federal job training grants and urban redevelopment funds. Even as need remained high, garden funding began to dry up under 1980s cuts to federal social services. Gardening leaders turned to nonprofit fund-raising and aligned with community institutions. A national conference of garden leaders spawned the American Community Gardens Association, which today estimates about eighteen thousand active community gardens in the United States.[53]

As interest in locally grown food surged in the late 1990s and early 2000s, Americans again adapted home gardening into their lifestyles, even in urban areas. Novella Carpenter's 2009 book *Farm City* chronicles her adventures raising food—including rabbits and a pig—around her Oakland, California, home. Financial concerns, intensified by the long recession beginning in 2009, have encouraged home growing. More than half of respondents to a national survey said they gardened to "save money on food." But an equal number said they garden to have "better tasting" and "better quality" food.[54] Others pointed to personal benefits or environmental principles. In April 2014 the National Gardening Association reported that a new high of 35 percent of all households (with Millennials the fastest-growing segment) were growing at least some of their own food.[55]

Food Fights for Freedom

A 1943 Office of War Information poster declared, "Food is a weapon!" A critical war resource in a global economy, food could be shipped to allies to shore up their strength, or blockaded to weaken an enemy. In World Wars I and II as well as during the Cold War, Americans began to see food as a strategic asset.

To minimize shortages in World War I, President Woodrow Wilson created a new agency, the U.S. Food Administration, appointing Herbert Hoover as its head. Hoover disapproved of rationing, believing it would cause shortages and hoarding; he hoped a spirit of "American patriotism and voluntarism" would prevail. Americans were asked to can their own foods, observe "Meatless Mondays" and "Wheatless Wednesdays," and bake "Victory Bread," supplementing wheat with another grain. The Food Administration spoke in the language of nutritionism: cottage cheese was as rich in protein as meat, and cookbooks tried to "make the case for using meat substitutes by providing elaborate and comparative nutritional information" for lentils and peanuts. Americans got used to swapping foods for others with similar nutrient profiles. Peer pressure encouraged compliance. Fourteen million people signed "pledge cards" promising they would eat within the guidelines. Pledgers received signs to put in their windows to "demonstrate their own patriotic feelings and to implicitly pressure their neighborhoods to support the government's initiatives . . . what a family chose to eat for dinner could be interpreted as a reflection of their degree of loyalty to the United States."[56] Poor people, who had never had much meat to begin with, were irritated by the Food Administration's hectoring. Flush with cash from war work, they ate more meat during the war years than they had before.

The experiences of World War I informed approaches to managing the food system in World War II. Rationing was planned from the outset to prevent disruptions, limit inflation, and forestall hoarding. Citizens were told that rationing was needed not because they would take too much, but because their neighbors might: propaganda featured characters like greedy Mrs. George Grabwell and sugar hoarder Miss Miranda Glucose. Roosevelt's rationing programs preserved an aspect of peacetime consumerism: the element of choice.[57] The inherent fairness of receiving a per-person allotment but choosing the specific items you wanted to eat appealed to individualism as well as patriotic spirit. At the same time, a hearty infusion of rhetoric was needed to "recruit" Americans into planned and managed hardship. By recasting buying, cooking, and eating as "military behavior, the entire population could be depicted as being directly a part of the war effort." The housewife was "a soldier and her kitchen a combination frontline bunker and rear-echelon miniature war plant."[58]

Limits on meat caused the greatest frustration. In managing America's favorite food, the government's Office of Price Administration "frequently, publicly, fell flat on its face," unable to deal with "chicanery, elaborate evasiveness or just plain passive noncompliance all along the chain of distribution." The meat industry was rife with kickbacks, skimming, and manipulation. Butchers complained they had to "cut by ruler," wasting the odd scraps. In California, a produce shortage resulted, ironically, from the internment of Japanese American farmers, who had raised a third of the vegetable crop. Milk and butter were scarce; most was processed into more cheese to send to allies, and butter all but disappeared except for those willing to spend a whole week's red points for half a pound. As a substitute, Americans tolerated oleomargarine, an unnaturally white synthetic fat they could mix at home with yellow food dye.[59]

Rationing was not just a set of limits but also a challenging and constantly changing accounting system. Point values shifted weekly. Shoppers learned "double budgeting" as stores posted two item prices, in cash and points. In theory, even if you had the money, no amount of pleading would allow you to purchase goods for which you had no stamps. But the idealism of the system provided no immunity to human frailty. The black market operated in both small-time ways and large, from shorting weights on a butcher's scale to disappearing entire shipments with the stroke of a pen. After the war, a sociologist found that charges of "illicit transactions" had been leveled at one out of fifteen businesses; many more were only cautioned and never charged—at the rate of one out of every five. As much as Americans valued cooperation, self-sacrifice, and patriotism, many also rewarded cleverness, favoritism, and opportunism.[60]

In the postwar period, with decades of Depression and war seemingly behind them, Americans with the means enjoyed an expanding world of choice. American largesse contrasted starkly with the long, slow recovery in Europe, Russia, and Asia. Wallach describes a clash over the symbolism of American foodways at the 1959 American National Exhibition in Moscow. Vice president Richard Nixon and Soviet premier Nikita Khrushchev took a diplomatic stroll through a demonstration ranch-style house, built to showcase the high standard of American living. A skeptical Khrushchev challenged Nixon on whether average American workers could really afford state-of-the-art appliances, and called the houses cheap and shoddy, saying they would barely last twenty years. Nixon responded that "after twenty years, many Americans want a new house or a new kitchen. Their kitchen is obsolete by that time. . . . The American system is designed to take advantage of new inventions and new techniques."[61] When the Russian leader tired of hearing about labor-saving devices, he asked Nixon, "Don't you have a machine that puts food in the mouth and pushes it down?" The discussion, broadcast over major networks in the United States, reinforced Americans' sense of economic and cultural superiority.

Betty Crocker went to Russia, too. General Mills and General Foods sent a team of demonstrators and seven tons of cake and brownie mix to the American National Exhibition. Making up to forty cakes a day for fair audiences, the demonstration cooks extolled the convenience and flavor of their products, but they were not allowed by Soviet hosts to distribute samples. Margaret Duehring, supervisor of the Betty Crocker kitchen staff, noted that "once in a while a package or a plate of brownies disappears, much to our delight." Duehring's cooks learned to turn their backs on the crowd periodically, so that when they turned around, the cake was gone.[62] American convenience and ever-advancing home technology were cultural weapons on the Cold War. Contrasted with Soviet scarcities and limited choice, patriotic messages of food underscored the strengths of capitalism and democracy.

Figure 6.3. American kitchens became propaganda at the 1959 American National Exhibition in Moscow. (Library of Congress/Thomas J. O'Halloran, photographer)

Liberating Food: Countercultural Cuisines

Social activists in the 1960s and 1970s used food to make statements about politics. Every food became politicized: at one extreme, products of the industrial food system represented dubious motives, environmental practices, labor conditions, and advertising; at the other, elemental foods connoted workers' cuisines, developing-world cultures, and a rough, unprocessed humility and purity. Barbara Haber remembers joining a student-led occupation at Harvard in the early 1970s. Though she endorsed demands to create a women's center and low-income housing, she recalls "an enormous vat of brown rice, fortified with raisins and chopped almonds, that I saw in the kitchen, giving me the impression that the students were preparing for a long siege. . . . Cheap, sustaining, and unpretentious, it was the food of choice for the counterculture of the late sixties and the seventies, a symbol of protest against the establishment and of a commitment to the poor and disenfranchised."[63] Children who had grown up on Cold War convenience food were seeking out fresher, less processed foods in what food historian Warren Belasco has termed the "countercuisine."[64] The zeitgeist produced culinary heroes like chef and local food advocate Alice Waters, a participant in the 1964–1965 free speech movement in Berkeley, California. Waters, who studied in France during college, saw a link between sexual liberation and the hedonistic pleasures of food in French culture. There was some tension between perspectives like Waters's and those of other revolutionaries: she was "decidedly a sensualist and a flavorist who had no truck with the puritanical types who saw nobility in deprivation."[65] Waters asked her peers to consider the idea that people in all economic strata deserved to eat and enjoy fresh, delicious, healthy food.

Decolonizing Diet: Food Sovereignty

Movements for Native American civil rights and tribal sovereignty found deep symbolic value in food. The late 1960s and early 1970s saw a surge in pan–Native American political action. High-visibility events such as the 1969 to 1970 occupation of Alcatraz Island, the 1972 Trail of Broken Treaties march to Washington, D.C., to occupy the offices of the Bureau of Indian Affairs headquarters, and the 1973 occupation of Wounded Knee, South Dakota, fostered intertribal political collaboration and engaged the American public on the issue of the historical violence against, and continuing oppression of, Native people. In the decades preceding these actions, federal policies supported relocation, which separated Native people from homelands, forced changes in lifeways, and weakened processes of cultural transmission. Government policies pushed Native communities to abandon traditional farming, fishing, and hunting practices for modern consumer lifestyles, undermining not only food traditions but also fundamental principles of tribal social organization. The right to grow, harvest, eat, and celebrate traditional foods—and to protect the natural systems that made those foods available—became a political issue. The Alcatraz occupiers declared that one of their goals was to establish on the island a "museum which will depict our native food and other cultural contributions we have given to the world."[66]

Some Native American leaders developed a focus on *food sovereignty*. That term, arising from international activism by working-class farmers, denotes the democratic right of peoples to "define their own food, agriculture, livestock and fisheries systems."[67] Food sovereignty promotes a vision of tribal communities "controlling and managing all of the factors that contribute to a sustainable food system: environmental assets, economic assets [and] cultural assets." Organizations such as Native Seeds/SEARCH, founded in 1983, worked to increase food sovereignty by saving, storing, and distributing seeds for more than two thousand native foods of the Southwest. The organization began when volunteers on a garden-building project in the Tohono O'odham nation heard from tribal elders that they wanted "seeds for the foods our grandparents used to grow."[68] In 1989, writer, cultural leader, and environmentalist Winona LaDuke (Anishinaabe) founded the White Earth Land Recovery Project, seeking to buy back land once part of the Anishinaabe territory and use it to cultivate "native seeds, heritage crops, naturally-grown fruits, animals, wild plants, traditions, and knowledge of our Indigenous and land-based communities."[69] The Native American Food Sovereignty Alliance formed in 2012, "dedicated to restoring the indigenous food systems that support indigenous self-determination, wellness, cultures, values, communities, economies, languages, families, and rebuild relationships with the land, water, plants and animals that sustain us."[70] For these Native activists, food is not only a tool for economic development but also an expression of community unity, power, and connection to history.

Food Politics Today

The intermingling of politics and food is nothing new under the American sun. Today, people with the wealth to choose from many foods are seeing their consumption as reflective of morality, ideology, and local, regional, or national affiliation. Many Americans are seeking out foods made locally in small-scale enterprises, noting reduced "food miles" and a positive impact on local economic development and community relationships. "Locavores" aim to eat food grown within a tightly defined range, like the radius Alisa Smith and James Bernard MacKinnon adhered to in their best-selling book *The 100–Mile Diet.* Others insist on organic food, expressing a primary concern over the potential dangers of agricultural chemicals. Vegetarianism and veganism are choices driven by anticruelty ethics and environmentalism. Movements for cultural empowerment explore and embrace community food histories. Many of these personal affinities translate into political activism—at the community level, the national level, and everything in between. In 2014, science writer Michael Pollan and food writer Mark Bittman cowrote an op-ed in the *Washington Post* calling for a National Food Policy to eliminate contradictions and provide coherence to a scattered and often conflicting set of regulations currently in place in many separate agencies.[71]

Best Practices: Interpreting Food Politics

- Trace histories of local and community involvement with food-related political movements. Were there boycotts, protests, and debates about access, policy, labor, or safety?
- Learn whether characters in your interpretation participated in a gardening movement. Also, investigate the history of period gardens. Do they represent an unbroken practice of gardening by that family or community, or later moments at which idealism and activism drove people to create new gardens?
- Develop interpretive discussions about the economics of food—pricing, competition, and national policy—which can connect to issues in farm policy today.
- Interpret the food labor force—farmers, fishermen, cooks, waiters, pieceworkers, caterers, business owners, herders, and others. What concerns about fairness, wages, and opportunity were on their minds?
- Contextualize today's food movement as part of a recurring historical phenomenon, and food movements in general as responses to persistent problems in producing and distributing a food supply.
- Establish connections with local food organizations and involve them in programming and interpretive planning.
- Consider hosting a community garden or period demonstration garden on your site.
- Seek advisory support from university programs in agricultural, economic, and political history.
- Include stories of the impacts of impure food, food reform, and producer protests.

Discussion Starter: Food Politics, Ripped from the Headlines

Discover the historical roots of food politics that affect your museum, site, or audience. To begin, ask your discussion group to scan newspaper headlines, Facebook posts, and local news for food-related issues popping up in your region. Bring the topics or clippings to a scheduled discussion. Write a few keywords about each issue on an index card; then work with the group to sort and classify the issues under headings such as:

Food labor
Food safety
Farming and agricultural policy
Urban agriculture
Food quality
Hunger and food insecurity
Food sovereignty and social justice
Ethics and humane practice
Boycotts or buycotts

Then discuss. Are there relationships between these contemporary concerns and your own site's food history? How can you make interpretive connections between hot-button issues of the day and ideas in your interpretive scope? Brainstorm a list of tactics for connecting past to present. To go beyond this discussion, you might choose one or two issues to research for an op-ed, program series, or public conversation offering historic context on a current issue.

Notes

1. Gregory Alexander Donofrio, "Feeding the City," *Gastronomica: The Journal of Food and Culture* 7, no. 4 (2007): 35.
2. Elspeth Hay, "Milk Lately: The History of Milk-Borne Diseases," *Edible Vineyard* 9 (2011), web magazine accessed April 26, 2015.
3. Jennifer Jensen Wallach, *How America Eats: A Social History of U.S. Food and Culture* (Lanham, MD: Rowman & Littlefield, 2013), 145.
4. Felipe Fernández-Armesto, *Near a Thousand Tables: A History of Food* (New York: Free Press, 2002), 216.
5. Marion Nestle, *Food Politics: How the Food Industry Influences Nutrition and Health* (Berkeley: University of California Press, 2002), 111–32. Marion Nestle identifies gaps between the regulatory responsibilities of the FDA and the USDA, resulting in inadequate protections, while opponents of regulation see wider inspection programs as a potential burden to manufacturers. Debate over the role of government in food oversight continues.
6. Fernández-Armesto, *Near a Thousand Tables*, 219.
7. Reay Tannahill, *Food in History* (New York: Three Rivers Press, 1989), 293.
8. Wallach, *How America Eats*, 145.

9. Tannahill, *Food in History*, 293–94.

10. "The American Chamber of Horrors," *Histories of Product Regulation*, United States Food and Drug Administration website, May 30, 2013, accessed April 26, 2015, http://www.fda.gov/AboutFDA/WhatWeDo/History/ProductRegulation/ucm132791.htm.

11. Hemi Weingarten, "1862–2014: A Brief History of Food and Nutrition Labeling," *Fooducate* (blog), October 25, 2008, accessed April 26, 2015, http://blog.fooducate.com/2008/10/25/1862-2008-a-brief-history-of-food-and-nutrition-labeling/.

12. Tannahill, *Food in History*, 343–44.

13. Mark McWilliams, "Distant Tables: Food and the Novel in Early America," *Early American Literature* 38, no. 3 (2003): 374.

14. Michael Tortorello, "Making Tea from Plants Grown in the Backyard," *New York Times*, July 21, 2010.

15. Lawrence B. Glickman, "'Buy for the Sake of the Slave': Abolitionism and the Origins of American Consumer Activism," *American Quarterly* 56, no. 4 (2004): 905.

16. Carol Faulkner, "The Root of the Evil: Free Produce and Radical Antislavery, 1820–1860," *Journal of the Early Republic* 27, no. 3 (2007): 379.

17. Faulkner, "The Root of the Evil," 388.

18. Lawrence B. Glickman, *Buying Power: A History of Consumer Activism in America* (Chicago: University of Chicago Press, 2009), 64.

19. Glickman, "'Buy for the Sake of the Slave,'" 892.

20. Glickman, "'Buy for the Sake of the Slave,'" 901.

21. Faulkner, "The Root of the Evil," 403.

22. Glickman, *Buying Power*, 61.

23. Bernice McNair Barnett, "Black Women's Collectivist Movement Organizations: Their Struggles during the 'Doldrums,'" *Feminist Organizations: Harvest of the New Women's Movement*, ed. Myra Marx Ferree and Patricia Yancey Martin (Philadelphia: Temple University Press, 1995), 211–12.

24. Enrico Beltramini, "Operation Breadbasket in Chicago: Between Civil Rights and Black Capitalism," *The Economic Civil Rights Movement: African Americans and the Struggle for Economic Power*, ed. Michael Ezra (New York: Routledge, 2013), 141.

25. "Operation Breadbasket 1962–1972," *Encyclopedia of Martin Luther King and the Global Freedom Struggle*, The Martin Luther King Jr. Research and Education Institute website, Stanford University, accessed April 26, 2015, http://mlk-kpp01.stanford.edu/index.php/encyclopedia/encyclopedia/enc_operation_breadbasket/.

26. "The Little Strike That Grew to La Causa," *Time Magazine*, July 4, 1969, accessed April 26, 2015, through Farmworker Movement Documentation Project, the Library of the University of California at San Diego, https://libraries.ucsd.edu/farmworkermovement/; Paradigm Productions, website of *The Fight in the Fields: Cesar Chavez and the Farmworkers Struggle* (film), accessed April 26, 2015, http://www.pbs.org/itvs/fightfields/resources.html.

27. "Boycotts," *GLBTQ: An Encyclopedia of Gay, Lesbian, Bisexual, Transgender, and Queer Culture*, website accessed April 26, 2015, http://www.glbtq.com/social-sciences/boycotts.html.

28. Tannahill, *Food in History*, 350.

29. "Politics of the 1870s and 1880s: Indiana History 1860–1900," Conner Prairie website, accessed April 26, 2015, https://www.connerprairie.org/Education-Research/Indiana-History-1860-1900/Politics-of-the-1870s-and-1880s.

30. Jayme L. Job, "Farm Holiday Association," *Dakota Datebook*, Prairie Public Radio broadcast November 30, 2011, Prairie Public Radio website accessed April 26, 2015.

31. Charles Vollan, "Farmers Holiday Association," *Encyclopedia of the Great Plains*, ed. David J. Wishart, University of Nebraska at Lincoln website, accessed April 26, 2015, http://plainshumanities.unl.edu/encyclopedia/doc/egp.pd.020.

32. Sam Brasch, "When Tractors Invaded D.C.," *Modern Farmer* magazine website, February 5, 2014, accessed April 26, 2015, http://modernfarmer.com/2014/02/living-legacy-d-c-tractorcade-35-years-later/.

33. American Agriculture Movement, Inc., "History of the American Agriculture Movement," American Agriculture Movement, Inc., website, accessed April 26, 2015, http://www.aaminc.org/history.htm.

34. Philip Ackerman-Leist, *Rebuilding the Foodshed: How to Create Local, Sustainable, Secure Food Systems* (White River Junction, VT: Chelsea Green, 2013), 149–52.

35. Bren Smith, "Don't Let Your Children Grow Up to Be Farmers," *New York Times*, August 9, 2014.

36. "Food and Beverage Manufacturing," United States Department of Agriculture Economic Research Service website, October 27, 2014, accessed April 26, 2015, http://www.ers.usda.gov/topics/food-markets-prices/processing-marketing/manufacturing.aspx.

37. Ackerman-Leist, *Rebuilding the Foodshed*, 156.

38. "Food and Beverage Manufacturing," United States Department of Agriculture Economic Research Service website.

39. Ackerman-Leist, *Rebuilding the Foodshed*, 178.

40. The Aspen Institute, "The Restaurant Workforce in the United States," Workforce Strategies Initiative at the Aspen Institute website, accessed April 26, 2015, http://www.aspenwsi.org/wordpress/wp-content/uploads/The-Restaurant-Workforce-in-the-United-States.pdf.

41. "Retailing and Wholesaling," *Food Markets and Prices*, United States Department of Agriculture Economic Research Service website, October 27, 2014, accessed April 26, 2015, http://www.ers.usda.gov/topics/food-markets-prices/retailing-wholesaling.aspx.

42. Smith, "Don't Let Your Children Grow Up to Be Farmers."

43. Boston's Putnam School garden, founded in 1891, served as a model for scores of similar projects across the country.

44. Laura Lawson, "A Brief History of Urban Garden Programs in the United States," October 2009, Laura Lawson website, accessed April 26, 2015, http://ljlawson.rutgers.edu/assets/pdf/UGPlecture.pdf.

45. Society of American Florists and Ornamental Horticulturists, "Story of the Landscape Gardening Work Being Done by the National Cash Register Company," August 24, 1906, *Dayton History Books Online* website, accessed April 26, 2015, http://www.daytonhistory-books.com/page/page/4542597.htm.

46. "History of Urban Agriculture: Potato Patches (1890–1930)," *Sprouts in the Sidewalk* (blog), April 13, 2008, accessed April 26, 2015, https://sidewalksprouts.wordpress.com/history/pp/.

47. "History of Urban Agriculture: First World War Liberty Gardens: 1917–1919," *Sprouts in the Sidewalk* (blog), April 13, 2008, accessed April 26, 2015, https://sidewalksprouts.wordpress.com/history/vg/.

48. United States Department of Agriculture, *Guide for Planning the Local Victory Garden Program*, United States Office of Civilian Defense (Washington, DC, 1941), accessed

on the Internet Archive, April 26, 2015, https://archive.org/details/GuideForPlanning TheLocalVictoryGardenProgram.

49. Amy Bentley, *Eating for Victory: Food Rationing and the Politics of Domesticity* (Urbana: University of Illinois Press, 1998), 117; Wallach, *How America Eats*, 163.

50. Bentley, *Eating for Victory*, 119.

51. Steve Brooks and Gerry Marten, "'Green Guerillas' Revitalizing Urban Neighborhoods with Community Gardens," *The Eco Tipping Points Project* website, June 2005, accessed April 26, 2015, http://www.ecotippingpoints.org/our-stories/indepth/usa-new-york-community-garden-urban-renewal.html.

52. Greg C. Watson, "Dare to Be Naïve: Boston Urban Gardeners," *12 Degrees of Freedom* (blog), accessed April 26, 2015, http://12degreesoffreedom.org/bostonurbangardeners.html.

53. American Community Gardening Association website, accessed April 26, 2015, https://communitygarden.org/.

54. Bruce Butterfield, "The Impact of Home and Community Gardening in America," National Gardening Association, 2009.

55. "Food Gardening at Highest Levels in More Than a Decade," Garden.org website, April 2, 2014, http://assoc.garden.org/press/press.php?q=show&pr=pr_nga&id=3819.

56. Wallach, *How America Eats*, 159.

57. Wallach, *How America Eats*, 161.

58. Richard Lingeman, *Don't You Know There's a War On? The American Home Front, 1941–1945*, 2nd edition (New York: Thunder's Mouth Press/Nation Books, 2003), 247–48.

59. Lingeman, *Don't You Know There's a War On?* 256–60.

60. Lingeman, *Don't You Know There's a War On?* 267–69.

61. "The Kitchen Debate," transcript, *Teaching American History* website, accessed April 26, 2015, http://teachingamericanhistory.org/library/document/the-kitchen-debate/.

62. Monte Olmsted, "Nixon, Kruschev, and Betty Crocker at the 1959 'Kitchen Debate,'" *Taste of General Mills* (blog), July 24, 2013, accessed April 26, 2015, http://www.blog.generalmills.com/2013/07/nixon-khrushchev-and-betty-crocker-at-the-1959-kitchen-debate/.

63. Barbara Haber, *From Hard Tack to Home Fries: An Uncommon History of American Cooks and Meals* (New York: Free Press, 2002), 2.

64. David Kamp, *United States of Arugula: The Sun-Dried, Cold-Pressed, Dark-Roasted, Extra Virgin Story of the American Food Revolution* (New York: Broadway Books, 2006), 132.

65. Kamp, *United States of Arugula*, 130.

66. "Islands-Alcatraz Occupation," Oakland Museum of California lesson plan, Oakland Museum website, accessed April 26, 2015, https://www.museumca.org/teacher-resources#quickset-curriculum=3.

67. "What Is Food Sovereignty?" US Food Sovereignty Alliance website, accessed April 26, 2015, http://usfoodsovereigntyalliance.org/what-is-food-sovereignty/.

68. "History and Mission," Native Seeds/SEARCH website, accessed April 26, 2015, http://www.nativeseeds.org/about-us/historymission.

69. "White Earth Land Recovery Project," White Earth Land Recovery Project Website, September 10, 2013, accessed April 26, 2015, http://welrp.org/.

70. "NAFSA's Call to Action," Native American Food Sovereignty Alliance website, http://www.nativefoodsystems.org/about/nafsa.

71. Mark Bittman, Michael Pollan, Ricardo Salvador, and Olivier De Schutter, "How a National Food Policy Could Save Millions of American Lives," *Washington Post*, November 7, 2014.

CHAPTER 7

Food Interpretation: The Raw Ingredients

Do museums really matter? Can and do museums make a difference?

—Stephen Weil[1]

WHEN IT COMES TO contemporary understanding of and appreciation of food, museums really can make a meaningful difference. Food is the stuff of which history is made. Using the resources of historic sites and museums, we can, with our audiences, explore the past for perspectives and resources that will help us all, together, build a stronger future. Food experiences can help us imagine away the barriers of time, getting a little bit closer to inhabiting the thoughts and experiences of people in the past. The intimate, daily, and very personal world of food—what people ate and thought they should eat, the sensory pleasures and public identities food afforded them—can create a kind of communion with the past, an understanding of how people thought and felt about the times in which they lived. Few aspects of social history have the power to tell us as much about power relationships, limitations, hopes, and hungers, literal and physical. And few of them offer so many immediately visible applications to the problems and hopes of our own lifetimes.

The current cultural trend toward food awareness is good for history museums. Food programming promises to develop human capacities and historical understandings, and also to increase institutional sustainability as it brings new audiences, increased visitation, and higher visitor satisfaction. Backyard chickens, home canning, and making your own beef jerky are no longer bizarre hobbies, and a whole generation of Americans has come of age watching the Food Network. Interpretation can now address food issues of greater complexity, range, depth, and even difficulty than ever before. Audiences are ready.

Museum and historic site food interpretation is just beginning to realize its potential for reaching new audiences and making a lasting and powerful impact on our communities as we creatively reimagine our collective future. With any luck, this book will soon be outdated as more and more museums use their own archives, collections, and interpretation power to tell compelling and meaningful stories of American food. Let's begin the feast.

For museums ready to introduce new food interpretations, or revise existing ones, this chapter contains some practical guidance. It's all well and good to understand broad social history themes and how they are expressed in food, but what does the visitor see, do, feel, taste? The next few pages outline four steps museums and historic sites can take to develop or enhance food interpretation.

Take a BITE: Developing Food Interpretation

Interpretation is a process, not a product. In a lively, engaged museum, it begins, but never really ends. Each interpretive conversation and experience informs the next. Interpreters may read food history and independently integrate some of its ideas and themes into their daily interactions with visitors. But even stronger, more consistent, and more memorable interpretation can result from a planning process that marries topics in food history with each museum or site's mission and interpretive goals.

Interpreting food is not really different from any other kind of interpretive planning. Museums and historic sites are used to undertaking research, developing themes, putting staff and resources into place, providing training, and presenting to the public. The difference is that many have not been used to applying those processes so intentionally with food and making changes in practice that meaningful engagement with food demands. When incorporating a food history approach, it can be helpful to discuss specific aspects of interpretive planning that are especially important when it comes to food. In this section, I suggest four stages that interpreters, planners, and exhibit developers might use to guide food interpretation research and projects. To make them easier to remember (and have a little fun) they're grouped under the acronym BITE:

- **B**egin with Evidence
- **I**nterpret Evidence and Develop Themes
- **T**arget Audiences and Partners
- **E**ngage

Begin with Evidence

Almost any strong interpretation begins with an analysis of your project's scope, strengths, or special messages. It's the same with food. Stepping back to look at your museum or site, think together about where the content you have to share sits within the history of the broader food system. Do you have an amazing collection of candy molds? An operational cider press? Gardens, farms, and kitchens? Biographical links to industries or activism? The answers to your questions about strong messages within your scope can help determine how you might encourage and contribute to your participants' food dialogue and practice. Perhaps you are a place to learn historical information from an intellectual orientation, or perhaps a place to learn real, practical skills. Maybe you can create encounters with contemporary chefs working with food traditions, or convene neighborhood potlucks with site-grown produce. Almost every history museum can connect, in some way, to the broad themes presented here, beginning with the strengths of your setting.

Next, begin gathering evidence. And for food interpretation, you will need good evidence. Apocrypha abounds, and real detective work may be required to reconstruct past food exchange systems or understand the demands of producing a particular item. Below are some guidelines for research.

Don't Generalize

Find as many specific sources as you can, getting as close to the bull's-eye of your topic as possible. Use more general or related sources as "resources," in Kathleen Wall's formulation, and seek to flesh out or corroborate them with primary research.

Explore Material Culture

Think broadly. Kitchen utensils and diningware are obvious subjects of research, but don't ignore product packaging, agricultural and industrial tools, appliances, cleaning supplies, shipping containers, and food gathering equipment. Analyze the material culture record for gaps, and compare it to inventories when possible. Look for contextual understanding and comparatives beyond your own institution's collection.

Dig into the Documentary Record

Material to support food interpretation can certainly be found in recipes, but cookbooks will never reveal the fullest picture of food culture. Material that may be more representative of what was cooked, eaten, loved, and hated is more likely to be found in other sources, many of them unexpected. Historian Megan Elias advises that

> even sites like courthouses that appear to have no connection to food are haunted by food ghosts. Consulting local business directories or newspapers can give a good idea of what kinds of establishments in the close vicinity of a public building might have served the men and women who worked within it. Record books may even show accounts kept at local establishments. Because much of public life involves food, one is likely to find connections to production or consumption in a wide variety of sites. A nineteenth-century firehouse, for example, would have been the site of communal cooking by men but also would have provided emergency response to many fires started in kitchens.[2]

Some of the sources worth exploring are:

- diaries and letters
- receipts
- home and business account books
- reports by reformers and public health workers
- travelogues, guidebooks, WPA materials
- slave narratives

- oral history
- historic photography
- seed and merchandise catalogues
- tourist brochures
- farm bulletins
- club and association minutes
- fair and festival programs
- restaurant menus
- newspaper stories about food events and concerns

Of course, any sources must be read critically, and considered alongside other contextual material. Always consider who is doing the writing, their perspective and orientation, and their relationships with the subjects they document. Michael Twitty draws on an extremely wide variety of sources to complement and round out the narrowness of much of the written record when it comes to the foodways of enslaved people. Some content, he says, "can be gleaned from the remarks of slave traders, slave owners, and plantation visitors," but he notes that

> these observations have to be weighed against the cultural backgrounds of an enslaved community, the ethnicities they encountered, the available food in any given region, the accounts of enslaved people themselves, historic receipts, and not least the oral tradition, culinary traditions, and memories that have filtered down into the present. Culture bearers are important counter voices to academic pronouncements. To suggest that my 92-year-old grandfather has nothing valid to add to the discussion, despite his having lived in the rural South in an era not much different from the antebellum period or having been in the presence of his enslaved grandparents; or that the testimony of a West African immigrant or the ethnographic writings of the early colonial period are moot merely because they were not recorded during the eighteenth and nineteenth centuries, is ludicrous and arrogant. Checks and balances on the sources and accuracy of data are fairly intuitive. If nothing else I work with the dictum, "If you can't prove or prove it reasonable, don't say it or cook it."[3]

Experiment

On some food topics, evidence can be discovered partially, or only, through processes of recreation. Try working with historic cooking implements, and sourcing foods as similar as possible to those of the fast. This process can reveal mistakes in interpretation caused by modern assumptions about cooking methods or ingredient qualities. In addition, it can supply missing context and create empathy and knowledge of the bodily dimensions of food labor. Michael Twitty shares that cooking in historic settings with period equipment teaches much that is rarely recorded in documentary sources: "The lower back and feet ache from hours on brick kitchen floors. You learn the wisdom of the recipes for salves and cures listed in the same receipt books that provide inspiration for menus. Your arms will teach you about the heft needed to carry 40- and 60-pound pots and the stamina it takes to cook a large meal by the standard dinner hour of two or three p.m."[4]

Consult Experts

Responsible food history interpretation incorporates scholarly perspectives. These may come from food historians, but don't overlook insights from the chemical, agricultural and biological sciences, anthropology and ethnobotany, literature and music, ethnic studies, and beyond. Also, remember that not all food experts are in the academy. Farmers and other food producers, food journalists, chefs, and home cooks can all be excellent authorities whose perspectives can enrich interpretation.

Connect to the Contemporary

Look for continuing manifestations of topics you are uncovering through research. In the local or regional food scene, or on the topic you are exploring, what continuities and consistencies are there with the past? This can also work in reverse. Are there contemporary trends, concerns, movements, and discourses that you can explore in your resources about the past?

Because research can be fraught with pitfalls and roadblocks, two special risks of researching food are discussed next.

The Cookbook Trap

Our contemporary instinct, when we want to know how to cook something, is to rush to a cookbook (or an Internet version of one) for instructions. It can be all too easy to project that strategy into the past, assuming that if we can just find a period cookbook from our interpreted time frame, we'll know exactly what and how to cook. But cookbooks rarely work in such a simple way, and using them so unquestioningly can be risky. Cookbooks are usually not a record of what people actually ate on a regular basis. They are documents of the exceptional and the aspirational, often written to impress or make a point, to convey a social imperative, or to dwell for a while in a fantasy of escape.

Calling cookbooks "an imperfect, insufficient source of information about past foodways," Sandy Oliver cautions food interpreters that "they must be used together with other corroborating sources. They are, after all, prescriptive literature. They describe how, in at least one author's opinion, a dish ought to be prepared, but they do not necessarily describe what the results actually were." As an example of how cookbooks might steer us wrong, Oliver offers recipe suggestions for a peanut butter and jelly sandwich appearing in a 1965 *Fannie Farmer* cookbook: "'Peanut butter, plain or moistened with salad dressing. Or sprinkle lightly with sugar or spread with jam or jelly. Or sprinkle with chopped sweet pickle or crumbled crisp bacon' . . . please think about your last PB&J and how odd this set of instructions sounds. Then consider that the advice never even begins to hint at the importance of peanut butter and jelly sandwiches in the American diet, or the fact that hundreds of children and adults alike eat this sandwich with such frequency that grocery stores place peanut butter and jelly on their shelves in close proximity to each other and bread."[5] For most of history, most people made most meals without the help of written instructions. The content we find in cookbooks is exceptional, not everyday.

Cookbooks can be incredibly useful to food history interpreters, but it's wise to heed Oliver's cautions. When referring to cookbooks, use as many comparative and corroborating sources as possible to understand them in context. Use them to understand food culture, not just recipes: cookbooks often reveal more about ideals for gender and family roles, home management, health, education, and class aspirations than they do about how people made and ate food. Use them and mine them for historical knowledge, but always be aware of their limitations as reflections of real food behavior.

Multiplying Myths

Many a myth lives on the historic house kitchen. The activities of food and cooking involve storytelling, shared memory, and cultural transmission, and they accumulate lore rapidly, both supported and unsupported by evidence. It can be difficult to tell the two apart, even with relatively recent myths. Sometimes a great deal of work is needed to peel back the accumulated layers of great stories burnished by Colonial Revival interpretations and simple misunderstandings.

A classic example is the inaccurate fact (still commonly repeated) that the most frequent cause of death for women in the colonial era was burning accidents, caused by their skirts catching fire as they cooked at the hearth. In her entertaining mythbusting book *Death by Petticoat*, Mary Theobold summarizes a lengthy debate on the topic by calling it a "huge exaggeration."[6] Not only did women observe fire safety practices ingrained in them since childhood (such as tying back skirts and never turning around without first stepping back from the fire), but their natural-fiber clothing—linen, wool, and heavy homespun—was also somewhat flame resistant. Research into causes of mortality in the colonial era reveals that deaths from disease and childbirth were far more common.

The kitchen is also home to many other, less grisly myths. Interpreters have been known to talk about how spices were used to mask the flavor of rotting meats—which would be unlikely, as spices were expensive and most meats were either fresher than ours today or thoroughly preserved—or how small cupboards built into the fireplace wall hid bottles of liquor from the prying eyes of the parson (really, they were just handy nooks, offering some protection from freezing because they were near to the fire). Even beyond the kitchen, stories too good to be true abound. Many of them are origin stories, like the one about Ruth Wakefield's invention of the chocolate chip cookie, or variations on stories about the introductions of the hot dog, ice cream cones, or the fortune cookie.

These misrepresentations can be hard to eradicate. But if they are embedded in interpretation, they offer an excellent chance for interpreters to reframe their understandings of what history is. Many of these stories have been revisited and revised in light of new evidence or focused inquiry—something anyone can undertake. If myths proliferate, interpreters can use them as the basis for discussion about what kinds of sources are credible and supported and how history is not a body of settled fact but a state of understanding arrived at by a given group of people at a given time. "Museumlore" can rarely be completely eliminated unless interpreters have the opportunity to be trained in history's processes and practices, changing their relationship to secondhand, overheard, and unreliable sources.

Interpret Evidence and Develop Themes

Once you have amassed a body of evidence about your topic or location, it's time to begin the process of interpretation: understanding what your evidence says and means that is of interest to your contemporary audience. This is the part of the process where your evidence should be brought together and viewed in light of your institution's mission and strategic goals. How can you see relationships between your institution's mission and the food history you are assembling? How can food experiences help you reach your institution's strategic goals, supporting that mission? This is the time to ask the question, "So what?" When you look at the body of evidence and supporting content you have developed, what does it say about people in the past and people today—and does anyone care? What about your discoveries has larger significance—to your visitors, your peers, and your community?

The next step is to begin drafting the interpretive plan. As described by the National Park Service, an interpretive plan is "a management document that outlines and guides decisions about a site's or region's interpretive programming."[7] An interpretive plan can also be created within a site, dealing with just one space or project at a time; for instance, a garden or an exhibition can have its own interpretive plan. Many models are available in the professional literature, but most interpretive plans:

- provide a bibliography of evidence and other content resources
- identify major themes and key messages
- develop interpretive goals for visitors encountering those themes and messages (for example, the interpretive goals included in this book)
- specify interpretive strategies and experiences that will be used to explore the themes and messages: for example, living history, discussion, participation activities, displays, and more
- describe the desired impact on the visitor: takeaways, responses, changes in behavior
- lay out the basics of an operational plan—who will do this work, and how they will accomplish it
- stipulate how the success of the interpretation will be evaluated

With food topics, information overload is always a risk. Food is fascinating. There's so much to know and say about it, and it can be overwhelming and intimidating. It's easy to become bogged down and lose sight of the big picture—what food means for people. This is why a strong interpretive structure with clear goals and strategies is important—it will focus interpretation on topics and experiences museums and historic sites are best positioned to explore.

Target Audiences and Partners

One of the distinguishing characteristics of food interpretation is that its nature is inclusive and expansive. Food connects us all. The interpretation of food history grows much stronger when careful thought is given to going beyond the traditional boundaries of museum practice and reaching out to groups and individuals who might offer new kinds of engagement with the museum. Targeting new audiences and partners can expand the museum's community and increase relevance and resilience.

Food history interpreters often mention that they glean as much from their encounters with visitors as visitors do with them, as people share stories, memories, questions, and wonderings about this topic so accessible and familiar to everyone. Strong food interpretation makes the most of this widely distributed knowledge and blurs the lines between "expert" and "novice." Devising experiences that allow visitors to share and contribute food knowledge, as well as discover and absorb it, results in richer two-way communication and an overall increase in knowledge and interpersonal connection. Food interpretation also allows museums and historic sites the opportunity to reconceive audiences. Rather than waiting passively for interested individuals to pay admission and visit the site, museums can reach out to people and communities with an identified interest in, or need for, food information with a historical slant. Create a "food systems map" to discover potential partners not currently engaged with your institution, thinking about the entire route food travels to, through, and beyond your community. Students, health support groups, gardening clubs, chefs and institutional cooks, locavore groups, parenting groups, CSA members, 4H and Future Farmers and Homemakers of America clubs, environmental sustainability groups, job-training programs (especially in hospitality and food service), book groups—there are many possibilities for expanding interpretation to reach audiences able to connect over a shared interest in food.

A second way to enrich and vary interpretive experiences is through partnering. In fact, I've come to doubt that strong food interpretation can really exist without venturing beyond the museum's walls to connect with unexpected partners in the contemporary world of food. Partners might be the experts and scholars engaged in the development of your food history evidence. They might be local chefs, gardeners, food and wine lovers, beer or cider makers, farmers, or cheesemakers. Or they might be nonprofits or businesses who share your interest in making a lasting impact on people's understandings of and interactions with food. Again, consult your community food map for partners across all the food sectors in your region. Invite them into the planning process, even if you're not sure yet what they might do for you. A farmer or gardener might grow historic varieties of food for you to cook and serve. A chef might borrow one of your historic recipes, or use a product grown on your site in the nightly specials.

Engage!

The final step in food interpretation is actively engaging your identified audiences and partners in the interpretive plans you've created. Sure, "engage" is a current buzzword, but an apt one, because it does not express any particular style of connection with a visitor. It doesn't presume a particular flavor of interpretation or relationship between interpreter and participant, so it allows interpreters and partners lots of imaginative freedom in conceiving of ways of interacting over food history in a museum or historic setting.

There are so many choices. The interpretive menu is a large one, and every item on it is strong in some ways, weaker in others. Some approaches are familiar and time tested, dating back to the earliest days of museum interpretation discussed in chapter 1. Others are innovative and often promising. Food interpretation today is most successful when it builds on, and creatively recombines, elements in the vocabulary of museum food interpretation. Contemporary audiences behave differently than those of the past. They prefer informality, value immediacy and access, enjoy participation, and pursue sensory experience. Interpretation should allow visitors to engage in these ways, and more. The following are a few ways of offering engagement, both old and new.

Exhibitions

History museums have presented food-focused exhibitions since at least 1958, when at Cooperstown, New York, the Farmers' Museum opened *The Farmer's Year*, a poetic and artistically designed exhibit that guided visitors month by month through the annual labors of New York State farmers.[8] But until the past two decades, food was not typically foregrounded as subject matter for an exhibition in its own right. Some of the earliest exhibitions of food topics appeared in virtual space. The New York Food Museum (www.nyfoodmuseum.org) began its digital presence in 1998, and it continues to curate digital collections and operate programs today. In 2005, food scientist and radio host Dave Arnold founded the Museum of Food and Drink (www.mofad.org), aiming to create a destination museum in New York City. MoFaD launched a series of traveling "pop-up" exhibitions in 2013 with the "Puffer Machine," an industrial steam-pressure grain-puffing gun essential to the development of commercial breakfast cereals and puffed snacks.[9] In New Orleans, the Southern Food and Beverage Museum (SoFaB) began in 2004 as a community of interest in the food of the American South, and in 2014, the museum was planning the ribbon cutting for its new space, to be shared with the associated Museum of the American Cocktail.

Museums with a wider mission are also presenting exhibitions on food. The flagship is the Smithsonian National Museum of American History's *FOOD: Transforming the American Table 1950–2000*, opened in 2012. Its centerpiece is Julia Child's kitchen, painstakingly transplanted to the galleries. This sweeping exhibition focuses on the post–World War II era, examining "innovations and new technologies" along with "social and cultural shifts."

Local and regional museums are also using exhibitions to highlight those stories in their own food cultures and economies. For instance, the Museum at the Castle in Appleton, Wisconsin, presents *Food: Who We Are and What We Eat*, inviting visitors to explore displays about "the area's most iconic food traditions, including fish fries, brandy old-fashioneds, frozen custard, lager beer and sausages," and even "spear a sturgeon in a virtual shanty!"[10] At the Adirondack Museum, the 2010 *Let's Eat! Adirondack Food Traditions* displayed "handwritten menus and journals" and "posters advertising turkey shoots, dances, and potluck suppers" to "offer insight into the ways that food has served as the centerpiece of social life in small, often isolated hamlets." The Adirondack Museum's exhibition also linked viewers to the region's contemporary food culture, presenting information about local farmer's markets, locavorism, and the rise of organic agriculture in the area.

Because the study of food is interdisciplinary, history museums are not alone in exhibiting food history. In 2012, the American Museum of Natural History (NYC) presented the enormous *Our Global Kitchen: Food, Nature, Culture*, arranged around systemic analyses of how food is produced and transported globally. Regular demonstrations in a working gallery-kitchen offered audiences a chance to taste products like cheese and bread while learning about food chemistry and the perception of taste. In Connecticut, the Peabody Museum of Natural History collaborated with the Yale School of Public Health and the Rudd Center for Food Policy and Obesity to develop the 2012 exhibition *Big Food: Health, Culture, and the Evolution of Eating*, which opened with "a startling visual of the amount of food the average American eats and finishe[d] with a challenge for visitors to reflect on their role in personal and community health and the sustainability of our food system."

Even art museums are exhibiting food. New York City's Drawing Center hosted a 2014 show titled *Ferran Adrià: Notes on Creativity*, in which the famed chef of the internationally influential restaurant El Bulli shares the drawings and notes he created in his quest to transform food into an art form.[11] Meanwhile, the Portland Art Museum selected a set of prints, posters, and artist-designed menus from between 1850 and the present for the 2014 *Feast and Famine: The Pleasures and Politics of Food*. Asserting that artists have used food to convey messages "from prehistoric cave paintings depicting wild game to lavish still lifes documenting the bounty and wealth of an urban society," the show's curators intended to "question how artists use the topic of food and drink as a means to explore society, examine ritual, and advocate politically."[12]

For history museums, gallery-based exhibitions can be excellent platforms for food interpretation. They offer the opportunity to incorporate documentary and photographic sources, show fragile and valuable objects, and integrate video and other media. Innovative design approaches can even create food tasting and sharing spaces within exhibition settings, and planned spaces can allow for performance stages for cooking demonstrations or classes, discussion groups, or formal dinners. For museums whose sites offer mostly indoor spaces, or a combination of indoor-outdoor spaces, exhibitions on food topics can allow audiences to experience food-related collection objects in a variety of ways, providing food for thought.

Live Interpretation

In many museums, exhibitions do only part of the work of interpretation. Facilitated experiences are often central to the interface between visitor and museum, especially at living history, outdoor, and historic house sites. Lively, fully interactive, and compelling, human presence is a powerful tool for delivering interpretation, whether the presenter is lecturing, demonstrating, guiding a tour, wordlessly completing a routine task, or just chatting informally. Museologist Timothy Ambrose calls live interpretation the "oldest, most natural and most common presentation technique of all," pausing to caution that "it can also be the best, but only when the person involved is really well informed, skilled at the technique he or she is using, and in tune with the audience. Using people needs as careful planning as using any other technique."[13] As a topic, food is particularly well suited to live interpretation, because food knowledge is typically developed and shared socially, in personal interactions.

Demonstration

The demonstration is the classic warhorse of food interpretation, in which interpreters move through some portion of the process of harvesting or preparing food in a way consistent with the interpretive goals. The interpreter may narrate the process, naming tools and offering information about ingredients, methods, and other contextual detail. Visitors are usually welcome to ask questions and make observations, which interpreters ideally respond to in a way designed to build further exploration and encourage curiosity. Visitors are sometimes invited to take part in a portion of the process, such as rolling dough, seeding raisins, or cutting biscuits, but they are generally not permitted to work with cooking fires, change or vary the process, participate for great lengths of time, or develop their own projects. Many museums are experimenting with ways to invite visitors to participate more fully in the process of their demonstrations, whether on a drop-in basis or through specially scheduled classes and events. Most regrettable, at many sites viewers are unable to taste the results of the processes they've just seen; the regulatory environment and/or an abundance of caution prevents many museums from sharing food. Other challenges of the demonstration technique can be blending conversation with visitors with the demands of completing the task. Interpreters often develop a sense of urgency and personal investment about their food projects, but good interpreters and managers always remember that the visitor is the reason they are there to do the work, and since they are not actually in a self-sufficient survival economy, it's likely that the corn husking or cheese washing can wait while the educational purposes of the demonstration—visitor learning and enjoyment—are fulfilled.

Living History

Living history can be thought of as a highly elaborated version of demonstration. In the movement toward living history as an interpretive technique, interpreters envisioned period rooms and demonstrations in a new way, linking them with performance to create a simulation of a community untouched by time. Food is not set apart but integrated into an illusion of day-to-day life. In living history museums, food demonstration becomes an anthropological experience, lacking the easy conversational bridge offered by third-person interpretation and expecting visitors to limit themselves mostly to observation and questioning. Interpreters may not thoroughly narrate what they are doing, as it could seem to be an overly artificial way to interact with a guest. At the same time, food offers a visible and familiar touchpoint for visitors looking for ways to engage with interpreters, a way of cutting through the barriers posed by the method. Elaborate living history interpretations may also have the benefit of including more scope of the process of food procurement, from sowing, growing, and harvesting to preserving, processing, serving, and disposing of waste.

Facilitated Programs

Many museums and historic sites present facilitated experiences. These offer the personal touch of informed and prepared presenters focused on participants, and they have the advantage of being responsive to group interests, skills, and preferences. There is a wide variety of possible formats, and all can be used effectively in food interpretation.

Tours

Tours are a very common form of facilitated program. Tours should not be walking lecture, but instead maximize shared discovery. Tours can explore a single aspect of a historic sites' food information, such as the historic gardens tour at Strawbery Banke Museum in Portsmouth, New Hampshire, or a walk through time that compares and contrasts plants and gardening styles from precontact through a re-created 1940s Victory Garden. Tours may even leave the museum grounds to explore the surrounding neighborhood's food history, as does the Lower East Side Tenement Museum's neighborhood tour "Foods of the Lower East Side."

Talks and Discussions

Among the oldest forms of communication, lectures, talks, and group discussions can still make for powerful museum experiences. Increasingly, museums are experimenting with speaking programs that combine information delivery with facilitated conversation. Point/counterpoint, lecture and response, small-group discussions, forum and townhall-style experiences, and multiple perspective talks are great ways to present and explore a range of ideas and perspectives.

Classes and Workshops

These are overtly didactic and outcome oriented: audiences expect to learn something useful to take away with them. Workshops usually involve active participation on the part of the user. These special opportunities, marketed in advance, usually involve a fee for participation and are typically limited to smaller groups. The scale and scheduling allow audiences to get behind barriers, use equipment, and learn real skills along with accompanying wisdom and practical knowledge. Workshops tend to take a topical, narrow focus, such as jam making or beer brewing, and to concentrate on culinary history—the ingredients, utensils, and methods used to produce a particular kind of food. Though well loved by participants, offering deeper and more participatory engagement, workshops can be challenging to offer. They rarely generate a great deal of revenue, and they demand a fair amount of staff time to research, plan, oversee, and clean up. However, a reputation for great workshops can enhance a museum's identification as a source for food history. Historic Deerfield, for example, is legendary for its historic bread-baking programs.

Food-Focused Events

These events can bring participants flocking. Historically themed banquets have appeared in popular culture for centuries, but they made their way into museums during the 1970s and 1980s as a way of indulging in the celebratory aspects of food history in a less rigorous format, offering some freedom to edit menus to contemporary taste. The meals tend to represent a hybrid of food and beverage palatable to a high-end diner of today while linking foods served to ideas and events from the site interpretation. These dinners often include a speaker, chef's talk, or other form of interpretation, and they sometimes add music, performance, role playing characters, or period entertainments. In recent years, museums have delved into food events in formats like festivals and connoisseurship events—beer tasting nights, seafood festivals, chocolate tastings, and so on. A third type of food event might feature cultural celebrations or presentations.

Research

Quite recently, museums have started finding ways to share their own evolving understandings with visitors, rather than presenting interpretive understandings as fait accompli. Visitors can be drawn into culinary experiments, archaeological investigations, and archival explorations, and at times they may help advance knowledge through their contributions. They will also develop stronger understandings of the challenges of researching food history: "Among the most valuable statements a visitor can hear in a living history museum are 'historians do not know for sure what the answer to that question is' and 'historians disagree in their interpretation of that subject.'"[14]

Museum Theater and Performing Arts

Not all food interpretation has to directly involve food. Music, dance, and theater programming can link to the thematics of food interpretation. For example, at Mystic Seaport, traditional "chanteymen," or maritime musicians, perform a song titled "Salt Horse" as a way of showing how sailors living for months at a time on salted meat expressed their displeasure at monotony in musical form. Role playing and participatory museum theater can dramatize food debates or powerful interchanges, producing empathy and insights not possible in using less poetic methods.

Other Strategies

As museums and historic sites innovate to connect with today's audiences, they are developing new, often mixed and hybrid program formats. Today, we understand that not everyone learns and experiences information in the same way, and emerging program ideas reflect this. Museums are hosting farmer's markets and community gardens, participating in seed banks and heirloom cultivation projects, and entering into more authentic and long-term relationships with their own food communities. Geolocation and augmented reality have drawn some museums into creating food history layers over existing maps, suggesting "a sense of the edible context in which any particular site existed at different times in the past,"[15] or creating experiential "trails" through a geographical area in or outside of the museum. For instance, Gloucester, Massachusetts's HarborWalk is a museum of local history and culture with no walls. Visitors use a smartphone app and/or a printed map to navigate along the city's historic waterfront, learning about fish-packing plants and the annual Feast of St. Joseph (a stop that includes a traditional Sicilian fettucine recipe), among many other topics. Food tours, too, are popping up in many cities. These fee-based experiences combine travel, tasting, and background information about local food, present and past. They are historical to varying degrees, but in many cases they are open to part-nering and collaborating with museums on content and tastings. Another way to share and develop food history is to use the Internet to create e-learning resources (such as the Jane Addams Hull House's free PDF manuals on canning and preserving), recipes, plant listings, essays, or directories, or hosting two-way food dialogues or hashtag campaigns on social media.

Inspiration from an Emerging Network

Museums and historic sites with a food interpretation focus are only just beginning to meet and talk with one another about what they do. Each year there are a few sessions at history museum conferences, and word of new ideas in programming and interpretation passes through the grapevine. Opportunities for further professional discussion and benchmark-ing will likely emerge over the next few years. In the meantime, often the best way to learn about next practices in history museum food interpretation is to visit museums, explore their websites, and follow them—and the energetic, forward-thinking interpreters who are innovating food interpretation—on social media. Here are few examples of programs that blend strategies old and new with food history themes to produce meaningful outcomes for their participants.

- Billings Farm Museum in Woodstock, Vermont, updates traditional farm museum interpretation with *Foodways Fridays*, combining a different featured heirloom pro-duce each week with a food demonstration in a historic kitchen, takeaway recipes, a visit to the garden, and a garden tour. Visitors are invited to discover "Ladies Cabbage, Flemish Carrots, Cymling Pudding, or Pink Velvet Soup."
- The Jane Addams Hull House in Chicago has been a leader in food and social justice programming with its *Re-Thinking Soup* series, a monthly soup lunch paired with provocative and relevant talks on food justice, food sovereignty, hunger and food waste, and food labor, and the Hull House Farm, a working farm that grows food for museum canning and preserving programs, supports farm-to-school programs and a chef collaboration, and hosts tours and other programs.
- The Homestead Museum in City of Industry, California, offers a lively food series including talks, lectures, and festivals on topics ranging from Native wild plants of the Kizh Nation to chili, chilies, and hot sauce to viticulture, furthering its mission to explore the history of the Los Angeles area from 1830 to 1930.
- Conner Prairie, in Fishers, Indiana, works with local chefs and brewers on a program titled *Prairie Plates*, serving contemporary meals inspired by site food history in his-toric buildings and structures. One was a progressive dinner in the 1836 Prairietown, featuring craft beers brewed especially for the evening with herbs collected from the museum's gardens. A late fall event paired a butchering workshop with a supper featuring the Indiana pork fabricated by workshop students.
- The Freeport Historical Society in Freeport, Maine, tweets entries from dairy farmer Maggie Pettengill's 1921 diary. @Miss_Pettengill shares brief food notes like

"Mr. Ringrose here to butcher" (January), "I cook a sirup" and "Hauled ice all day" (February), and "We had clams today" (March), revealing calendar day for calendar day the food events in a rural Maine year.[16]

- The Maine State Historical Society developed the exhibition *Sugar and Spice: Our Vintage Recipes* to showcase recipes from the Federal period through recent years. Curator Jamie Kingman Rice explained the rationale of the exhibition as follows: "We really want to document Maine: Maine ingredients, traditional or regional recipes like brown bread, things that have been passed down in families, or even things that have become more modern regional favorites. . . . What does it mean to be the quintessential New England recipe in 1975?"[17]

Making It Happen: Managing Food Interpretation

Once an interpretive plan is in place, how are food projects implemented? Just like other museum programs, for the most part. But food interpretation, especially where it involves real cooking and eating, does have some of its own unique requirements. Sometimes doing food interpretation means doing things differently, creating institutional change. It can mean tackling obstacles, winning buy-in, and troubleshooting and problem-solving together. Let's look at some common challenges and potential solutions.

Training and Staffing

Warren Leon and Margaret Piatt have observed that one of the biggest challenges to live interpretation is "to develop a staff capable of transmitting a sophisticated message to the public."[18] Representing food history can be complicated, and sometimes, the research and practice required can be at odds with the realities of the interpretive workforce. Seasonal and part-time interpreters and volunteers might not have the time to gain depth of knowledge, and they might not be compensated for the time it takes to learn and present food history interpretation and might not be rewarded for increasing degrees of skill and mastery.

Interpreters can only be as good as the body of information they have to work with. For planners and site managers, the planning of training and preparation of study material is worth the investment of time. Many historic sites and museums consider "interpreter training" to be something that happens in an initial phase of a few days or weeks, or a short period of apprenticeship with other interpreters. In reality, training is neverending. After mastering basics, food history interpreters benefit from ongoing experiences like reading and discussion groups, field trips, talks and visits from outside experts, research experiments, preparation for special events, and participation in internal opportunities like collections-based experiences. All of these experiences can be rolled into the regular schedule, making the experience of being a museum food interpreter one of ongoing learning and continually developing mastery. Constant infusions of new ideas can help keep interpreters engaged—especially when they are actively involved in developing their own curriculum for ongoing learning.

This book has talked about visitors' tendency to romanticize the past. Sometimes, however, it is interpreters who want to be "time travelers," all but dwelling within the past.

Leon and Piatt have noted that this idea can cut both ways: "Their desire to experience the past often gives them an admirable dedication to authenticity in the details of material culture,"[19] but they may also be the ones most likely to avoid details that represent the past as difficult, unpleasant, or unfair. One way to keep the focus on the present is to encourage faithful attention to visitor interactions. Museum audiences exist in the present, and it's their ideas, interests, and needs that should guide interpretive responses, not the other way around. Interpretation managers should gather and share as much data as possible—quantified and anecdotal—about how visitors experience sites and make sense of what they have seen and done. They should keep events and trends in the wider culture before interpreters' eyes, always considering the possibility of making interpretive connections between past and present. The training activities at the end of each thematic chapter of this book offer ways of sparking interpretive discussions that link the personal to the contextual, past to present.

Regulation Roadblocks

One of the most common challenges facing history institutions who want to do food interpretation are the regulations put in place at all governmental levels to protect health and safety. Across the country, many state and local laws define acceptable practices in food production and service. Local boards of health also oversee adherence to standards, often in a very close and detailed way. Quite often, these regulations make it clear that cooks and food producers in museums are not to sell or give away the food they are presenting, since it has not been prepared according to contemporary safety standards. This puts interpreters in the miserable position of denying visitors, even when they lodge mournful pleas.

How to navigate this regulatory environment? First, take these regulations seriously; municipalities certainly do. Outbreaks of foodborne illness are something every community wants to avoid. Don't take risks or practice a "look the other way" strategy. It's impossible to know when something might be off, or when one of your guests has an unknown allergy or compromised immune system that calls attention to lax practices.

But, at the same time, don't assume that there is no way to work within the standards of your health codes. As Deb Friedman describes in her "Fresh Ideas" in chapter 5, most local agencies are willing to work with museums and historical sites, recognizing that they provide a cultural and educational service. Long before making any plans to serve food to visitors, meet with local officials, share your hopes and ambitions, and ask for their help and collaboration. Brainstorming together can reveal solutions you may not have imagined on your own, and health officers may have resources within their networks that can be of help to you. Using this process, museums have found ways to achieve their food interpretation goals. For instance, for the preparation of historic recipes for visitors to sample, some museums partner with a health-certified local culinary school, incubator kitchen, restaurant, school cafeteria, church or community kitchen, or licensed food truck or mobile kitchen. Another strategy may be to relocate smaller-group programs or special events to offsite locations where certified kitchens already exist, such as partnering with a chef on presenting a historically themed dinner in his or her restaurant rather than on museum grounds. Finally, it may also be possible to certify museum staff as food handlers. Even if it means they occasionally have to don a nonhistoric plastic glove, visitors are likely to overlook small anachronisms if it means they can enjoy the total experience of tasting what they have seen in preparation.

Negotiating Politics

As we saw in chapter 7, the edible is political. There may be times when food politics affects the scope or content of interpretive projects. As nonprofit organizations, most museums are unable to campaign for a candidate or a specific piece of legislation. However, they can help people understand the decisions facing them by historicizing them. Interpreters may use contemporary issues as jumping-off points, writing blog entries or op-eds sharing a historical perspective, offering talks to local policy councils or advocacy groups, and being present at places of public debate. The ideal of museum as public forum is ascendant, and museums can serve a civic role as places to explore and discuss complex issues, using the intellectual resources underlying interpretation to inform public discussions.

This can be more challenging than it may at first sound. Historical institutions have many stakeholders. The negotiation of what is presented on a historical site can include board members, donors, descendants, neighbors, advisors, corporate partners, grantors, advocacy groups, and volunteers, to name just a few people who care about the interpretive experience. What programs and exhibitions say and do passes before many sets of eyes, and those consulted must overtly or tacitly agree with the messages and means of presentation. Because many food issues are inherently political and/or personal, this can sometimes be a sticky process. Relationships and tight social networks—especially in local and regional institutions—can resist change for fear of losing goodwill. Taking the time to build new relationships, cultivate existing ones, and achieve a working consensus is essential to success. If at first you don't succeed in having a new food history interpretation plan approved, keep at it. Clarity of communication can help interpreters and other stakeholders arrive at a shared understanding of how messages will be framed and questions explored.

Also, history organizations, like all human organizations, have biases. In the world of historic sites and museums, there is a strong and often useful bias toward reliance on evidence and a less defensible bias toward being seen as places with all the answers. Together, these often amount to a stated or unstated goal of presenting only the most "accurate" information. Scott Magelssen mounts a strong critique of "accuracy" as an uncomplicated value for museum practice. The notion of accuracy, he contends, is troubled by assumptions that the past is wholly knowable; that time proceeds in a direct, linear fashion; that effects can always be traced to visible causes; and that all important thoughts, events, and perspectives have been sufficiently documented to be represented with the certainty of truth. At best, he argues, history institutions can draw on historical detail and the evidentiary record to explore questions of contemporary fascination, but they can never honestly propose to offer an "accurate" experience of history. A true and full representation of the past as it was lived, he asserts, is beyond our power to produce.[20] Andrew Haley, in his essay "The Nation before Taste," expresses related concerns. He worries that the public devotion to food may cause historic sites to frame the tasting of a recipe from a historical document as an experience of the past itself. Describing the "thrall of food" as "both a blessing and a curse," Haley argues that our present-day experience of food, exquisitely focused on flavor and texture, is a relatively recent phenomenon. Because our understanding of the role of food is entirely different from that of people in the past, their perspective on food, their very orientation to the act of eating, is unavailable to us. Yet food interpreters have trouble resisting the claim that a taste can "bring the past to life." Contesting that notion as naive, Haley says that "it is no more possible to re-create an apple pie from the mid-nineteenth century than it is to know exactly what was going through the mind of Abraham Lincoln as he walked up to the platform to give the Gettysburg address. Yet in the first instance, we persist in believing that a complete understanding of the past is perfectly attainable, and in the second, historians largely agree that our understanding of the past is never complete."[21] For most people, the closest we can get is to use the food to build more empathy with people of the past, being able to imagine their lives in greater detail. To borrow an apt phrasing from literature scholar Hester Blum, we don't *know*, but we know *better*.[22]

The unknowability of the past is only one problem with accuracy in food interpretation. Another is the unresolved nature of so many of our most complex questions about the food supply. Where food issues are concerned, there are few things one can say with certainty—on many issues, our data (and questions) are still developing and answers are not yet, and may never be, completely clear. For example, GMOs have proponents and detractors, all of whom can marshal a body of serious evidence in favor of their cases. The question of whether GMOs will offer the world benefits that are worth their potential costs, or destroy the genetic commons and put health at risk, is not a settled one in the public mind. As museums, we can raise questions and probe the issues with historical inquiry into plant genetics and breeding practices, but we can't necessarily reflect an "accurate" stance on them based on evidence from the past. Then, as now, plant variety development was a topic of debate and constant change. It should be no surprise that those issues continue to evolve. The stories we can tell about the past are not likely to provide hard-and-fast answers, but they can certainly help us have smarter, more interesting conversations. As history practitioners, good food interpretation may require us to grow beyond the comfortable role of absolute arbiter of settled fact. We might instead aspire to be authoritative on certain food topics most relevant to our sites, today and in the past, serving our audiences best by being a reliable and interesting place to gather information and pursue further exploration.

Many political obstacles are in the process of falling. This is not so much because of a revolution within our field—though some people have been hard at work to set museums on a new course for food interpretation—but because of our audiences, who are hungry for change. Conner Prairie CEO Ellen Rosenthal puts it quite simply: "Our visitors are asking us for this."[23]

Managing the Logistics

Food interpretation can get messy. Interpreters of food want to do things that give curators and CEOs nightmares: cook on open flames, have food in exhibition spaces, keep livestock. Though museums and historic sites have inherent limitations, many sites can do much more than they might initially think, especially where collaborative processes focus on generating solutions rather than assuming impossibility.

Fire and Flame

In many settings, the possibility of cooking is totally precluded because of a prohibition on open flame. The first step in addressing this is to discover whether this prohibition is penetrable. Begin by asking: What is the source of this prohibition? Is it buildings and grounds policy, collections concerns, worker safety issues, municipal law, or something else? Once the principal obstacles are surfaced, look at each separately. If the problem is building safety, bring in professional voices. Consult with a chimney company to evaluate chimneys, hearths, and stovepipes. Discuss programmatic wishes with insurance company risk managers. If cooking can't happen daily, could it happen seasonally, or a certain number of days a year? Would a sprinkler system or management protocol reduce concerns? If the prohibition results from a concern for collections, explore whether vulnerable objects can be relocated to different rooms or buildings. Perhaps spaces can be reinterpreted so they are no longer naturalistic settings but practical workspaces for a focus on culinary activities. In some cases, museums may be able to remodel or build a separate facility for cooking programs that mimics the hearth or stove technology in a historic exhibit. Wherever progress seems impossible, reach out to other institutions in the region that have active cooking programs. Most have faced similar challenges and worked out solutions that others can learn from.

No matter where a fire-based cooking program takes place, it should, of course, be handled with the utmost care for safety. Work with the person responsible for workplace safety on your site to establish protocols. At a minimum, fire extinguishers and escape routes should meet or exceed local code. Interpreters who work near a fire should receive specific training on fire management, safety, and risk prevention. Many sites require cooks to wear natural fibers, flame-resistant aprons, or other protective clothing. Also, protect visitors—especially young children who may not know iron cookstoves are hot or might stumble toward open flames. Create naturalistic barriers with furniture and equipment, and arrange kitchen spaces so as to protect the active zone around the heat source from unexpected activity. Fire safety protocols should include clear procedures and responsibilities for starting the fire each day and putting it out. Flammable materials should be stored as far away as possible, and woodboxes, matches, and tinderboxes stored at a safe distance. First-aid materials and a lightning-fast method of contact (phone, walkie-talkie) for emergency assistance are essential. If cooking with heat is just not possible after exhaustive problem solving, don't despair. With creativity and ingenuity, food interpreters can find ways to activate other spaces—porches, dining rooms, storefronts, taverns, gardens, galleries, even snack bars—with food activity.

Livestock

Many an upstaged interpreter can tell you that few things are as compelling as live animals. Historic breeds of fowl, pigs, goats, and cows can enliven farms and historic sites with the sights, sounds, and scents of animal husbandry, common everywhere well into the last century. There are many good reasons to have livestock on sites, but husbandry is a big commitment, requiring careful planning and staffing. Livestock don't shut down during holidays or sleep in when the museum is closed. Reliable staff must always be available to feed and water them—every single day. Animal health is also a constant concern. Livestock housing must be kept very clean to prevent infections and vermin. An on-call or consulting veterinarian is essential. Veterinary care can be expensive, but it is necessary for the health and humane treatment of the animals, as well as to protect human health and prevent the spread of infection and disease. Visitors will certainly ask about how animals are cared for; it can be wise to have a prepared FAQ statement or interpreter brief on animal care routines. Occasionally, visitors or community members with a special concern for animal rights may voice public objection to a museum's keeping livestock. These events are rare, but it is wise to think through in advance how you might handle them. Museums must also plan for the whole life cycle of the animal—including the end of life. Will chickens, pigs, and cattle be killed for food, or will they be allowed to live until geriatric (humane in some ways, but beset with complications and historically extremely rare)? What about animal products? Will interpretive projects absorb eggs and milk when available? What will happen to the products when museum programs are not in session? How will using raw milk affect your ability to eat or serve food products? Make sure you seek expert consultation before beginning a new livestock interpretation program. It may even be possible to present animals on your site without taking on the considerable responsibilities of owning them. Historic New England's Spencer-Peirce-Little Farm, for instance, fosters surrendered farm animals for the local SPCA. The shelter provides care and oversight, while the farm's visitors enjoy their interactions with Big Dave, the Yorkshire mix pig, and Sukey, the quarter horse.

Provisioning

Programs that involve cooking also involve gathering food to cook. It's certainly easiest to stop at the twenty-four-hour grocery to pick up food for historic cooking demonstrations, but more learning and a richer experience would result from using historic food varieties. We can never really know what a 1930 backyard-raised egg or a nineteenth-century apple tasted like, but we can come close using products from the same genetic stock, raised under similar conditions. A good way to begin is to become familiar with historic regional plant and animal varieties. The Slow Food Ark of Taste and RAFT Collaborative's Lists of Foods at Risk are excellent places to find varieties common in the past but rare in supermarket produce sections today. Another way to source historically appropriate food is to visit the farmer's market and connect with local farmers. Let them know your interests and needs. Some may be raising plant varieties you need, which you can buy in season at reasonable cost (sometimes even lower than the grocery store). Farmers are often happy to arrange bulk buys for preservation projects or storage. Making friends with farmers is likely to advance your food interpretation no matter what you buy from them. Farmers know regional climates and seasonal variations intimately, and in many cases they have troves of information about characteristic local varieties. Sometimes, if a farmer knows you have an interest in and a commitment to buy a particular product, they will grow it especially for your programs. Another option for produce sourcing is to grow your own. Establish kitchen and dooryard gardens on your site, or take out a community garden plot somewhere nearby to cultivate needed varieties. Museum volunteers might also be willing to grow desired plants. When it comes to meat, fish, and game, connect to food producers and processors for guidance. Butchers will often be willing to save "off" cuts or break down primal cuts in historic ways no longer common in commercial butchering. They may enjoy partnering with you on special projects involving salting or curing methods not common today. Local fishermen will often be willing to save uncut fish or unusual species for museum presentations, as will hunters. Some museums have even cultivated relationships with local public works departments so that they can be offered roadkill deer, turkeys, and other food animals!

Final Words: Toward Resilience

If you've made it to the end of this book, your head is most likely swimming with the rich possibilities of museum food interpretation. There are so many directions to go, all of them much deeper and more moving than simple illustration. Armed with an awareness of key themes in food history, you can help to lead interpretation of food at your site into exciting, serious, and transformative directions.

Exploring food with visitors is about so much more than enjoyment, sensory pleasure, and nostalgia. It is a topic that links us together profoundly—and intimately. Food—getting enough of it, making sure it is safe, using it to maintain our interpersonal connections—is a social challenge we must work together to solve. Museum food interpreters have the enviable position of presenting a topic that breaks through the barriers of time, connecting to compelling interests today as well as to the shaping forces of the past.

I hope that by describing some of the far-reaching impacts of food in history that this book has inspired you to take your food interpretation to a deeper level. Perhaps you can now see ways to use the food interpretation at your museum or historic site to connect to dynamic contemporary issues and communities. The skills, knowledge, flavors, and perspectives you steward as a museum have the potential for vital and meaningful application to pressing concerns and social needs of our own day; and the content you seek to share can be more deeply informed by a connection with food producers active in the present. Food interpretation offers museums the opportunity to make a difference, today and for the future, and to invite broader constituencies of people into the museum community. With well-planned, sophisticated food interpretation, museums can broaden their base of support and demonstrate the utility of history in understanding the perennial challenges—and potential solutions—of getting good, healthy, delicious food on the plates of citizens. Having set the table, I look forward to the continuing development of food interpretation in museums and historic sites. Together, as colleagues seeking to connect contemporary food culture and food history in museum settings, we can bring a new and vital seriousness to food interpretation. I look forward to the feast.

Notes

1. Stephen Weil, *Making Museums Matter* (Washington, DC: Smithsonian Books, 2002), 55.
2. Megan Elias, "Summoning the Food Ghosts: Food History as Public History," *The Public Historian* 34, no. 2 (2012): 28.
3. Michael Twitty, "The Unbearable Taste: Early African American Foodways," *Commonplace* 11, no. 3 (2011).

4. Twitty, "The Unbearable Taste."
5. Sandra Oliver, "Ruminations on the State of American Food History," *Gastronomica* 6, no. 4 (2006): 95.
6. Mary Miley Theobald, "Revisited Myth #2: Burning to death from their long petticoats catching fire was the leading cause of death for colonial American women, after childbirth," *History Myths Debunked* (blog), January 25, 2014, accessed April 26, 2015, https://historymyths. wordpress.com/2014/01/25/revisited-myth-2-burning-to-death-from-their-long-petticoats-catching-fire-was-the-leading-cause-of-death-for-colonial-american-women-after-childbirth/.
7. U.S. Department of the Interior, National Park Service, "Interpretive Planning Tools for Heritage Areas, Historic Trails, and Gateways," July 2010, http://www.nps.gov/heritageareas/toolbox/management.htm#planning.
8. Gary Kulik, "Designing the Past: History Museum Exhibitions from Peale to the Present," in *History Museums in the United States: A Critical Assessment*, ed. Warren Leon and Roy Rosenzweig (Urbana: University of Illinois Press, 1989), 23–26.
9. Elva Ramirez, "Have Puffer Gun, Will Travel," *Wall Street Journal*, August 14, 2013.
10. "Whet Your Appetite!" History Museum at the Castle website, accessed April 26, 2014, http://www.myhistorymuseum.org/food.html.
11. George Embiricos, "Food Arts: Ferran Adrià Museum Exhibition to Open in New York City," FoodRepublic.com, January 6, 2014, http://www.foodrepublic.com/2014/01/06/food-arts-ferran-adria-museum-exhibition-open-new.
12. "Feast and Famine: The Pleasures and Politics of Food," Portland Art Museum website, accessed April 26, 2015, http://portlandartmuseum.org/exhibitions/feast-famine/.
13. Timothy Ambrose and Crispin Paine, *Museum Basics*, 3rd edition (New York: Routledge, 2012), 88.
14. Warren Leon and Margaret Piatt, "Living History Museums," in *History Museums in the United States: A Critical Assessment*, ed. Warren Leon and Roy Rosenzweig (Urbana: University of Illinois Press, 1989), 89.
15. Elias, "Summoning the Food Ghosts," 28.
16. Larry Grard, "Through Twitter, Daily Doses of Farm Life," *Tri-Town Weekly* [Westbrook, ME], March 3, 2015, *Tri-Town Weekly* website, accessed April 26, 2015, http://www.keepmecurrent.com/tri_town_weekly/through-twitter-daily-doses-of-farm-life/article_f71e66ee-c1b5-11e4-a2e5-676bb0d98f0c.html.
17. Peggy Grodinsky, "Recipe Exhibit at Maine Historical Society Shows State's Changing Tastes," *Portland Press Herald* (Portland, ME), April 22, 2015.
18. Leon and Piatt, "Living History Museums," 79.
19. Leon and Piatt, "Living History Museums," 83.
20. Scott Magelssen, *Living History Museums: Undoing History through Performance* (Lanham, MD: Scarecrow Press, 2007), xiii–xiv.
21. Andrew P. Haley, "The Nation before Taste: The Challenges of American Culinary History," *Public Historian* 34, no. 2 (2012): 56.
22. Hester Blum, "18 Hours Before the Mast," *Los Angeles Review of Books*, August 3, 2014.
23. Ellen Rosenthal, correspondence with the author, November 9, 2014.

Bibliography

Books

Ackerman-Leist, Philip. *Rebuilding the Foodshed: How to Create Local, Sustainable, Secure Food Systems.* White River Junction, VT: Chelsea Green, 2013.

Albala, Ken. *Routledge International Handbook of Food Studies.* New York: Routledge, 2013.

Alexander, Edward P., and Mary Alexander. *Museums in Motion: An Introduction to the History and Functions of Museums.* 2nd ed. Lanham, MD: AltaMira Press, 2008.

Belasco, Warren. *Meals to Come: A History of the Future of Food.* Berkeley: University of California Press, 2006.

Davidson, Alan. *The Oxford Companion to Food.* 3rd edition. New York: Oxford University Press, 2014.

Denker, Joel. *The World on a Plate: A Tour through the History of America's Ethnic Cuisine.* Boulder, CO: Westview Press, 2003.

Diner, Hasia. *Hungering for America: Italian, Irish, and Jewish Foodways in the Age of Immigration.* Cambridge, MA: Harvard University Press, 2001.

Fernández-Armesto, Felipe. *Near a Thousand Tables: A History of Food.* New York: Free Press, 2002.

Fraser, Evan D. G., and Andrew Rimas. *Empires of Food: Feast, Famine, and the Rise and Fall of Civilizations.* New York: Free Press, 2010.

Freedman, Paul, ed. *Food: The History of Taste.* Berkeley and Los Angeles: University of California Press, 2007.

Freidberg, Susanne. *Fresh: A Perishable History.* Cambridge, MA: Harvard University Press, 2009.

Glickman, Lawrence B. *Buying Power: A History of Consumer Activism in America.* Chicago: University of Chicago Press, 2009.

Haber, Barbara. *From Hard Tack to Home Fries: An Uncommon History of American Cooks and Meals.* New York: Free Press, 2002.

Kamp, David. *United States of Arugula: The Sun-Dried, Cold-Pressed, Dark-Roasted, Extra Virgin Story of the American Food Revolution.* New York: Broadway Books, 2006.

Kiple, Kenneth F., ed. *Cambridge World History of Food.* New York: Cambridge University Press, 2000.

Kurlansky, Mark. *Cod: A Biography of the Fish That Changed the World.* New York: Walker, 1997.

———. *The Food of a Younger Land.* New York: Riverhead Books, 2009.

Lee, Jennifer 8. *The Fortune Cookie Chronicles: Adventures in the World of Chinese Food*. New York: Twelve, 2008.

Levenstein, Harvey. *Fear of Food: A History of Why We Worry about What We Eat*. Chicago: The University of Chicago Press, 2012.

Magelssen, Scott. *Living History Museums: Undoing History through Performance*. Lanham, MD: Scarecrow Press, 2007.

Mintz, Sidney Wilfred. *Sweetness and Power: The Place of Sugar in Modern History*. New York: Viking, 1985.

Nabhan, Gary Paul, ed. *Renewing American's Food Traditions: Saving and Savoring the Continent's Most Endangered Foods*. White River Junction, VT: Chelsea Green, 2008.

Nestle, Marion. *Food Politics: How the Food Industry Influences Nutrition and Health*. Berkeley: University of California Press, 2002.

Nylander, Jane. *Our Own Snug Fireside: Images of the New England Home, 1760–1860*. New Haven, CT: Yale University Press, 1994.

Pollan, Michael. *In Defense of Food: An Eater's Manifesto*. New York: Penguin Group, 2008.

———. *The Omnivore's Dilemma: A Natural History of Four Meals*. New York: Penguin Press, 2006.

Rees, Jonathan. *Refrigeration Nation: A History of Ice, Appliances, and Enterprise in America*. Baltimore: Johns Hopkins University Press, 2013.

Schenone, Laura. *The Lost Ravioli Recipes of Hoboken: A Search for Food and Family*. New York: Norton, 2008.

Shapiro, Laura. *Perfection Salad: Women and Cooking at the Turn of the Century*. New York: Farrar, Straus, and Giroux, 1986.

Shephard, Sue. *Pickled, Potted, and Canned: How the Art and Science of Food Preserving Changed the World*. New York: Simon and Schuster, 2000.

Smith, Andrew, ed. *Oxford Companion to American Food and Drink*. New York: Oxford University Press, 2007.

Smith, Betty. *A Tree Grows in Brooklyn* (1943). New York: Harper Perennial Modern Classics, 2001.

Spencer, Colin. *Vegetarianism: A History*. New York: Four Walls Eight Windows, 2000.

Strasser, Susan. *Never Done: A History of American Housework*. New York: Pantheon, 1982.

Tannahill, Reay. *Food in History*. New York: Three Rivers Press, 1989.

Visser, Margaret. *The Rituals of Dinner: The Origins, Evolution, Eccentricities, and Meaning of Table Manners*. Toronto: HarperCollins, 1992.

Wallach, Jennifer Jensen. *How America Eats: A Social History of U.S. Food and Culture*. Lanham, MD: Rowman & Littlefield, 2013.

Willard, Pat. *America Eats! On the Road with the WPA*. New York: Bloomsbury, 2008.

Williams, Susan. *Savory Suppers and Fashionable Feasts: Dining in Victorian America*. New York: Pantheon Books in Association with the Margaret Woodbury Strong Museum, 1985.

Williams-Forson, Psyche A. *Building Houses out of Chicken Legs: Black Women, Food and Power*. Chapel Hill: University of North Carolina Press, 2006.

Woolcott, Victoria W. *Remaking Respectability: African American Women in Interwar Detroit*. Chapel Hill: University of North Carolina Press, 2001.

Woodard, Colin. *The Lobster Coast: Rebels, Rusticators, and the Struggle for a Forgotten Frontier*. New York: Penguin, 2004.

Ziegelman, Jane. *97 Orchard: An Edible History of Five Families in One New York Tenement*. New York: Smithsonian Books/HarperCollins, 2010.

Articles

Adler, Thomas A. "Making Pancakes on Sunday: The Male Cook in Family Tradition." *Western Folklore* 40, no. 1 (1981): 45–54.

Albala, Ken. "History on the Plate: The Current State of Food History." *Historically Speaking* 10, no. 5 (2009): 6–8.

Ayers, Edward. "Introduction." In *All Over the Map: Rethinking American Regionalism*, ed. Edward Ayers, Patricia Nelson Limerick, Stephen Nissembaum, and Peter Onuf. Baltimore: Johns Hopkins University Press, 1996.

Barbas, Samantha. "Just Like Home: 'Home Cooking' and the Domestication of the American Restaurant." *Gastronomica: The Journal of Food and Culture* 2, no. 4 (2002): 43–52.

Carroll, Abigail. "Of Kettles and Cranes: Colonial Revival Kitchens and the Performance of National Identity." *Winterthur Portfolio* 43, no 4 (2009): 335–64.

Elias, Megan. "Summoning the Food Ghosts: Food History as Public History." *The Public Historian* 34, no. 2 (2012): 13–29.

"Feeding the Spirit Cookbook: A Resource and Discussion Guide on Museums, Food, and Community." Edited by Elizabeth Merritt. Washington, DC: American Association of Museums, 2012.

Ferguson, Kennan. "Intensifying Taste, Intensifying Identity: Connectivity through Community Cookbooks." *Signs* 37, no. 3 (2012): 695–717.

Fitts, Robert K. "The Archaeology of Middle-Class Domesticity and Gentility in Victorian Brooklyn." *Historical Archaeology* 33, no. 1 (1999): 39–62.

Fitzgerald, Gerard T., and Gabriella M. Petrick. "In Good Taste: Rethinking American History with Our Palates." *Journal of American History* 95, no. 2 (2008): 392–404.

Glickman, Lawrence B. "'Buy for the Sake of the Slave': Abolitionism and the Origins of American Consumer Activism." *American Quarterly* 56, no. 4 (2004): 889–912.

Grodinsky, Peggy. "Recipe Exhibit at Maine Historical Society Shows State's Changing Tastes." *Portland Press Herald* (Portland, ME), April 22, 2015.

Haley, Andrew P. "The Nation before Taste: The Challenges of American Culinary History." *Public Historian* 34, no. 2 (2012): 53–78.

Kulik, Gary. "Designing the Past: History Museum Exhibitions from Peale to the Present." In *History Museums in the United States: A Critical Assessment*, ed. Warren Leon and Roy Rosenzweig. Urbana: University of Illinois Press, 1989.

Levinson, Mark. "How the A&P Changed the Way We Shop." Interview by Terry Gross, *Fresh Air from WHYY, National Public Radio*. August 23, 2011. http://www.npr.org/2011/08/23/139761274/how-the-a-p-changed-the-way-we-shop.

Litoff, Judy Barrett, and David C. Smith. "To the Rescue of the Crops: The Women's Land Army during World War II." *Prologue* (magazine of the National Archives and Records Administration) 25, no. 4 (1993).

Lowenthal, David. "Pioneer Museums." In *History Museums in the United States: A Critical Assessment*, ed. Warren Leon and Roy Rosenzweig. Urbana: University of Illinois Press, 1989.

Magelssen, Scott. "Resuscitating the Extinct: The Backbreeding of Historic Animals at U.S. Living History Museums." *TDR: The Drama Review* 47, no. 4 (2003): 98–109.

Markel, Howard, and Alexandra Minna Stern. "The Foreignness of Germs: The Persistent Association of Immigrants and Disease in American Society." *Millbank Quarterly* 80, no. 4 (2002): 757–88.

McWilliams, Mark. "Distant Tables: Food and the Novel in Early America." *Early American Literature* 38, no. 3 (2003): 365–93.

Melosh, Barbara. "Speaking of Women: Museums' Representations of Women's History." In *History Museums in the United States: A Critical Assessment*, ed. Warren Leon and Roy Rosenzweig. Urbana: University of Illinois Press, 1989.

Moon, Michelle, and Cathy Stanton. "The First Course: A Case for Locating Public History within 'The Food Movement.'" *Public Historian* 36, no. 3 (2014): 109–29.

Oliver, Sandra. "Ruminations on the State of American Food History." *Gastronomica* 6, no. 4 (2006): 91–98.

Oyangen, Knut. "The Gastrodynamics of Displacement: Place-Making and Gustatory Identity in the Immigrants' Midwest." *Journal of Interdisciplinary History* 39, no. 3 (2009): 323–48.

Pierce, Stella Jean. "Kitchen Cache: The Hidden Meaning of Gender and Cooking in Twentieth-Century American Kitchens." Master's thesis, Appalachian State University, 2010.

Rahn, Millie. "Laying a Place at the Table: Creating Public Foodways Models from Scratch." *Journal of American Folklore* 119, no. 471 (2006): 30–46.

Skramstad, Harold. "An Agenda for Museums in the Twenty-First Century." In *Reinventing the Museum: Historical and Contemporary Perspectives on the Paradigm Shift*, ed. Gail Anderson. Lanham, MD: AltaMira Press, 2004.

Stanton, Cathy. "Serving Up Culture: Heritage and Its Discontents at an Industrial History Site." *International Journal of Heritage Studies* 11, no. 5 (2005): 415–31.

Trotter, Joe William, Jr. "African Americans and the Industrial Revolution." *OAH Magazine of History* 15, no. 1 (2000): 19–23.

Twitty, Michael. "The Unbearable Taste: Early African American Foodways." *Common-Place* 11, no. 3 (2011). http://www.common-place.org/vol-11/no-03/twitty/.

Wallace, Michael. "Mickey Mouse History: Portraying the Past at Disney World." In *History Museums in the United States: A Critical Assessment*, ed. Warren Leon and Roy Rosenzweig. Urbana: University of Illinois Press, 1989.

Weaver, William Woys. "The Dark Side of Culinary Ephemera: The Portrayal of African Americans." *Gastronomica: The Journal of Critical Food Studies* 6, no. 3 (2006): 76–81.

Wilkening, Susie. "Do Museums Need to Care About Foodies?" *Center for the Future of Museums* (blog), September 22, 2011.

Blogs, Digital Collections, and Online Resources

Afroculinaria blog, edited by Michael Twitty: www.afroculinaria.com

Civil Eats blog, edited by Naomi Starkman: www.civileats.com

Cornell University Library, Food, Wine, and Culinary History Resources: rmc.library.cornell.edu/collections/food_wine.html

Digest: A Journal of Foodways and Culture, American Folklore Society, journal edited by Diane Tye and Michael Lange: http://www.afsnet.org/?page=Digest

Edible Geography blog, edited by Nicola Twilley: www.ediblegeography.com

Feeding America: The Historic American Cookbook Project digitized cookbook collection: digital.lib.msu.edu/projects/cookbooks

Food History Jottings blog, edited by Ivan Day: www.foodhistorjottings.blogspot.com

Food History News, website and publication edited by Sandy Oliver: www.foodhistorynews.com

The Food Museum website: www.foodmuseum.com

Food Politics blog, edited by Marion Nestle: www.foodpolitics.com

The Food Timeline hyperlinked food history notes, www.foodtimeline.org

Four Pounds Flour: Historic Gastronomy blog, edited by Sarah Lohman: www.fourpoundsflour.com

Gastronomica journal, edited by Melissa Caldwell: http://www.gastronomica.org/

Getting Started in Food History, by Rachel Laudan: www.rachellaudan.com/getting-started-in-food-history

History Is Served blog, edited by Colonial Williamsburg Department of Historic Foodways: http://recipes.history.org/

The History Kitchen blog, edited by Tori Avey: www.pbs.org/food/blogs/the-history-kitchen

Johnson and Wales University Culinary Arts Museum website: www.culinary.org

Ken Albala's Food Rant blog, edited by Ken Albala: www.kenalbala.blogspot.com

Kitchen Historic blog, edited by Anje Merkies: www.kitchenhistoric.blogspot.com

Library of Congress Science Tracer, Food History: www.loc.gov/rr/scitech/tracer-bullets/foodhistorytb.html

MADFeed website and symposium: www.madfeed.co

New York Public Library Culinary History Resources: www.nypl.org/node/5629

Sprouts in the Sidewalk: https://sidewalksprouts.wordpress.com/

United States Department of Agriculture Food and Nutrition Service: www.fns.usda.gov

United States Department of Health and Human Services, Food Safety: www.foodsafety.gov

United States Food and Drug Administration: www.fda.gov/Food

Food Organizations

Agriculture, Food, and Human Values Society: afhvs.wildapricot.org

Agricultural History Society: www.aghistorysociety.org

American Community Gardening Association: communitygarden.org/

Association for Living History, Farm, and Agricultural Museums: www.alhfam.org

Association for the Study of Food and Society: www.food-culture.org

Chefs Collaborative: www.chefscollaborative.org

Culinary Historians groups: www.culinaryhistoriansny.org

Food Studies Knowledge Community: food-studies.com

The Herb Society of America: www.herbsociety.org

International Association of Culinary Professionals: www.iacp.com/

The Livestock Conservancy: www.livestockconservancy.org

Native American Food Sovereignty Alliance: www.nativefoodsystems.org/about/news/fsa

Native Seeds/SEARCH: www.nativeseeds.org/

Oxford Symposium on Food and Cookery: www.oxfordsymposium.org.uk/

RAFT Alliance and Foods at Risk: www.albc-usa.org/RAFT

Slow Food USA: www.slowfoodusa.org

Southern Foodways Alliance: www.southernfoodways.org

US Food Sovereignty Alliance: usfoodsovereigntyalliance.org

Index

Page references for figures are italicized.

Pack, Charles Lathrop, 162. *See also* gardens/
    gardening
Pingree, Hazen, 162
Plimoth Plantation, 20, 23, 25–26, 31–34, 88
Plymouth Colony, 10, 43
Post, Charles, 92
poverty, 164, 166; and diet, 72; and diet-related
    disease, 131; food and, 67–70; food insecurity
    in, 73; and food recovery, 68; and food
    relief, 69–70, 113; and gardening, 162; and
    immigration, 55; and reformers, 17, 20, 152
Pure Food and Drug Act, 153

rationing, wartime, 61, 89, 164–65
recipes, 2, 44, 50–51, 63, 68, 107, 112–13, 143.
    See also cookbooks
reform movements, 9, 16–20, 54–55, 152
refrigeration, 129, 130, 133
relief, 69–70, 162; food stamp program, 69,
    73; New Deal, 113, 158; and surplus
    commodities, 69
religion and food, 77, 97–98, 120
restaurants, 56, 59, 61, 63, 137–39; and African
    Americans, 66, 49, 138–39; Automat, 138;
    chain, 116, 157; Chinese, 52, 53; delicatessen,
    51; Delmonico's, 137; diners, 138; fast food,
    48, 110, 138, 157; and gender, 61, 66, 137–38;
    "home cooking" style, 60–61; Italian, 52;
    Julien's Restarator, 137; and segregation, 49,
    138. *See also* dining out
retailing: and food safety, 152–53; and gender,
    59; immigrants in, 51; supermarkets, 130,
    135–37, 157
Richards, Ellen Swallow, 16–17, 18–19, 20
Rockefeller, John D., 21. *See also* Colonial
    Williamsburg
Roosevelt, Franklin D., 158
Rorer, Sarah Tyson, 17, 92, 93

Salisbury, James H., 90–91
Sanitary Fairs, 15, *16*, 112. *See also* exhibitions,
    industrial and agricultural
Saunders, Clarence, 136
Settlement House movement, 18
Shakers (religious community), 27, 97
slavery, 44–45, 49, 71, 77; food as product
    of, 44, 45, 132; and free produce

movement, 155; at Mount Vernon, 11;
    in museum interpretation, 13, 22, 76, 176
slave trade, food in, 43
Southern Christian Leadership Conference.
    See civil rights movement
sugar, 44, 128; dietary, 94; maple, 43, 116,
    117–18, 155; and slavery, 44
Sugar Act of 1764, 155
supermarkets. *See* retailing

technology, 60, 125–32; food transportation,
    131–32, 152, 160, 161; industrial, 14, 15, 52;
    retail, 136–37. *See also* fire and fireplaces;
    cooking, technology; food preservation;
    refrigeration
Tilden, Freeman, 22
Toll House cookie. *See* Wakefield, Ruth
Townsend, John Trowbridge, 11

U.S. Sanitary Commission, 15, 37n30, 64
United Farm Workers, 156–57

vegetarianism, 91, 97, 168
Victory Gardens. *See* World War II,
    gardening in
vitamins, 89, 93, 102n10

Wakefield, Ruth, 133, 178
Waters, Alice, 166–67
wealth, 67, 168; and dining, 71–72; and travel,
    108; and voluntary austerity, 72
Wilson, Woodrow, 162, 164
women and food, 16–20, 77, 82n100, 93,
    94, 112, 113; in historic preservation
    movement, 10, 15, *16*; as professional cooks,
    45, 48, 63, 66; as wage laborers, 62–63;
    in World Wars I and II, 61. *See also* cooking,
    by women; domestic service; gender;
    reform movements
Women's Land Army, 61, *62*
Works Progress Administration, 114
World War I, 61, 94; gardening in, 162; food
    rationing in, 164
World War II, 61, 94, 134, 158; gardening in,
    162–63; food rationing in, 164–65

xenophobia, 50, 53, 111

About the Author

Michelle Moon oversees adult learning and develops interpretation at the Peabody Essex Museum (PEM) in Salem, Massachusetts, a museum of global art, culture, and history. A founder of Slow Food Seacoast and New England regional governor for Slow Food USA, she frequently speaks to professional audiences and college and graduate students on topics in museum interpretation, adult learning in museums, and food history.